Knowledge Commercialization and Valorization in Regional Economic Development

Knowledge Commercialization and Valorization in Regional Economic Development

Edited by

Tüzin Baycan

Professor of Urban and Regional Planning, Istanbul Technical University, Turkey

Edward Elgar

Cheltenham, UK • Northampton, MA, USA

Published by
Edward Elgar Publishing Limited
The Lypiatts
15 Lansdown Road
Cheltenham
Glos GL50 2JA
UK

Edward Elgar Publishing, Inc.
William Pratt House
9 Dewey Court
Northampton
Massachusetts 01060
USA

A catalogue record for this book
is available from the British Library

Library of Congress Control Number: 2012949785

This book is available electronically in the ElgarOnline.com
Economics Subject Collection, E-ISBN 978 1 78100 407 4

ISBN 978 1 78100 406 7

Typeset by Servis Filmsetting Ltd, Stockport, Cheshire
Printed and bound by MPG PRINTGROUP, UK

Contents

PART III   KNOWLEDGE AND TECHNOLOGY
           TRANSFER DYNAMICS AND REGIONAL
           ECONOMIC DEVELOPMENT

Contributors

Jonathan Aberman is the Founder and Managing Director of Amplifier Ventures, an early stage venture capital firm based in the Washington, DC region, Managing Director of the Mason Entrepreneurship Initiative, George Mason University, and a Lecturer at the Smith School of Business, University of Maryland. He is a nationally recognized expert on entrepreneurship and commercialization, currently engaged with state and local governments in creating programing to promote regional economic development and company creation. Jonathan's published works include research papers on technology clustering, venture capital, entrepreneurship and entrepreneurial characteristics and merger and acquisition trends. In addition to his career as a venture investor and academic, Jonathan was an international corporate lawyer and managing partner for a number of national law firms, including Pillsbury and Fenwick & West, and an investment banker and trader for firms including Goldman Sachs and Diawa Securities.

Zoltan J. Acs is University Professor at the School of Public Policy and Director of the Center for Entrepreneurship and Public Policy, Arlington, VA, USA. He is co-editor and founder of *Small Business Economics*, the leading entrepreneurship and small business publication in the world. Acs is the co-author of the *Global Entrepreneurship and Development Index*. He is also a visiting professor at Imperial College Business School in London. His career has focused on the link between innovation and entrepreneurship in industries, cities, and worldwide.

Tüzin Baycan is Professor of Urban and Regional Planning at Istanbul Technical University, Istanbul, Turkey. She is a Fellow of the Academia Europaea, panel member of ERC Advanced Grants for Social Science and Humanities: Environment and Society, and editorial/advisory board member of the *International Journal of Sustainable Society*, *Studies in Regional Science*, *Romanian Journal of Regional Science*, *Journal of Independent Studies and Research-Management: Social Sciences and Economics* and A/Z ITU *Journal of Faculty of Architecture*. Baycan is also co-editor of *Sustainable City and Creativity: Promoting Creative Urban Initiatives* (2011) and *Classics in Planning: Urban Planning* (2008), and author of many scientific papers and book chapters. Her main research interests cover urban and regional development and planning; urban systems; environment; sustainable development; creativity, innovation and entrepreneurship; diversity and multiculturalism.

Toon Buddingh' is serial entrepreneur and incubator manager at New Energy Docks, ESA-BIC and BViT, Amsterdam, Netherlands. His main focus is creating business and startups in the domain of government-research-entrepreneurship. He has founded seven incubators and three shared facility buildings, and helped almost 200 startups. In 2006 he was second in the Best Science Based Incubator election, worldwide. He developed multiple courses for entrepreneurs and one minor for bachelor level. He has been teaching at bachelor level for several years and is guest teacher at master level.

Manuel Fernández-Esquinas is a research scientist at the Institute for Advanced Social Studies (IESA), an official centre of the Spanish National Research Council (CSIC), Amsterdam, Netherlands. He has worked as an applied sociologist conducting extensive studies on public opinion polls, public policy analysis, social problems and programme evaluation. He has also worked as evaluator and consultant for the Spanish Ministry for Science and Innovation and several regional governments. He is currently Vice-president for Research of the Spanish Sociological Association, and Spanish delegate at the OECD Committee for Science and Technology Policy. His main research interests are on university-industry relationships, entrepreneurship and the effects of knowledge transfer on firm innovation. Currently he explores the socioeconomic impacts of public research organizations and the emergence of collaborative research centres. He has written books on research training, science policy and entrepreneurship. His latest articles are in *Science and Public Policy*, *Higher Education* and *Public Understanding of Science*.

Edward Feser is Dean of the College of Fine and Applied Arts at the University of Illinois at Urbana-Champaign, USA; Visiting Professor at the Manchester Business School, University of Manchester, UK; and Senior Research Fellow with the Center for Regional Economic Competitiveness, Arlington, Virginia, USA. His research focuses on technology-based regional economic development; industry clusters and regional growth; institutional design, innovation and policy implementation in public sector economic development organizations; the development of methods for detecting distinctive regional economic specializations; and policies supporting entrepreneurial business formation and growth in cities and regions.

Marina van Geenhuizen is Professor of Innovation and Innovation Policy in Urban Economies, in the Faculty of Technology, Policy and

Management, at Delft University of Technology, Delft, The Netherlands. She holds a PhD from Erasmus University in Rotterdam, Faculty of Economics. She is author of 90 reviewed journal articles and chief editor of six international volumes. Her main research activity is in theory and practice of commercialization of knowledge from university and research institutes, including spin-off firms, and policy instruments to enhance commercialization, including those of cities and regions. Her focus is on life sciences, sustainable energy technology, and information and communication technology. Her latest edited volumes (as chief editor) are *Technological Innovation across Nations* with Chihiro Watanabe, Vinnie Jauhari and Enno Masurel (Springer), *Energy and Innovation* with William Nuttall, David Gibson and Eline Oftedal (Purdue University Press), and *Creative Knowledge Cities, Myths, Visions and Realities* with Peter Nijkamp (Edward Elgar).

Harvey Goldstein is Professor and Dean of the Program in Public Governance and Management and Vice-Rector at MODUL University, Vienna, Austria. His research has spanned many dimensions of regional economic development, regional labour markets, innovation, entrepreneurship, science/technology parks, industrial clusters, and the governance of development. Prior to moving to Austria, he served on the faculties of Columbia University and the University of North Carolina at Chapel Hill. He has received numerous awards and honours for his research and teaching including a Fulbright Senior Scholarship in 2000 and selection as a Kauffman Entrepreneurship Faculty Fellow in 2006. Goldstein completed his undergraduate education at Columbia University and holds two master's degrees and a PhD from the University of Pennsylvania.

Vadim Grinevich is a Lecturer in Management, Business and Enterprise at the University Campus Suffolk Business School, Ipswich, United Kingdom. He is also a Research Associate with the Martin Centre for Architectural and Urban Studies at the University of Cambridge Cambridge, United Kingdom. His research interests include academic entrepreneurship, university-industry links, regional spatial development, sectoral and regional systems of innovation and productivity growth. He has worked on research projects funded by UK Research Councils and collaborated with the Japanese National Institute of Advanced Industrial Science and Technology, the Australian Business Foundation, the UK Department of Innovation, Universities and Skills, the UK National Endowment for Science, Technology and the Arts, and the Department of Enterprise, Trade and Investment in Northern Ireland.

Patricia van Hemert has been working as a researcher at the VU University Amsterdam, Center of Entrepreneurship since 2005 on several European and national research projects. Since 2007, she has been working on a PhD-thesis on innovation networks of small and medium-sized enterprises and their role on innovation performance. This thesis has been successfully defended in spring 2012. She has published in a number of international journals. At the moment she is working on a project involving scenario analysis for the Amsterdam Metropolitan region that is commissioned by the Amsterdam Economic Board.

Maria Ljunggren is a PhD student at the Department of Urban Planning and Environment at the Swedish Royal Institute for Technology, Stockholm, Sweden. Her primary research interests cover higher education institutions and their collaboration with the public and private sector, social capital building, and the effect collaboration has on undergraduate education. She is also a Senior Auditor at the Swedish National Audit Office, focusing her work on performance auditing in the area of research and education.

Enno Masurel is Professor in Sustainable Entrepreneurship and the director of the Amsterdam Center for Entrepreneurship at VU (ACE@VU), Amsterdam, The Netherlands. His main research focus is Entrepreneurship and Small and Medium-Sized Enterprises (SMEs), with special reference to innovation. He has attended many international seminars and published in a number of international journals. In an analysis by *Technovation* (2006) concerning publications in the field of entrepreneurship he was in the Dutch Top 3 and the World Top 8. He teaches entrepreneurship at both bachelor level and master level. He is also supervisor of PhDs in the field of entrepreneurship.

Xian-fei Meng is Vice-Director of the Office of Scientific Research and Development, Tsinghua University, Beijing, China. His academic research focuses on S&T policy and patent management.

David J. Miller is a PhD candidate in the School of Public Policy at George Mason University, an Adjunct Professor in the School of Management, and Director of Entrepreneurship at the Mason Center for Social Entrepreneurship, Arlington, USA. His research focuses on high impact firms created by students at US universities and colleges. He writes about this topic at http://www.campusentrepreneurship.com.

Peter Nijkamp is Professor of Regional, Urban and Environmental Economics and in Economic Geography at the VU University, Amsterdam, The Netherlands. His main research interests cover quantitative plan evaluation, regional and urban modelling, multicriteria analysis, transport systems analysis, mathematical systems modelling, technological innovation, entrepreneurship, environmental and resource management, and sustainable development. In all these fields he has published many books and numerous articles. He is member of editorial/advisory boards of more than 30 journals. According to the RePec list he belongs to the top 30 of well-known economists world-wide. He is past president of the European Regional Science Association and of the Regional Science Association International. He is also fellow of the Royal Netherlands Academy of Sciences, and past vice-president of this organization. From 2002 to 2009 he served as president of the governing board of the Netherlands Research Council (NWO). In addition, he is past president of the European Heads of Research Councils (EUROHORCs). He is also a fellow of the Academia Europaea, and member of many international scientific organizations. In 1996, he was awarded the most prestigious scientific prize in the Netherlands, the Spinoza award. At present, he is honorary university professor.

Gregor H.F. Noltes is a MSc Business Administration graduate and Business Manager at Rockstart, Amsterdam, The Netherlands. In 2012, Rockstart was elected Best Investor at the Dutch Startup Awards. His main focus is the organization of mutual exchange of coaching support among startups and businesses. Noltes is a public speaker and a guest teacher at master level in the field of entrepreneurship.

Andrea Piccaluga is Professor of Innovation Management at Istituto di Management, Scuola Superiore Sant'Anna, Pisa, Italy. He is the Coordinator of the PhD Program in Management at Scuola Superiore Sant'Anna, is on the Editorial Advisory Board of *R&D Management Journal*, and is Associate Editor of the *Creativity and Innovation Management Journal*. He is also author of many scientific papers and book chapters. His academic research focuses on innovation management.

Hugo Pinto is a post-doctoral research fellow at the Centre for Social Studies, University of Coimbra, Portugal. He is an associate member of the Research Centre on Spatial and Organizational Dynamics and invited Assistant Professor at the University of Algarve. In 2010, he was visiting scholar at the Institute of Advanced Social Studies, Spanish National Research Council (Spain). Previously, Hugo was European project manager (University of Algarve, Centre of Marine Sciences, and BIC Algarve-Huelva). His main research interests are innovation systems and knowledge transfer. He is also interested in the debate on economics as a science and economic turbulence. Recent articles include 'Efficiency of innovation systems in Europe' (*European Planning Studies*, Routledge) and 'The role of econometrics in economic science' (*Journal of Socio-Economics*, Elsevier).

Kai Rao graduated from a PhD programme of innovation management at Istituto di Management, Scuola Superiore Sant'Anna, Pisa, Italy. Now he is an Assistant Professor at the International Business School of Sen Yat-sen University, China. His academic research focuses on technology transfer, IP management, science and technology policy, and academic entrepreneurship.

Alexander Rehbogen studied political science and sociology at the University of Salzburg, Salzburg, Austria and finished a post-graduate degree (MBA) in Public Governance and Management at MODUL-University Vienna, Austria. Since 2010 he has worked for the Austrian Energy Agency, where he is involved in the management of Austria's national climate protection initiative, klima:aktiv.

Roger R. Stough is Vice President for Research and Economic Development, George Mason University and NOVA Endowed Chair, Eminent Scholar and Professor of Public Policy. His education includes a BS in International Trade, Ohio State University; MA in Economic Geography, University of South Carolina; and PhD in Geography and Environmental Engineering, Johns Hopkins University. He also holds an *Honoris Causa* Doctor degree from Jönköping University, Jönköping, Sweden. His research specializations include leadership and entrepreneurship in regional economic development, regional economic modelling and transport analysis and planning. During the past 12 years Dr Stough has been heavily involved in development related research in China and India and in the development of entrepreneurship training and education programmes, including advising enterprise development and incubation centres there.

Paul Vulto is Senior Scientist at the Leiden/Amsterdam Centre for Drug Discovery, the Netherlands. He specialized in microfluidics and Lab-on-a-chip technology, for which he received his PhD *cum Laude* from the University of Freiburg, Germany. He worked as an engineer for the high-tech company Silicon Biosystems in Bologna, Italy and headed the diagnostic microsystems group at IMTEK, Germany. Prior to his return to academia, Paul was general manager of The Technopolicy Network and co-founded the consulting company ScienceWorks. Paul is (co-)author of five international patent applications and 15 peer reviewed journal publications. His current research efforts focus on microfluidics for metabolomics and drug screening. In addition to his academic activities, he is involved in spin-off company MIMETAS, which is developing micro-organs on-a-chip for better, more personalized development of medicines.

Hans Westlund is Professor in Regional Planning and Head of the Department of Urban Planning and Environment at KTH (Royal Institute of Technology), Stockholm, Sweden and Professor in Entrepreneurship at Jönköping International Business School, Jönköping, Sweden. He is also connected to the Institute for Developmental and Strategic Analysis (IRSA), Ljubljana, Slovenia. He holds a PhD in Economic History from the University of Umeå, Sweden. He has been Visiting Professor of Tokyo University and Kyoto University, Japan. Westlund is President 2013/14 of the Western Regional Science Association (USA) and he was Chairman of the European Regional Science Association's (ERSA) 50th Anniversary Congress 2010. He has a broad research interest in regional development issues across the world. His recent works deal with social capital, multidimensional entrepreneurship and innovation in regional contexts.

Acknowledgements

The idea for this volume came about at George Mason University, Fairfax, Virginia, USA where I spent a one-year sabbatical in 2011. During my sabbatical in the Office for Research & Economic Development at Mason, I observed Mason's transformation into a more entrepreneurial university. While I worked on knowledge commercialization, the university's technology transfer program transformed from an internally focused 'patent-centric' design to an externally focused 'company-centric' orientation in practice. I attended several meetings and discussions during this transformation process. I would like to express my appreciation and thanks to George Mason University for its inspiring research environment and great hospitality. However, there is one special person who created this inspiring atmosphere and who has been my 'muse' for this volume: Roger R. Stough. His unlimited energy, enthusiasm and excitement provided excellent motivation. I wish to express my sincere gratitude to Roger R. Stough for his support and encouragement.

I would like to thank all of the contributors for their dedication and hard work, which was often done in difficult circumstances. During this project two baby girls were born: one in Sweden and one in the Netherlands. I wish to thank in particular Maria Ljunggren and Patricia van Hemert for their hard work at the final stages of their pregnancies and the very beginning of their motherhood journeys. I would also like to thank the many referees who carefully judged the quality of the contributions. Finally, I wish to thank Matthew Pitman and Laura Seward (Edward Elgar, Cheltenham, UK) for their support and kind cooperation.

Tüzin Baycan, August 2012
Istanbul, Turkey

xiv

PART I

Introduction

1. Knowledge commercialization and valorization in regional economic development: new perspectives and challenges

Tüzin Baycan

1. KNOWLEDGE COMMERCIALIZATION AND VALORIZATION: INTERNATIONAL PERSPECTIVES

In recent years, commercialization and valorization of knowledge has come to be seen as an important stimulant of economic growth (Agrawal, 2001; Baycan and Stough, 2012; Bok, 2003; Etzkowitz, 1990, 2002; Litan et al., 2007; Viale and Etzkowitz, 2010), particularly for improving the development capabilities and economic performance of regions (Duch et al., 2011; Goldstein and Renault, 2004; Shane, 2004). In parallel, the traditional mission of universities including teaching and research has gradually changed, with new perspectives on the role of the university in the system of knowledge production, and has expanded in order to take over a 'third mission', namely commercial activities including patenting, licensing and company formation (Baldini, 2006; Owen-Smith and Powell, 2003; Rasmussen et al., 2006). Universities are now expected not only to sustain or to support economic growth but also to generate economic growth through producing new knowledge and human capital, licensing innovations and creating new companies.

These developments have led to the emergence of new phenomena called 'entrepreneurial universities' (Baldini, 2006; Etzkowitz et al., 2000; Jacob et al., 2003; Powers, 2004; Smilor et al., 1993) and 'academic entrepreneurship' (Bercovitz and Feldmann, 2008; Meyer, 2003; Shane, 2004, Wright et al., 2007). The transformation of universities towards a more entrepreneurial restructuring is leading to new types of relations and governance systems such as the 'triple helix' model of university-industry-government relations (Etzkowitz and Leydesdorff, 1996 and 2000). Today, this model of university-industry-government relations plays a variety of roles in different combinations in the process of knowledge commercialization.

The acceptance of knowledge commercialization as a 'third mission' can be viewed as an 'academic revolution' that is having enormous impacts on economic development. Academic knowledge commercialization first became part of the economic development agenda in the United States in the 1980s.[1] Later, in the 1990s, it spread to European countries. The Bayh-Dole Act in 1980 has been a milestone in the adoption of commercialization of knowledge in the US. Following the passage of the Bayh-Dole Act, US universities increased their efforts in technology transfer, licensing and investments in new firms. In the following 20 years, the number of universities engaged in technology licensing increased eightfold and the volume of university patents increased fourfold (Mowery and Shane, 2002). The number of universities that created technology licencing and transfer offices increased from 20 in 1980 to 200 in 1990 and by 2000 nearly every research university had at least one technology transfer office (Colyvas et al., 2002). From 1980 until 2000, 3376 academic spinoff companies were established (Pressman, 2002). According to the Association of University Technology Managers (AUTM), from 1980 to 1999, American university spinoffs generated $33.5 billion in economic value added. In the same period, these spinoffs generated 280,000 jobs, at an average of 83 jobs per spinoff. According to Cohen (2000), this rate of job creation shows that the average university spinoff creates more jobs than the average small business founded in the United States.

This transformation has been followed in many other countries. The US Bayh-Dole Act has become a benchmark model for knowledge commercialization. Knowledge commercialization has been recognized as the 'third mission' of universities in various European countries as well (Charles and Howells, 1992; van Geenhuizen, 2010; Goldfarb and Henrekson, 2003; Howells and McKinlay, 1999; Muscio and Geuna, 2008; PriceWaterhouseCooper, 2007). This rather new role started to grow in Europe in the early 1980s (Charles and Howells, 1992; Howells and McKinlay, 1999). Commercialization of knowledge first started in the UK in the early 1980s (Wright et al., 2002), and then spread to the continent, first in the Netherlands, then to other northern European countries and more recently to southern European countries like France and Italy (Muscio and Geuna, 2008). In the 1990s, technology commercialization efforts accelerated in many European countries. A decrease in public research funding at universities, a public debate about the role that universities have to play in society and a Bayh-Dole type of Act adopted by many countries played an important role in this process (Wright et al., 2007). In the UK, with the establishment of university technology transfer offices (Wright et al., 2002), and in Sweden with major changes in research policy and the 'university teachers' exemption' that gave intellectual property rights (IPRs) to researchers, university technology commercialization activities accelerated (Goldfarb and Henrekson, 2003; Kitagawa and Wigren, 2010). Therefore, following the change in American universities in the 1980s, the universities in Europe have also changed dramatically since the mid-1990s.

2. KNOWLEDGE VALORIZATION VERSUS KNOWLEDGE COMMERCIALIZATION

Although European countries have followed the US in bridging academic or scientific knowledge to commercialization and the US Bayh-Dole Act has become a benchmark model for knowledge commercialization, the literature shows the use of different concepts especially by American and European scholars in order to refer to the same phenomenon. Despite the increasing importance of the phenomenon, a conceptual consensus has not been provided yet. There are three major approaches to the concept of transforming knowledge in universities to a state of economically useful knowledge. In Europe the concept of the 'valorization of knowledge' is commonly used, whereas in the US the concept of 'commercialization' is more common. A third concept called 'knowledge capitalization' is also used by some scholars (for a comprehensive evaluation of emerging concepts we refer to Baycan and Stough, 2012).

'Knowledge valorization' is a relatively new term that refers to the need to turn knowledge into value in the knowledge-based economy. The concept of this term is broader than that of knowledge commercialization in that the concept of 'value' is in terms of a societal benchmark rather than just commercial or private sector profit. 'Knowledge valorization' is often used in a more narrow sense within the context of the 'knowledge paradox', which describes the situation that exists in many countries in Europe, where there is both considerable knowledge and the capacity to produce large amounts of it – especially within universities – that are not used (Andriessen, 2005; Audretsch and Aldridge, 2009).

Although knowledge valorization and knowledge commercialization are commonly used in order to refer to the same phenomenon – the transfer of knowledge into economically useful knowledge – the meaning of these two concepts is different. While 'knowledge valorization' is described as 'the transfer of knowledge from one party to another for economic benefit' (Andriessen, 2005: 1), 'knowledge commercialization' refers to the 'the process of making money from knowledge with or without a knowledge transfer' (Andriessen, 2005: 2). The third concept, 'knowledge capitalization', on the other hand, is defined as '. . . culture, including science, becomes capital when it generates a stream of income' (Etzkowitz, 1990: 118). As can be seen from these definitions, although these three concepts (knowledge valorization, knowledge commercialization and knowledge capitalization) refer to the same phenomenon, they consider different features and components. While transfer of knowledge is a necessary condition for knowledge valorization, knowledge commercialization and capitalization consider monetary values such as making money or generating income unnecessary to the transfer of knowledge.

The chapters in this collection use concepts of both 'knowledge commercialization' and 'knowledge valorization'. While contributors from the US use the concept 'knowledge commercialization', contributors from European countries prefer to use the concept 'knowledge valorization'. Therefore, the volume investigates 'knowledge commercialization' in the US, 'knowledge valorization' in Europe and 'technology transfer dynamics' in China.

3. 'KNOWLEDGE COMMERCIALIZATION' IN THE US, 'KNOWLEDGE VALORIZATION' IN EUROPE AND TECHNOLOGY TRANSFER DYNAMICS IN CHINA

This collection investigates the emerging factors in bridging knowledge to commercialization from an international perspective and highlights the research agenda and the challenges for the academy, industry and government. While focusing especially on the new role of universities in regional economic development through knowledge commercialization as well as the university-industry interaction and factors that influence knowledge and technology transfer, the volume addresses 'knowledge commercialization' in the US, 'knowledge valorization' in Europe, and technology transfer dynamics in China and provides a forum for discussion of whether, why, and how commercialization and valorization of knowledge can lead to higher levels of innovation and economic development from an international perspective.

The collection of chapters in this volume considers commercialization and valorization of knowledge as an essential element of regional innovation systems and economic development. Therefore, the volume addresses modern theories and concepts related to research on knowledge commercialization and valorization and provides a valuable overview and introduction to this fascinating and rapidly emerging field for academics, policy-makers, entrepreneurs, researchers and students who share a common interest and commitment to knowledge commercialization and valorization.

The volume consists of two main parts which map out the most important issues and challenges. After this introductory Chapter 1 by Tüzin Baycan, addressing knowledge commercialization and valorization in regional economic development and highlighting new perspectives and challenges, Part II investigates knowledge commercialization and valorization from the university perspective, whereas Part III addresses knowledge and technology transfer dynamics at the university-industry interface. In other words, while the chapters of the former 'look in' the university and reveal the critical factors from an 'internal perspective', the chapters of the latter 'look out' the university as well as 'look from outside' at the university and examine the university-industry interaction from an 'external perspective'. Parts II and Part III both offer an 'international perspective' as well as a better understanding of knowledge commercialization and valorization in different countries including the US, Sweden, UK, Netherlands, Spain and China. This diversity of country experiences from different parts of the world leads the volume to reveal critical factors in knowledge commercialization and valorization from American, European and Chinese perspectives. Detailed descriptions of Part II and Part III as well as summaries of the chapters are given in the next sections.

3.1 University Engagement, Knowledge Commercialization and Regional Economic Development

The first part of the volume puts the debate on knowledge commercialization and valorization into context from the university perspective. This part highlights: (i) different commercialization models; (ii) university engagement and faculty attitudes to knowledge commercialization and valorization; (iii) transformation of technology transfer program; and (iv) entrepreneurship education in the research-intensive entrepreneurial university. This part consists of five chapters. The first three chapters address 'knowledge commercialization' experiences in the US, whereas the following two chapters reflect the European approach of 'knowledge valorization' on the basis of two case studies from Sweden and the UK. Therefore, this part of the volume offers an international perspective to better understand knowledge commercialization and valorization in different countries. Especially the findings of two chapters, Chapter 4 and Chapter 5, offer very interesting results from a comparative evaluation perspective as they have similarly examined university engagement and faculty attitudes in the US and Sweden.

The first chapter of Part II, Chapter 2 by David J. Miller and Zoltan J. Acs, explores contemporary policy responses to demands for knowledge commercialization at US research universities, contrasting them with various entrepreneurial mechanisms from outside of the campus. The chapter employs interpretive analysis in order to examine and assess past and recent developments in knowledge commercialization in the US and provide an alternative framework, based on historical precedent and contemporary economic realities, for considering commercialization of knowledge in an entrepreneurial age. On the basis of their interpretive analysis, Miller and Acs argue that though current practices have many advocates, their focus is incongruent with an entrepreneurial economy, and will be contrasted with some flexible, non-campus models evolving in growth sectors. Underlining that higher education in the US has a history of supporting importation of new models, they shed light on commercialization in an entrepreneurial economy, and emphasize that the criticism and call for reform of Bayh-Dole highlight just one small area where new models of distribution are needed. These new models of knowledge commercialization would also underscore the need to return to empowering individuals as opposed to institutions. Against the limitations of the current 'organization centric commercialization model', they suggest the need for 'methods and models focused on supporting individuals'.

Next, Chapter 3 by Roger R. Stough, Jonathan Aberman, Tüzin Baycan and Paul Vulto examines the concept of the knowledge economy and the barriers to the transformation of knowledge into economically useful knowledge or into commercially valuable products and services by universities at the regional level. The chapter explicates the notion of barriers to this conversion with a discussion of the knowledge filter and knowledge absorption concepts, and introduces for the first time the 'innovation column' model of knowledge conversion. A case study of the transformation of the George Mason University technology transfer program is presented to illustrate how these three concepts help understand where barriers to the creation of economically useful knowledge are and how such efforts influence knowledge commercialization by easing constraints in the knowledge filter.

Chapter 4 by Harvey Goldstein and Alexander Rehbogen investigates university engagement and knowledge commercialization and analyzes faculty attitudes towards academic entrepreneurship. Goldstein and Rehbogen discuss the multi-faceted aspect of the 'entrepreneurial turn' within research universities including on the one hand the pressure for universities to become more active in stimulating and assisting economic growth and development through patenting, licensing and university-based start-up companies, and on the other hand, a growing movement for universities to enhance their 'engagement' activities. They emphasize that while these activities represent a third mission of universities after the generation of new knowledge and teaching, knowledge commercialization tends to be considerably more controversial because it is perceived to be in conflict with the Mertonian norms of 'open science'. Using the results of a web-based survey of US faculty attitudes towards academic entrepreneurship and the application of factor analysis to the survey data, they explore to what extent faculty perceive these types of activities independently, and the association of attitudes towards each activity with attitudes towards Mertonian norms and various types of conflicts of interest within the academy.

In Chapter 5, Maria Ljunggren and Hans Westlund examine professors' attitude to collaboration and central infrastructure for collaboration in Sweden. Although collaboration between higher education institutions and industry has gained an increasing importance in the development of economic and educational policy, the majority of research analyzing collaboration has neglected the issue of policy development for collaboration within the higher education institutions and its potential effect on members of the academic community. Ljunggren and Westlund address this neglected issue in order to better understand collaboration and the potential differences in attitude and ambition to participate in collaboration activities within the academic community. They use social capital theory as a framework and as a theory of the social infrastructure and norms that govern the exchange of knowledge and technology between higher education institutions and external actors, and they analyze professors' attitudes towards collaboration and interfaculty differences in attitude to collaboration. Using the results of a web-based survey, they explore that collaboration is seen as useful for the quality of research and education among all faculties, but that the actual participation in collaboration projects differs among faculties, with a low participation rate among professors from the humanities and a high participation rate among professors from the technical faculty. They further explore that collaboration is a path-dependent and bottom-up process and that establishing and initiating external social capital building through public policy is complex.

The last chapter of Part II, Chapter 6 by Edward Feser, investigates entrepreneurship education in the research-intensive entrepreneurial university. Although 'entrepreneurial turn' and 'entrepreneurial university' have attracted much attention in the literature, entrepreneurship education, especially the link between entrepreneurial university and entrepreneurship education, has been a neglected issue. The chapter by Feser addresses this neglected issue and explores the interface between commercial engagement and entrepreneurship education. Feser argues that entrepreneurship education programs have tended to develop in parallel to 'entrepreneurial university' initiatives, rather than in intentional alignment with them and this is reflected in the research literature as well, where the analysis of the 'entrepreneurial university' and studies of entrepreneurship education have little overlap. Feser examines the evolution of the entrepreneurship education initiative of a single research-intensive institution – the University of Manchester in the United Kingdom – and the ways in which that initiative have contributed to the broader entrepreneurial and commercial engagement objectives of the university. The Manchester case suggests that research-intensive universities that wish to bring entrepreneurship education and knowledge commercialization and commodification into effective and beneficial alignment face challenges that require determined strategies to overcome.

3.2 Knowledge and Technology Transfer Dynamics and Regional Economic Development

The final part of the volume addresses knowledge and technology transfer dynamics and regional development. This part highlights: (i) 'knowledge paradox' and the barriers in valorization of academic knowledge; (ii) university-industry interaction and factors that influence knowledge and technology transfer; (iii) regional innovation system; (iv) innovation performance of SMEs; and (v) the role of business incubators in knowledge valorization. This part consists of six chapters. The first two chapters address knowledge valorization experiences in the Netherlands, the following two chapters explore knowledge transfer dynamics in the UK and Spain, the next chapter offers empirical evidence from Europe on the performance of business incubators in different European countries, whereas the last chapter highlights technology transfer activities in China. Therefore, this part of the volume mainly reflects the European countries' experiences in knowledge and technology transfer activities while including also an exceptional country, China.

The first chapter of Part III, Chapter 7 by Marina van Geenhuizen addresses 'knowledge paradox' and the barriers to valorization of university knowledge and investigates whether 'living labs' can provide solutions. In order to better understand the 'knowledge paradox', the chapter first explores the extent of failure/success in valorization at universities and factors that hinder valorization. While focusing on collaboration of university and firms in research projects, which has received relatively little attention to date, the chapter examines the development of university R&D projects in the Netherlands in terms of success, delay and failure, and identifies major obstacles to reaching success. Next, the chapter draws attention to the concept of 'living labs', currently in vogue in enhancing knowledge valorization by involving groups of users in the creation/design and testing of new product and process. Following a state-of-the-art analysis of key characteristics of living labs as a tool, the chapter offers an inventory of what is not known about the tool and its application but should be known to get living labs properly structured and implemented. Finally, the chapter assesses the benefits of living labs, providing solutions to factors hindering valorization in university-business interaction.

Chapter 8 by Patricia van Hemert, Peter Nijkamp and Enno Masurel explores whether relationships exist between the key subsystems of the regional innovation system and the innovation performance of Dutch SMEs and how these relations are affected by cross-border knowledge interactions. Although the regional innovation system focuses on local interactions generally, the chapter is especially interested in the cross-border knowledge interactions of SMEs, as increasingly the idea is gaining ground that, more often than not, a regional innovation system is inserted into a complex web of relations to national and international organizations and innovation systems. Focusing in particular on the moderating effect of cross-border activity of Dutch SMEs, the chapter aims to contribute to a better understanding of how cross-border relations may moderate the relationship between knowledge subsystems and innovation performance. Using the results of a survey among Dutch SMEs that participated in a government subsidy program ('innovation vouchers programme') which aimed to improve knowledge relations between universities and other knowledge institutions and SMEs, and deploying a moderated hierarchical regression approach and structural equation modeling, the chapter analyzes the moderating effect of cross-border knowledge relations and the mediating effect of cross-border knowledge interaction of SMEs. The results support the significant effect of cross-border knowledge interactions on the relationship between knowledge generation and diffusion subsystems and innovation performance of SMEs, but this effect is negative. Further, there is no mediation effect of cross-border knowledge interactions, which suggests that knowledge exploitation interactions are more likely local and national rather than international for SMEs.

Chapter 9 by Vadim Grinevich addresses region-specific effects of the university-industry interface and investigates whether the region-specific extent of industry-university interactions can be linked to the size of sectoral productivity gains achieved at a regional level. The chapter analyzes region-specific productivity competitiveness of industry in combination with the patterns of university-industry links. Assuming that the extent to which sector-specific needs for knowledge and technology are met by the university may vary across regions, depending on the local history of university-industry links, the local policy context and the structure and quality of the local university system, the chapter examines whether these deviations from region-invariant patterns of university-industry links are significant enough to contribute to region-specific competitiveness effects. The results of the analysis suggest that relatively high levels of industry interconnectedness with multiple innovation system players, including the university, have a positive effect on region-specific competitiveness. In terms of policy implications the results indicate that the emphasis should be on enhancing business skills and expertise with regard to sustainable innovation network building, with the university concentrating on the quality of its academic research.

Chapter 10 by Hugo Pinto and Manuel Fernández-Esquinas focuses on the dynamics of knowledge valorization in regional development by exploring a diversified set of interactions between firms and the academic sector. Pinto and Fernández-Esquinas describe knowledge transfer as a diversified process that includes the most science-intensive mechanisms, such as patenting, collaborative projects and research contracts, but they also stress the importance of services and personal interactions. Their analysis pays special attention to several key aspects of the dynamics of knowledge transfer: the breadth of university-industry interactions, the intensity of the interactions and the importance of informal relations, and their statistical exploration identifies the main features of firms and research teams that influence these dynamics. Using two surveys representing innovative firms and university research groups, they explore the crucial factors that increment science and industry collaborations in Andalusia, a catching-up region in Spanish and European context. Their econometric findings support many of the influences suggested by current research, but also offer a number of specific patterns as well as some contrasts between knowledge-transfer dynamics in companies and research groups. Their estimated regressions create a mirror image between these two institutional spheres, stressing aspects that are more relevant in each reality to stimulate the existence, intensity, breadth and informality of knowledge transfer. Their results provide insights for knowledge transfer policies in technology moderate-intensive South European regions and underline the need to develop specific instruments to incentivize university-industry interactions from the company's and the university's perspective.

Chapter 11 by Gregor H.F. Noltes, Enno Masurel and Toon Buddingh' investigates different types of business incubators (BIs) in Europe and measures the performance of BIs and their incubatees. In order to answer the question 'Does type matter?', Noltes, Masurel and

Buddingh' distinguish five types of BIs: Business Innovation Centres (BICs), University Business Incubators (UBIs), Independent Business Incubators (IBIs), Corporate Private Incubators (CPIs), and Green Business Incubators (GBIs), and examine whether different types of BIs and their incubatees perform differently. Although they distinguish five types, as only one GBI joined their research and CBIs were not represented at all, they compare the performance of BICs, UBIs and IBIs. Their empirical research among 51 European BIs shows that the differences between the types of BIs and their incubatees are very limited and that the majority of the few differences are economic by nature. Based on these findings they recommend for future research that this typology should not be distinguished a priori, but that characteristics should be collected for distinguishing a new typology.

Undoubtedly, an important dimension of knowledge transfer dynamics is human resources factors. University human resources factors are considered as the determinant of active university technology transfer activities, but researches on university technology transfer activities are focused on western countries and our knowledge about non-western countries, including China, is quite limited. There is a gap of comprehensive investigation of Chinese universities and their technology transfer activities in the literature. The limited number of studies are mostly qualitative and a few quantitative studies investigate universities according to their institutional structure and reputation. To meet this need, the last chapter of the book addresses China and technology transfer activities in Chinese universities. Chapter 12 by Kai Rao, Andrea Piccaluga and Xian-fei Meng examines the impact of human resources factors on university patent technology transfer activities in China. Based on the analysis of provincial panel data from 2004 to 2010 on Chinese universities, the chapter reveals that the factors related to the quantity of university human resources can significantly promote university patent technology transfer activities, whereas the factors of quality do not show similar significance. The results also show that there are some differences among regions that influence university patent technology transfer activities. The chapter enriches the literature on Chinese university technology transfer activities and provides some references for decision-makers in government, industry and universities.

4. NEW PERSPECTIVES AND CHALLENGES

Knowledge commercialization and valorization is a complex and a multi-faceted phenomenon. Despite the positive implications, there are several bottlenecks. However, there are also many challenges for academia, industry and governments. The overall conclusion of this volume is that research in the field of knowledge commercialization and valorization does significantly contribute to a better understanding of the complexity of the issues concerned and has contributed to the development of relevant policies for knowledge-based economic growth. The volume suggests a form of change that generates productive improvements and enhanced performance, but also entrepreneurial and innovative growth and development, and emphasizes the crucial role of university-industry-government interaction in innovative policies. The volume also provides important insights into the ongoing transformation of universities to become more dynamic and entrepreneurial institutions. All in all, the volume offers a wealth of refreshing studies with a high value for academia, industry and government and suggests a set of challenges, summarized below, from different regional and structural perspectives:

- University knowledge commercialization in an entrepreneurial economy requires viewing the campus and its knowledge commercialization from a broader perspective and taking into consideration entrepreneurial mechanisms outside of the campus as well as non-campus models evolving in growth sectors. As mentioned by Miller and Acs (Chapter 2), a university-governed system is not an efficient model in the entrepreneurial age and there is a need for an 'individual-centric commercialization model' rather than an 'organization-centric commercialization model'. Therefore, the first challenge emerges in governance systems of knowledge commercialization, to find methods and models focused on supporting individuals to unleash their knowledge to solve local and regional challenges.
- There are various barriers to the transformation of knowledge into commercially valuable products and services by universities that can be explicated by the concepts of knowledge filter and knowledge absorption. Understanding and modeling the barriers to knowledge transformation requires linking these concepts and providing a synthesizing framework. The 'innovation column model' introduced by Stough, Aberman, Baycan and Vulto (Chapter 3) offers a useful framework to illustrate where the barriers are and how to ease the constraints in the knowledge filter, therefore reducing the barriers to knowledge conversion. This new synthesizing framework challenges further applications and development of the innovation column model.

- Another challenge stems from a case study of the transformation of the George Mason University technology transfer program from an internally focused design to an externally focused orientation. Using the innovation column model framework Stough, Aberman, Baycan and Vulto highlight the contributions of the transformation from a 'patent-centric' to a 'company-centric' orientation in reducing the barriers to knowledge commercialization in the region. Therefore, the experience of George Mason University presents the challenge of an external orientation.
- The 'entrepreneurial turn' of universities is a complex and multi-faceted phenomenon including the favorable or unfavorable attitudes towards engagement and collaboration, the different levels of conflicts or threats perceived by faculties and a set of norms of open science, highlighted by Goldstein and Rehbogen (Chapter 4) and Ljunggren and Westlund (Chapter 5). Arising from this complexity is the challenge of a better understanding of differences in attitude towards engagement and collaboration and the role of social capital which govern the knowledge and technology exchange between higher education institutions and external actors.
- Entrepreneurship education is a crucial component of the entrepreneurial university development. However, entrepreneurial university and entrepreneurship education constitute two separate streams in the literature. As emphasized also by Feser (Chapter 6), there is a need to properly integrate entrepreneurship education and entrepreneurial university strategies.
- There are many barriers that hinder university-industry interaction and collaboration, such as cognitive distance, differences in value systems between university and industry, and regional factors such as shortcomings in financial arrangements, markets and financial risks. Overcoming these barriers requires the development of bridging activities between university and industry. As suggested by Marina van Geenhuizen (Chapter 7), living labs seem to enable the smoothing of university-industry relationships through an increased mutual understanding of differences in values and needs and through emerging changes in attitudes. Living labs as a user-driven open innovation model appear to have great potential to overcome barriers to valorization, through which cognitive distance between universities and firms may be reduced, and market and financial risks may be more equally distributed. Therefore, the challenge is to use living labs as a tool in order to achieve higher efficiency in knowledge valorization processes.

- Although the regional innovation system literature acknowledges that knowledge interactions with international partners and knowledge sources are important, the studies that explore the question of whether and under which conditions a regional innovation system can transcend national borders have been very limited. As underlined also by van Hemert, Nijkamp and Masurel (Chapter 8), cross-border interactions are indeed a reality that deserve research attention, because they can lead to a stronger regional innovation system. In order to better understand the complex web of relations to national and international organizations and innovation systems, the challenge for future research is to pay more attention to the extent and the nature of trans-border linkages and to evaluate the development potential and future prospects of cross-border regional innovation systems.
- Industry-university linkage as a mechanism of enhancing innovation and improving productivity competitiveness of local industries is an important issue from a policy perspective. The literature reports that high levels of industry interconnectedness with multiple innovation system players, including the university, have a positive effect on region-specific competitiveness. Therefore, the first challenge from a policy perspective is to promote networks and to increase interconnectivity among multiple innovation system players, both locally and externally. Nevertheless, region-specific productivity competitiveness of industry can be idiosyncratic as Vadim Grinevich highlights (Chapter 9), and therefore can only be attributed to a unique combination of regional, sectoral and temporal effects. Regarding this idiosyncratic nature of region-specific competitiveness, the second challenge from a policy perspective is to carefully design a regional policy that takes into consideration every aspect of regional geographic, historical, institutional and resource conditions that may enhance regional competitiveness and productivity growth performance. In addition, as the patterns discovered are very complex, there is a need for more research on the mechanisms by which the university, through engagement with business innovation, can affect regional economic performance.
- Knowledge valorization is diverse and occurs through several channels such as patenting, licensing, spin-off creation, human-resources training, use of university facilities, contract research, consultancy, public–private partnerships, collaborative projects, exchange of personnel, and also informal interpersonal contacts. As Pinto and Fernández-Esquinas report (Chapter 10), empirical results show that personal contacts are the most frequent interactions, followed

by other relevant links related to human resources and to R&D services. Therefore, the challenge is to investigate the conditions that favor the diversity of contacts and collaborative activities between sectors. There is also a need to develop specific instruments to incentivize university-industry interactions from the company's and the university's perspective.

- Business Incubators (BIs) as organizations which promote innovation and entrepreneurship play an important role in knowledge transfer processes. As Noltes, Masurel and Buddingh' highlight (Chapter 11), beyond providing a shared-space office facility, an infrastructure and a mission statement to their incubatees, BIs contribute to knowledge commercialization and valorization by offering also access to networks including universities, research institutes, industry contacts, investors, and government agencies. However, there is a need for further empirical research to better understand the characteristics of BIs and their role in promoting knowledge valorization.
- University human resources factors have significant influences on university patent technology transfer activities. However, these influences are not always the same, especially in different national and regional contexts. As Rao, Piccaluga and Meng explore (Chapter 12), for example, the quantity of human resources has significant influences on the performance of university patent technology transfer in China, whereas the quality of human resources does not show a significant positive impact on the quantity of the university patent technology transfer contracts and revenues. It seems that Chinese universities do not fully exploit the enormous potential of high quality human resources. Of course, this fact is not China-specific. Many universities in different countries face the same problem: they cannot fully exploit their potential of high quality human resources. Therefore, the challenge for universities is to fully exploit their potential of high quality human resources. There is also a need for further research especially from an internationally comparative evaluation perspective.

An overall evaluation of this volume highlights that there are neither single models nor simplistic solutions available for success. To foster knowledge commercialization and valorization requires a better understanding of the dynamics of change for universities, scientists/researchers, industry and governments/regions; a shift of mindset according to the new realities; being visionary, and re-balancing the risks; building consensus; and the creation of conditions for all stakeholders to become agents of change and drivers of economic development.

NOTE

1. Certainly universities in the US such as MIT and Stanford became leading examples of commercialization of knowledge in the mid-20th century but not until the Bayh-Dole Act in the early 1980s did this become more broadly recognized as a way for the university to contribute to its bottom line and to contribute more broadly to society via economic development that creates jobs, income and wealth.

REFERENCES

Agrawal, A. (2001), 'University-to-industry knowledge transfer: literature review and unanswered questions', *International Journal of Management Reviews*, **3** (4), 285–302.

Andriessen, D. (2005), 'Value, valuation, and valorisation', in S. Swarte (ed.), *Inspirerend innoveren; meerwarde door kennis*, Den Haag: Krie. (Available at www.weightlesswealth.com).

Audretsch, D.B., and Aldridge, T.T. (2009), 'Scientist commercialization as conduit of knowledge spillovers', *The Annals of Regional Science*, **43** (4), 897–905.

Baldini, N. (2006), 'The entrepreneurial university: a debate', http://ssrn.com/abstract=1097325.

Baycan, T., and Stough, R.R. (2012), 'Bridging knowledge to commercialization: the good, the bad, and the challenging', *Annals of Regional Studies*, DOI 10.1007/s00168-012-0510-8.

Bercovitz, J., and Feldmann, M. (2008), 'Academic entrepreneurs: organizational change at the individual level', *Organization Science*, **19** (1), 69–89.

Bok, D. (2003), *Universities in the Market Place: The Commercialization of Higher Education*, Princeton, NJ: Princeton University Press.

Charles, D., and Howells, J. (1992), *Technology Transfer in Europe: Public and Private Networks*, London: Belhaven Press.

Cohen, W. (2000), 'Taking care of business', ASEE Prism Online, January, 1–5.

Colyvas, J., Crow, M., Annetine, G., Mazzoleni, R., Nelson, R.R., Rosenberg, N., and Sampat, B.N. (2002), 'How do university inventions get into practice?', *Management Science*, **48** (1), 61–72.

Duch, N., García-Estévez, J., and Parellada, M. (2011), 'Universities and regional economic growth in Spanish regions', Document de treball de l'IEB 2011/6, Institut d'Economia de Barcelona.

Etzkowitz, H. (1990), 'The capitalization of knowledge: the decentralization of United States industrial and science policy from Washington to the States', *Theory and Society*, **19** (1), 107–121.

Etzkowitz, H. (2002), 'Bridging knowledge to commercialization: the American way', Science Policy Institute, State University of New York. http://www.fnir.nu/upload/Publications/Procee,dings/OE02/ABSTRACT-ETZKOWITZ.pdf.

Etzkowitz, H., and Leydesdorff, L. (1996), 'Emergence of a triple-helix of university-industry-government relations', *Science and Public Policy*, **23**, 279–86.

Etzkowitz, H., and Leydesdorff, L. (2000), 'The dynamics of innovation: from national systems and "Mode 2" to a triple helix of university-industry-government relations', *Research Policy*, **29**, 109–23.

Etzkowitz, H., Webster, A., Gebhardt, C., and Cantisano, B.R. (2000), 'The future of the university and the university of the future: evolution of ivory tower to entrepreneurial paradigm', *Research Policy*, **29**, 313–30.

Geenhuizen, M. van (2010), 'Patterns of knowledge commercialization at universities: project level results in The Netherlands', paper presented at ERSA Conference, 19–23 August, Jönköping, Sweden.

Goldfarb, B., and Henrekson, M. (2003), 'Bottom-up versus top-down policies towards the commercialization of university intellectual property', *Research Policy*, **32** (4), 639–58.

Goldstein, H.A., and Renault, C.S. (2004), 'Contributions of universities to regional economic development: a quasi-experimental approach', *Regional Studies*, **38** (7), 733–46.

Howells, J., and McKinlay, C. (1999), 'Commercialization of university research in Europe', Report to the Advisory Council on Science and Technology, Ontario, Canada.

Jacob, M., Lundqvist, M., and Hellsmark, H. (2003), 'Entrepreneurial transformations in the Swedish university system: the case of Chalmers University of Technology', *Research Policy*, **32** (9), 1555–68.

Kitagawa, F., and Wigren, C. (2010), 'From basic research to innovation: entrepreneurial intermediaries for research commercialization at Swedish "Strong Research Environments"', Center for Innovation, Research and Competence in the Learning Economy (CIRCLE), Paper No. 2010/02, Lund University, Sweden.

Litan, R.E., Mitchell, L., and Reedy, E.J. (2007), 'Commercializing university innovations: alternative approaches', *Innovation Policy and the Economy*, **8**, 31–57.

Meyer, M. (2003), 'Academic entrepreneurs or entrepreneurial academics? Research-based ventures and public support mechanisms', *R&D Management*, **33** (2), 107–15.

Mowery, D.C., and Shane, S. (2002), 'Introduction to the special issue on university entrepreneurship and technology transfer', *Management Science*, **48** (1), v–ix.

Muscio, A., and Geuna, A. (2008), 'Governance of university knowledge transfer in Europe', paper presented at the DRUID 25th Celebration Conference, 17–20 June, Copenhagen, Denmark.

Owen-Smith, J., and Powell, W. (2003), 'The expanding role of university patenting in the life sciences: assessing the importance of experience and connectivity', *Research Policy*, 32, 1695–711.

Powers, J.B. (2004), 'R&D funding sources and university technology transfer: what is stimulating universities to be more entrepreneurial?', *Research in Higher Education*, **45** (1), 1–23.

Pressman, L. (ed.) (2002), *AUTM Licensing Survey: FY 2001*, Northbrook, IL: Association of University Technology Managers.

PriceWaterhouseCooper (2007), *Staying In Control While Unlocking The Knowledge* (in cooperation with TechnoPartner).

Rasmussen, E., Moen, Ø., and Gulbrandsen, M. (2006), 'Initiatives to promote commercialization of university knowledge', *Technovation*, **26** (4), 518–33.

Shane, S.A. (2004), *Academic Entrepreneurship: University Spinoffs and Wealth Creation*, Cheltenham, UK and Northampton, MA, USA: Edward Elgar.

Smilor, R.W., Dietrich, G.B., and Gibson, D.V. (1993), 'The entrepreneurial university: the role of higher education in the United States in technology

commercialization and economic development', *International Social Science Journal*, **135**, 1–11.
Viale, R., and Etzkowitz, H. (eds) (2010), *The Capitalization of Knowledge: A Triple Helix of University-Industry-Government*, Cheltenham, UK and Northampton, MA, USA: Edward Elgar.
Wright, M., Vohora, A., and Lockett, A. (2002), *Annual UNICO–NUBS Survey on University Commercialisation Activities: Financial Year 2001*, Nottingham: Nottingham University Business School.
Wright, M., Clarysse, B., Mustar, P., and Lockett, A. (2007), *Academic Entrepreneurship in Europe*, Cheltenham, UK and Northampton, MA, USA: Edward Elgar.

PART II

University engagement, knowledge commercialization and regional economic development

2. Backing the horse or the jockey? University knowledge commercialization in the entrepreneurial age

David J. Miller and Zoltan J. Acs

INTRODUCTION

Practical and productive output has been demanded of US higher education since the founding of the first colleges in North America. The meaning of practical and productive has evolved over time and innovative educational, political, and philanthropic leaders have delivered by building higher education institutions and structures connected to local, regional, and national needs (Carlsson et al. 2007).

After World War II and especially in recent decades, universities have employed an organization centric model for commercializing knowledge and providing practical value to their constituents. In its wake, a higher education landscape full of technology transfer programs, triple-helixes, science parks, spin-offs, and commercial partnerships has been created. Many research universities perpetually struggle to become innovation and entrepreneurship leaders and while a few vivid outliers seem to have 'perfected' innovation, entrepreneurship, and commercialization, their fortunes are not easily replicated. In an entrepreneurial age, researchers and policy makers must view the campus and its knowledge commercialization from a broader perspective and return to the local roots of America's great universities (Audretsch 2007).

Today the practical and productive output expected of higher education is innovation and entrepreneurship (Etzkowitz 2008; Crow 2008). This has not always been the case. The expectations of policy makers and the public at large were not nearly as lofty just over 100 years ago when less than 4 percent of Americans attended college and much of the public mistrusted colleges and universities alike (Veysey 1965; Thelin 2004; Kamenetz 2010).

This chapter employs interpretive analysis to examine and assess past and recent developments in knowledge commercialization in the US and provide an alternative framework, based on historical precedent and contemporary economic realities, for considering commercialization of knowledge in an entrepreneurial age. The next section of this chapter reviews the higher education models imported by leaders in the US and the growth of these models in higher education. Next an exploration and examination of the ways in which these models were changed, evolved and integrated in the US by various local and regional leaders is presented.

The importation and evolution of foreign higher education models and the direct entrance of the federal government would eventually lead to the development of what Clark Kerr called the modern multiversity (Kerr 2001). Kerr's multiversity will be used to understand the contemporary innovation and entrepreneurship landscape in US higher education, including technology transfer programs, science parks, spin-offs, and corporate partnerships. While these organizations and systems have been in place for decades in many cases, the effectiveness at most universities is unclear, though the demand for more productive output continues (Bercovitz and Feldmann 2006).

The gap between the standard organization centric commercialization model in use today and the emerging entrepreneurial age will be discussed in the following section. Finally, some recommendations are presented based on previous higher education successes and off campus entrepreneurial models available to a higher education sector charged with commercializing knowledge. The evolution from an organization centric model to something more appropriate for today's society and economy is underway and will likely follow past eras of change and innovation in higher education marked by responsiveness and innovation.

INFLUENCE OF FOREIGN HIGHER EDUCATION MODELS IN AMERICA

The early introduction of colleges in North America highlights the desire by some early colonists for a North America that replicated Europe. There were nine colleges in existence by the time of the American Revolution, all of which exist today and all of which are considered to be among the best in the world (*Economist* 2005).[1]

Classic languages and philosophy dominated a curriculum that could be traced to ancient Greece and was provided for those who would be civic and religious leaders (Rudolph 1990; Thelin 2004). Institutional structures – a central location, master instructors with autonomy, examinations and degrees – dated to medieval Europe (Kerr 2001; Crow 2008).

Most colonial, revolutionary, and pre-Civil War colleges would follow the elite British model and a period of college building using this model occurred in the US through the 19th century (Rudolph 1990). With frontiers breached and new states entering the union, local leaders pushed for their own colleges, often with the help of business and political hands and often under the leadership of various religious denominations (Mardsen 1994). In establishing colleges, cities were competing with cities, states with other states, and denominations with other denominations in a race to 'civilize' the American Frontier. Professors were poorly paid and treated, students had few rights, and the value of the output was unclear, especially in an age of limitless possibilities on the American frontier (Veysey 1965). The course of studies varied by student, often with no set time or clear course of study for completion (Rudolph 1990).

Early colleges, whether Harvard or Miami of Ohio, were bare bone affairs, depending on donations and tuition and offering little value beyond serving as basic, elitist institutions, limiting their impact and offerings (Rudolph 1990; Kamenetz 2010).

Colleges sprouted across the land, but there was little there beyond a skeleton structure, a small number of students and a few supporters trying to establish some kind of elite tradition in a land where innovative structures, political, economic, and otherwise, were being created with each new frontier (Altbach et al 2001; Turner 2008; De Toqueville 2006). By the Civil War, there were 182 colleges in the United States, though most Americans did not know much about them or care to attend or send their children to them (Cole 2009).

As America grew its British style colleges, a new model for higher education was created when Prussian educator and state bureaucrat Von Humboldt founded Berlin University in 1809. Von Humboldt's innovation would alter the trajectory of higher education and directly impacts current universities, policies, and expectations (Flexner 1994; Veysey 1965; Kerr 2001).

Humboldt designed a graduate institution dedicated to teaching science and finding new knowledge; new fields would be explored and the university would offer the resources (i.e. laboratories, libraries) to support such efforts (Flexner 1994; Kerr 2001). This was the birth of the research university. Humboldt's university, the product of a bureaucrat, was designed to work for the benefit of an industrializing Germany and would be managed directly by state authorities.

Humboldt's institution was radically different from previous models in higher education (Flexner 1994; Kerr 2001; Goldstein and Buck 2010). According to Clark Kerr, former Chancellor of the University of

California and creator of the much copied California Master Plan for Postsecondary Education:[2]

> The emphasis was on philosophy and science, on research, on graduate instruction, on the freedom of professors and students (*Lehrfreihet* and *Lernfreiheit*). The department was created, and the institute. The professor was established as a great figure within and without the university. (Kerr 2001, p. 11)

The German model supported interdisciplinary studies through institutes and interacted with off campus sectors of society; scientific institutes were particularly important to the interactions with industry (Flexner 1994). Thus the research university and its scientific output could and would provide direct value to an emerging, industrializing Germany.

Like the British model before it, the German model would come to the US, but would be adapted by different institutions, leaders, and funders to meet the needs of the nation, specific states and cities, and even specific industries, social classes, and professions. Many reforming education leaders in the US spent time at German research universities and worked to import their structures and practices.

Post Civil-War America began in earnest to build universities based on the German model through the early part of the 21st century, with higher education and local leaders attempting to provide practical knowledge, tools, and graduates (Rudolph 1990; Thelin 2004).

Federal funding for higher education, through the Morrill Act of 1862 and the Hatch Act of 1887, set up broad frameworks for using research universities to achieve public, but local, goals. These were federal policies (or rather grants of land), but they allowed individual states and even private universities and their leaders to support research and technology to solve local needs (Rudolph 1990; Thelin 2004). This local control would be crucial to the eventual success of 'land grant' universities in output and connection to local populations.

The Hatch Act, for example, provided funding for agricultural research stations. Thelin (2004) recounts that German botanists were not trusted upon arrival at the University of Kentucky, but eventually won great praise as their methods for testing and certifying the quality of fertilizer provided direct benefits to the farmers of the state. Not only did these policies solve public needs, they helped build the trust of local populations by serving their needs (Rudolph 1990; Thelin 2004).

The value of higher education and the university would eventually become known not just in agriculture, but via engineering in manufacturing, via chemistry in industry, and also in the military (Carlsson et al. 2009; Thelin 2004). Over time, the new research universities, with the support of philanthropists and local and federal government would begin to prove their worth to society and economy. As with the college building era through the civil war, the research university era would employ higher education to help grow 'competitive' advantages of cities, states, and regions (Rudolph 1990; Kamenetz 2010).

AMERICANIZING FOREIGN IMPORTS AND THE RISE OF KERR'S MULTIVERSITY

When the British college model arrived in North America, there were immediate calls for reform, especially related to curriculum (Rudolph 1990; Thelin 2004). It was clear very quickly that England was different from North America and some early Americans realized that traditional European models would not work on the new continent, whether trapping fur in upstate New York, homesteading in Oklahoma, or building a college in Iowa (Turner 2008).

Reformers were present throughout the leadership and faculty of many colleges in the late 1700s and the early 1800s and much of their effort focused on evolving the curriculum to include more practical subjects such as math, science, and engineering (Rudolph 1990; Thelin 2004). Engineering and science had been taught in Europe since the middle of the 18th century and some reformers and college builders in the US took notice and action (Carlsson et al. 2007).

Ben Franklin's College of Philadelphia, opened in 1751, and Thomas Jefferson's University of Virginia, founded in 1819, hinted at the possibilities of offering students more practical subjects including sciences and math (Veysey 1965; Rudolph 1990). In his *Great American University* Cole writes,

> In 1749, Benjamin Franklin outlined a course of education in a pamphlet entitled Proposals for Education of Youth in Pensilvania. Students would be prepared for public service and business, quite a different mission from the ecclesiastical purposes outlined by Harvard and Yale. In keeping Franklin's interest in science and in promoting useful knowledge, the University of Pennsylvania was designed to produce men of practical affairs rather than scholars or ministers. About one-third of the three year curriculum was devoted to science and practical studies. (Cole 2009, p. 35)

Jefferson's University of Virginia offered multiple schools and points of leadership and students were free to choose their courses. This decision, according to Rudolph (1990), would forever change higher education. Rudolph explains, 'One of the most liberating regulations in the history of American higher education – indeed in the history of liberty in America – was the one adopted by the University of Virginia board of visitors in 1824: "Every student shall be free to attend the schools of his choice, and no other than he chooses'" (Rudolph 1990, p. 126). This undergraduate freedom (which would take decades to spread across the higher education landscape in America), combined with the research freedom introduced with the German model, would make US campuses liberating places for students at all levels.

It is important to note that American students, unlike their predecessors in Europe, played a central role in reforming the British college model in North America. By the early 1800s, students began to demand more than just recitation of classics, poor treatment from greybeard faculty members, and limited resources (Rudoph 1990; Thelin 2004; Kamenetz 2010). Living in dormitories in small, newly established towns (few other living arrangements existed) hastened rebellious thoughts and activities beyond the reach and rule of college leaders (Thelin 2004).

Literary societies and debating groups were the first student organizations to flourish, and in many cases provided resources such as speakers and libraries that early colleges did not furnish; Phi Beta Kappa was one of the first, radical, extra-curricular activities on campus (Rudolph 1990; Kamenetz 2010).

Fraternities would mushroom and vault to prominence in the life of the campus as would sports and a range of other extra-curricular activities (Rudolph 1990). Over time, the 'collegiate way' of life came to be seen as boorish, lazy, and rebellious, yet another reason for the general public not to value or trust colleges as the 19th century neared its end (Rudolph 2004; Kamenetz 2010).

A few institutions and leaders would attempt radical change, but most would move incrementally. The turn of the century cases of the University of Wisconsin and the University of Chicago are briefly discussed below to highlight cases where strong local leaders brought value to the public and began changing perceptions of the role of universities so that the public and policy makers would come to view research universities as central to civic and regional wellbeing.

Van Hise's University of Wisconsin and the 'Wisconsin Idea'

Like many of the emerging universities at the turn of the century, the University of Wisconsin was experimenting with new methods and means for providing value to society. Under the leadership of Charles Van Hise (president from 1903 to 1918), the university set about innovating and expanding with the stated goal of serving the entire population of the state (Curti and Carstensen 1949).

The 'Wisconsin Idea' set a high bar for public state universities. It meant that a university, in this case the University of Wisconsin at Madison, was to serve the entire state, literally up to the border (Curti and Carstensen 1949; Rudolph 1990; Thelin 2004). Van Hise supported the traditional roles of preparing undergraduates for work and civic life (teaching) and expanding knowledge (research), but added this third, public task of serving the entire population of the state.

According to Curti and Carstensen, Van Hise believed the university had to 'take knowledge to the people and to aid in its application to economic, social, and political problems' (Curti and Carstensen 1949, p. 87). The 'Wisconsin Idea' was predicated on the notion that all fields were worth pursuing because, Van Hise believed, 'It cannot be predicted at what distant nook of knowledge, apparently remote from any practical service, a brilliantly useful stream may spring' (quoted in Curti and Carstensen 1949, p. 88).

Driven by the 'Wisconsin Idea', the school offered practical and popular extension programs, built leading PhD programs, and forged relations with policy makers through the school's location in the state capital (Rudolph 1990; Thelin 2004). Van Hise thought like an entrepreneur and used commercial terms in explaining his goals and methods, likening the university's extension program to a retailer bringing products directly to consumers (Curti and Carstensen 1949).

William Harper and the University of Chicago

An interesting contrast to the public University of Wisconsin and Van Hise's 'Wisconsin Idea' was the growth of the privately funded University of Chicago under the leadership of William Harper. The University of Chicago was like many of the greenfield German style research universities being established near the turn of the century in that an industrial philanthropist, in this case John D. Rockefeller, was persuaded to support it.[3]

Beyond building a university focused on research and graduate work, Harper envisioned a role for it to represent the city of Chicago itself, which was clearly becoming the social and economic hub of the Midwest, as it transitioned from frontier life to densely populated, industrial and urban (Rudolph 1990).

Harper's goal was to make the University of Chicago a central asset, rallying point and representation of the entire city. Harper used the World's Fair of 1893 to erect stunning campus buildings in Beaux Arts architecture, and Rockefeller's Standard Oil built an oil rig on campus and offered postcards to visitors so that they would share the greatness of the University of Chicago, the city, and Standard Oil with family and friends all over the world (Thelin 2004). The 1893 World's Fair celebrated the 400th anniversary of Columbus' arrival in North America and, more importantly, the transition of the US into the industrial era. Harper, with the help of his funders, made sure the University of Chicago and the city would come to represent that emerging strength and the modern world. All of this before the school was properly functioning – it had been founded in 1892 (Storr 1966).

Harper raided other colleges and universities for star faculty and enticed Alonzo Stagg, the most famous football coach in the US, to leave Yale and lead the University of Chicago football team (Rudolph 1990). College football was wildly popular and the success of the team under Stagg created insatiable public demand for stories on the team (Rudolph 1990). Football success integrated the public, the city and the region with the university.

Harper, like Van Hise, innovated on the education front and expanded access to university knowledge through the creation of a junior college and summer school offerings. He pioneered for equality by welcoming large numbers of women to the University of Chicago so that by 1902 48 per-cent of U of C's students were female (Thelin 2004). Harper's university was there to support the growing city and its residents; the university was to be a resource and representation of Chicago and Chicagoans.

Harper made the University of Chicago a central leading institution for a dynamic, expanding metropolitan region and in many ways created a prototype for the modern American research university, heavily integrated into the surrounding social and economic fabric.

Making use of the Humboldt model to provide scientific and com-mercial influence, and integrating public goods through expanded edu-cational offerings, healthcare institutions, sports, exhibitions, and civic engagement would prove to be a hallmark of great American research universities. Many other universities such as Johns Hopkins in Baltimore and Cornell University in Ithaca, NY followed similar models, but each tailored and built a university to the needs and vision of university and local leaders, supporting philanthropists, and hosting populations.

US RESEARCH UNIVERSITIES IN THE ORGANIZATIONAL AGE: CLARK KERR'S 'MULTIVERSITY'

Some in the US would build new, research and graduate focused uni-versities modeled on Humboldt (Johns Hopkins University being the first), while most would weld German style research apparatus and graduate programs onto existing British style colleges. This would form a new hybrid kind of institution across America (University of Michigan, Stanford University, Harvard University, Emory University, etc.).

The German model was research focused and interdisciplinary; it evolved and mutated in the US as it merged with undergraduate colleges and local needs and culture. For example, student and professor worked collaboratively in US graduate schools, whereas in Germany, a master–apprentice relationship existed (Cole 2009).

Leaders such as Van Hise and Harper would graft new responsibilities and organizations onto the emerging hybrid American research university. Over time, with deeper integration into regional ecosystems, a new kind of institution would be born. Clark Kerr would call this the 'multiversity' (Kerr 2001).

The multiversity would expand in ever more directions and engage ever more stakeholders. Writing in 1963 Kerr describes the research intensive, undergraduate welcoming, socially and economically integrated universities, building on Abraham Flexner's influential studies on research universities in the US, Britain, and Germany. Kerr writes,

> Flexner thought of the university as an 'organism.' In an organism, the parts and the whole are inextricably bound together. Not so the multiversity – many parts can be added and subtracted with little effect on the whole or even little notice taken or any blood spilled. It is more a mechanism – a series of processes producing a series of results – a mechanism held together by administrative rules and powered by money. (Kerr 1991, p. 15)

Today's US research university, or Kerr's multiversity, is a modular institution. The British style undergraduate college and the German modeled graduate schools form the center base, but multiple institutions, professional schools, activities, organizations, and undertakings integrate or release from the core depending on the needs of the students, faculty, and regional communities. From regional science parks and entrepreneurial incubators to billion dollar athletic programs and hospital systems, the multiversity is deeply rooted in local ecosystems.

Towards a Federal Focus with a Local System

The contemporary demands for commercial productivity and output from higher education are not unprecedented. Colleges such as Jefferson's Virginia began to teach practical subjects and make undergraduates relevant, while research apparatus and graduate programs of German modeled research universities, pushed by the Morrill and Hatch Acts, would provide human capital and innovation for growing cities, regions, and companies for decades. However, the stated policy idea of employing universities for economic innovation in the US was crystallized by Vannevar Bush in the mid-20th century (Cole 2009).

Bush, an MIT trained engineer, former MIT engineering Dean, and founder of Raytheon, was summoned from Boston to Washington, DC by Franklin Roosevelt during World War II and managed over 6,000 scientists in applying technology, often university based, to the war effort (Thelin 2004; Cole 2009).

Bush, along with a handful of other university scientists, became the public face of American science and was introduced to the general public by *Life* and *Time* magazines as the brains behind the 'arsenal of democracy' during the war, growing citizens and policy makers' faith in research universities and science (Cole 2009).

Near the war's end, Bush released *Science: the Endless Frontier*,[4] a blueprint for a national science and technology innovation system that contained direct commercial and economic implications. Bush argued for unleashing the 'creative and productive energies of the American people' as a key asset in producing 'new and more attractive and cheaper products' (Bush 1945, Chapter 3, p. 2). Bush wondered in the report:

> Where will these new products come from? How will we find ways to make better products as lower cost? The answer is clear. There must be a stream of new scientific knowledge to turn the wheels of private and public enterprise. There must be plenty of men and women trained in science and technology for upon them depend both the creation of new knowledge and its application to practical purposes.
>
> More and better scientific research is essential to the achievement of our goal of full employment.

Much of Bush's blueprint would eventually be implemented to build a scientific innovation system of federal grants, peer review and competition as the drivers for knowledge creation at the university level (Cole 2009). The system has its flaws, but global rankings of US research, the migration of foreign scientists and students to American research universities, and the volume of international academic prizes awarded to US based and trained researchers is exceptional (*Economist* 2005; Cole 2009; Thorp and Goldstein 2010).

However, Bush's system represents the organizational age that birthed it, and WWII and the Cold War positioned the US federal government at the head. Decades of federal funded research followed, yet the federal effort did not appear to unleash the economic impact that Bush and other national and regional leaders envisioned in their blueprint.

In 1980, the Bayh-Dole act was passed and the fruits of federal largesse that Bush's structures supplied were expected to finally be harvested. In the decades following World War II the federal control over intellectual property came to be seen by many as a bottleneck to profitable commercialization of research (Etzkowitz 2008; Cole 2009). The Bayh-Dole act would allow universities, non-profits, small businesses, and inventors control over intellectual property supported by federal funds. It was meant to be a watershed change in policy that would unleash the commercial potential articulated by Bush.

In the years following Bayh-Dole a large majority of US universities have chosen to keep the commercialization responsibility inside of the university, empowering university administrators and staff to lead commercialization efforts, though other options were available (Markham et al. 2005). University technology transfer offices (TTOs) existed before Bayh-Dole, but passage of the act clarified practices and provided certainty surrounding intellectual property rights. Many technology commercialization and transfer offices and staff would be established in the United States as regional and university leaders drove for innovation and sustainable economic growth; the results would be mixed (Etzkowitz 2008; Markham et al. 2005).

A few universities, such as Stanford, Caltech, Johns Hopkins, and MIT performed well through this federal system and its various metrics (patents, license revenue and spin-offs) and set a high, technically led bar for employing university assets and human capital to support regional wealth creation.

But even the leading successes must be put into context as it took singular leaders such as Vannevar Bush and his student Frederick Terman (at Stanford) to lay the groundwork for today's successes in Silicon Valley and Boston; North Carolina's Research Triangle also has its own decades of local support and consistent growth and evolution to reach today's successes (Saxenian 1996; Florida et al. 2006; O'Shea et al. 2007).

The results of the last three decades of Bayh-Dole have been mixed, so much so that in 2010, as the thirtieth anniversary arrived, *Harvard Business Review* cited Robert E. Litan and Lesa Mitchell's (Kauffman Foundation) call for intellectual property reform a 'break through idea.' Litan and Mitchell argue for 'free agency' for inventors, allowing them choice in 'licensing' agents beyond the school's organization centric licensing process (Litan and Mitchell 2010). 'Perhaps it was not a bad idea to centralize their commercialization capabilities and give TTOs control of the process; they gained immediate organizational benefits and economies of scale. But this monopolistic model has since evolved into a major impediment,' explain Litan and Mitchell (2010, p. 53).

It is interesting to note that Stanford Provost John Etchemendy, speaking recently after Stanford's IP case against Roche Pharmaceuticals and the court's support of faculty members' right to assign IP, played down the importance of technology transfer revenues, minimizing the $45 million to $60 million in intellectual property revenue generated annually (Titus 2010). 'We're on the upper end, and that's on a $3.5 billion budget. It's not a major source of revenue,' stated Etchemendy (Titus 2010).

In another sign that TTO offices may distort commercialization efforts, Penn State University, a leading research university in the US, announced that it will no longer demand any intellectual property rights from commercial research partnerships, explaining,

> In short we are doing it because we consider the net present value of the interactions and relationships that our faculty and students have with industrial professionals to be very important and therefore greater than the apparent future value of the proceeds from such intellectual property. (Hank Foley, vice president for Research, Penn State University 2011

Today, the typical university TTO, muddling along, acts as the center and primary driver of commercialization efforts, interacting with professors, institutes, and commercial partners to commercialize the knowledge apparatus of the modular multiversity. Unfortunately, this organizational model, with university centric design and strategies, would seem to be of a past era and thus has not produced as expected in an entrepreneurial age.

ORGANIZATIONAL STRUCTURES IN AN ERA OF THE INDIVIDUAL

Clark Kerr's concept of the multiversity and Henry Etzkowitz's triple helix provide useful guides for understanding the evolution of research universities in the US and their attempts to commercialize knowledge over the past 60 years. Bayh-Dole was enacted because policy makers, university and regional leaders, and corporate leaders suspected that federal control over intellectual property was not effective in an entrepreneurial economy. The growth of TTO offices in recent years was a direct acknowledgement of the rise of the entrepreneurial economy, and recognition that local control and ownership might better encourage innovation and commercialization.

This shift from an industrial to an entrepreneurial economy, which the *Economist* noted in 1976 in a special survey titled *The Coming Entrepreneurial Revolution*, has been picked up on by Bell (1999), Drucker (1985), Florida (2002), and other social and economic observers.

Regardless of insights from various fields, university and regional leaders have been building for the last war – that of the commercialization of knowledge in the 'Fordist' or organizational age. As the *Economist* noted in 1976, 'It is gradually becoming clear that ownership of means of production is no longer a source of economic or political power, and may indeed now be a source of powerlessness' (*Economist* 1976, p.42). Ownership of the means of production is the position that universities and their regional partners find themselves in today with balance sheets full of economic and scientific assets.

However, what was overlooked was that the multiversity and the triple helix were organization centric models, not people centric, putting structures (or means of production) ahead of the human capital that would be producing the real value with those structures. Building on the modular nature of the modern research university, administrators and their partners have built technology transfer offices and other pieces of the triple helix (incubators, science parks, business development centers, economic development offices, etc.) across the United States with varying models and levels of success (Bercovitz and Feldmann 2006; Etkzowitz 2008).

Instead of universities and regions full of entrepreneurs and start-ups, in most places we have landscapes full of organizational units engaged in bureaucratic dances to little or marginal effect on regional development.

US universities have creative and innovative individuals (both faculty and students) expected to act entrepreneurially, but forced to interact with the market through institutional methods and timelines even though innovators and entrepreneurs globally use Facebook, LinkedIn, Twitter, Quora, texting, and Skype to connect with the market and make incredible impact. The next section will explore some of the recent structures and models that innovators are plugging into that are not congruent with current university practices.

SUCCESS IN THE ENTREPRENEURIAL AGE

This chapter has attempted to highlight that much of the success achieved by US higher education has been through two important strategies. One strategy is importing and evolving models from abroad. The second successful strategy has been using knowledge to solve societal needs: at the local and regional level during the post-civil war university building era and after World War II, employing the national innovation system laid out by Vannevar Bush. The current Bayh-Dole, multiversity model of connecting research professors through the university to both federal funding and potential commercial opportunities has its roots deep in Bush's system that made federal priorities the sun around which most research universities orbited.

The remainder of this chapter suggests that higher education leaders and policy makers revisit innovation themes from higher education history and create models for the commercialization of knowledge in an entrepreneurial age. This includes the early research university focus on the individual and local needs, the adoption and evolution of new models from outside, and the expansion in the conception of useful, commercial knowledge worth exploring and commercializing.

Individual Focus and Local Solution

From the founding of Harvard in 1636 through World War II, advances in higher education effectiveness and demand occurred when leaders such as Jefferson, Van Hise, and Harper focused on individuals and building relationships with individuals in their communities and states. Undergraduates gained freedom in classes and extra-curriculars, graduate students in sciences, and professional schools offered opportunities for individuals to chart their own paths in the marketplace. Higher education became directly relevant to citizens, businesses, and policy makers by building institutions and structures, at the undergraduate, professional, research, and regional levels that were responsive (Rudolph 1990; Cole 2009). World War II and Vannevar Bush changed all that with central planning and resource control for the achievement of national, not regional and local initiatives. It appears, however, that even those who did well under this system continued to tie their federal work to local firms and populations. Triple helix success follow in the path of Van Hise, Franklin, Harper and others who built effective universities by serving local populations, and solving regional problems, often of economic nature.

In her study of Silicon Valley and Route 128, Saxenian notes that Frederick Terman, as Dean of Engineering at Stanford, set up multiple levels of interaction between university students and professors and local engineers and their firms in the region (Saxenian 1996). Silicon Valley, Route 128, and North Carolina's Research Triangle all evolved beyond their early reliance on federal needs because leaders focused on connecting local individuals and set up multiple channels of interaction between people, not just organizations.

O'Shea et al.'s (2007) analysis of MIT's entrepreneurial culture highlights that multiple factors interacting over decades led to the institution's current success in knowledge commercialization. Similarly, North Carolina's research triangle was created to employ local assets, not to achieve federal goals, and took decades of action, during the organizational era, by local leaders worried about local economic development issues (Link and Scott 2003).

Today's 'ideal' cases of MIT, Stanford, and North Carolina were started over 50 years ago in an organizational age and made use of large-scale real estate development and early contracts and interactions with governments (Link and Scott 2003; O'Shea et al. 2007; Saxenian 1996). This strategy is not congruent with the entrepreneurial age and one can only conjecture what the early leaders in Boston, Silicon Valley, and North Carolina would do today if they were just starting out. It is unlikely they would build industrial parks over hundreds of acres of empty land and look to the federal government to determine which areas of research demanded exploration.

It should be noted that launching firms, perhaps the 'most' entrepreneurial of acts, is a commercialization model that most universities in the US do not choose, instead keeping control at the university level and choosing instead to use university offices to patent and license technology in the hope of a portfolio of cash streams (Markham et al: 2005). There is change around this goal and this will be discussed below.

As mentioned previously, ideas such as Litan and Mitchell's have tried to push policy makers and regional university leaders to think at the individual level rather than the organizational level. More must be done to reorient knowledge commercialization to the individual rather than institutional level as innovative higher education leaders have in the past.

Adoption and Evolution of New Models

US higher education leaders have been very successful through importing and evolving various models from abroad. And while US institutions are global leaders in higher education, new models should continue to be imported.

The criticism and call for reform of Bayh-Dole highlights just one small area where new models of distribution are needed. New models of knowledge commercialization would also underscore the previous need to return to empowering individuals as opposed to institutions.

For example, in private investing markets, a clear trend among venture investors looking for high impact is towards smaller, quicker startups that succeed or fail in a short period of time with very little investment. In 2005, venture capitalist Paul Graham introduced his innovation accelerator program Y Combinator. Through this program his team invests a small amount of money (less than $20,000) in a group of early stage ventures and takes the founding team through a 14 week acceleration program. Two cohorts have been through the program annually since Y Combinator's founding. A recent *TechCrunch* article states that Y Combinator has invested in 316 firms since its inception and values the top 21 startups in the portfolio at $4.7 billion dollars (Tsotsis 2011). Y Combinator accepted 64 firms in its most recent cohort (Tsotsis 2011). For comparison, in FY 2009, according to the Association of University Technology Managers (AUTM), all participating US universities, hospitals, and research institutes in the survey (181 institutions) created 596 new companies (AUTM 2010). The accelerator model, which places small amounts of capital behind many innovative ideas, is gathering steam quickly with many new accelerators emerging and focusing on specific regions or industries.

PayPal founder and billionaire Peter Thiel, a Silicon Valley legend and Stanford Law School graduate, offers another innovative model to explore. Thiel's foundation recently awarded up to $100,000 to 24 innovators age 20 or younger to allow them to leave the university structure and have the freedom and flexibility to push their innovation closer to commercialization and impact (MacMillan 2011). Many of the Thiel Fellows are students at leading universities and active in coursework and extra-curricular activities, including many that had participated in entrepreneurial activities.[5]

Both the Thiel and Y Combinator examples, from outside of the academy, highlight how private innovators are focusing on fast, small scale innovation, quite a contrast from the large scale, federally funded and processed path that most universities and regional leaders look to for knowledge commercialization.

Certain schools and regional leaders are picking up on this trend and are experimenting with new entrepreneurial age offerings. The University of Texas has recently launched the 1 Semester Startup program and Harvard Business School has introduced the Minimum Viable Product Fund.[6] Both attempt to stand up impactful companies quickly and at low cost – they focus on the individual and small team and their ideas and business models for commercial success.

Unfortunately, many of these activities are housed in particular schools (often business schools) and have not engaged individuals across the campus yet. Moreover, like Jefferson's radical idea of offering choice for undergraduates in 1819 or Van Hise's plan to educate fishermen in Minocqua, Wisconsin, most institutions of higher education and regional leaders are not ready to 'fund' small scale projects by non-technical, professional students such as MBA candidates and undergraduate music majors, instead placing large federal grants at the center of their commercialization efforts.

Reframing the starting point for commercialization towards models such as Y Combinator or the Minimum Viable Product Fund – small scale and individually driven – would be a dramatic change for universities and regional leaders, but importing and evolving models from the outside has always been crucial to higher education's relevance in the US.

In an interesting recent twist, the National Science Foundation has taken steps towards focusing on individuals and a new model is being explored. The creation of the National Science Foundation's Innovation Corps or I-Corps makes use of an entrepreneurship curriculum developed at Stanford's School of Engineering by Steve Blank.[7]

This importation of a new model, developed by entrepreneurs such as Steve Blank and Eric Ries in various real marketplaces, is a good thing; however, the I-Corps is funded through the grant making process whereby NSF leadership determines which ideas are worth pursuing. According to the I-Corps website, 'With the I-Corps grants, NSF will strategically identify these nascent concepts and leverage its investment in basic research for technology innovation. To do so successfully – and to address the national need for economic growth – will require a public–private partnership.' It is also worth noting that the Kauffman Foundation has played a role in funding the I-Corps and Lesa Mitchell is quoted in the press release announcing the launch of the initiative in early 2011, about a year after her TTO criticisms were highlighted in *Harvard Business Review*.

Moreover, for the team making the application, the reliance on a federal grant to get them acting entrepreneurially is somewhat against the spirit of the lean methodology as it is outlined by Eric Ries and Steve Blank. The movement, which has led to Ries's book *Lean Startup* becoming a best-seller, is called lean for a reason. The goal of lean startup is to help a team find a financially viable business model that provides value, not just a plan for finding funding streams (Blank 2007; Ries 2011).

Rethinking Commercial Knowledge

In our entrepreneurial economy, incredible wealth is and can be created with technology, but not always the credentialed patentable type that those pushing knowledge commercialization in higher education typically think of. The work of professors, PhD candidates and research fellows is impressive and has a long track record of creating regional and societal wealth, as evidenced by Google and Genentech. That said, those charged with commercializing knowledge must have a broader perspective in their understanding of what is commercializing.

While the creation of the I-Corps and its promotion of lean methods and minimum viable products are encouraging, the program is only open to teams that have active NSF awards or one that was active in the last five years (National Science Foundation 2011). This means that the NSF is only willing to 'double down' on ideas it has already picked, becoming in fact more focused and putting more resources into ideas that have yet to be validated. Would the I-Corps have been more innovative if it were only open to first time NSF applicants or those who haven't applied for at least five years?

Another limitation, beyond focusing on federally charted routes of discovery, that commercialization leaders make is ignoring the fact that technological knowledge is but one of the methods employed by entrepreneurs in unleashing change and creating regional wealth. Bill Gates was an extraordinary undergraduate at Harvard, working with his buddy Paul Allen, an undergrad drop out from Washington State University, on their own projects, not federally funded research, when they founded Microsoft (Allen 2010).

Michael Dell and his radical PC manufacturing and distribution ideas were birthed in a dorm room, not a research lab, at the University of Texas. Frederick W. Smith introduced the idea for an overnight package delivery system in an undergraduate economics paper at Yale. University of Maryland football player Kevin Plank built prototypes for his Under Armour perspiration wicking performance apparel while an undergraduate and is now CEO of a global sports apparel giant valued at over $4 billion. These individuals were working on problems and opportunities they uncovered, not those of the National Science Foundation or departmental leaders. Most importantly, their ideas, innovations, and improvements were driven by their creative thinking about business models and markets, not perceptions on patentable science from national policy makers. In our entrepreneurial era, new business models, services, and content, for example, are of incredible economic value.

Groupon, a group buying website founded in 2008, which had revenues over $600 million dollars in Q1 2011 and has gone from 37 employees to over 7,100 employees in less than 2 years,[8] was recently called the 'fastest growing company in history,' by *Forbes Magazine* (Steiner 2010).

Andrew Mason, Groupon's founder, was a first year graduate student at the University of Chicago's Harris School of Public Policy when he began working on the first iterations of a collective action website. While the campus clearly offered Mason the freedom and support to work on his idea to leverage technology for group action, the type of innovation and entrepreneurial impact he unleashed is not congruent with the dominant commercialization strategies of policy makers and university leaders. Mason, for example, ended up leaving campus to work with private investors on his idea.

Those charged with the integration of universities and regional economies must think creatively when analyzing the entrepreneurial assets in the university and the opportunities for creating commercial value. Van Hise, Harper, and Franklin all thought broadly when viewing the avenues of impact their universities could have on regional economies and quality of life.

Many institutions have responded by increasing their entrepreneurship offerings and infrastructure – including classes, entrepreneurship centers, and business plan competitions.

Once described as 'capitalist beauty contests' (Lehman-Haupt 2000), business contests have evolved to become a regular feature on multiversity and other campuses and also among economic developers.

The business plan competition, an extra-curricular activity in which students write business plans for new ventures and are judged by 'real world' investors, has become a standard practice across entrepreneurship education (Gartner and Vesper 1994; Katz 2008). The business plan contest was created in 1982 by students at the University of Texas at Austin business school in their quest for an efficient and fun extracurricular activity (Cadenhead 2002). Bo Fishback of the Kauffman Foundation estimates there are more than 700 business plan competitions today (Farrell 2010). The University of Chicago, which has offered its New Venture Challenge for 15 years through its Booth School of Business, now takes equity in winning companies in exchange for the funding won by competitors.[9]

Regional leaders and university officials must find and promote entrepreneurship by offering individuals across the university the freedom to experiment just as innovators like Jefferson gave individual students freedom in choosing what they would study, thus allowing individuals to guide how institutions could provide real value to society. Duke University, in recognition of this need, recently appointed Microsoft Education Division Founder Kimberly Jenkins as special assistant to the President and Provost for Innovation and Entrepreneurship. While innovation occurs frequently on university campuses, the entrepreneur, or driver for commercial impact, is not always in the lab and leaders focused on knowledge commercialization must be aware of this when viewing their modular institutions.

CONCLUSION

With greater economic uncertainty and governmental budgets under pressure, the commercialization of university knowledge is getting as much attention as ever. It's clear, through an interpretive analysis of the evolution of US higher education, that periods of responsiveness to society have been its most productive for higher education institutions and their communities.

In an entrepreneurial economy university and regional leaders must understand the path from Bush to Bayh-Dole centers around institutional leadership, not entrepreneurial opportunity. Industries from media and finance to retail and shipping have seen fundamental reordering in the entrepreneurial era. Commercialization of university knowledge cannot be insulated from these economic realities.

The move from an organization centric model to something more appropriate will likely follow past eras of change and innovation in higher education. Various regional and local leaders, inside and outside of the campus, will take innovative steps and experiment with new models. As noted above, this has already begun in some places. The models that achieve success will be replicated to varying levels of success. Like technology transfer offices and Bayh-Dole, followers will likely try to become replicas of leaders after the fact, rather than unleashing locally created entrepreneurial methods for knowledge commercialization.

The challenge for regional and university leadership is clear: find methods and models focused on supporting individuals in unleashing their knowledge to solve local and regional challenges. If the problems are real and the solutions are effective, they will be applicable across many regions and markets. Today suburban soccer players, immigrant roofers, and $100 million professional athletes all consume a sports drink formulated for college football players at the University of Florida in the late 1960s. When Gatorade was first being created and tested, the university didn't want to engage with the professors working on the project; many decades and a few law suits later, Gatorade has provided more than $80 million to the University of Florida (Rovell 2006). For university and regional leaders, the lesson from Gatorade and countless others is obvious: it is time to back the jockeys that come through campus and not the horses that we assign them to ride while they are there.

NOTES

1. The nine colleges on the eve of the American Revolution were: Harvard (1636), William & Mary (1693), Yale (1701), Pennsylvania (1740), Princeton (1746), Columbia (1754), Brown (1764), Rutgers (1766), and Dartmouth (1769). See Rudolph (1990) for an extensive discussion of the founding and founders behind each of these colleges. Universities, colleges, professional schools, and even departments have all become part of various 'rankings games' that try to rank the best globally. Examples include *US News and World Report*, *FT Business School*, *Times Higher Education World University Rankings*, and *QS Global Rankings*.
2. The California Master Plan for Higher Education sets distinct roles for various

campuses – including research, college, and community college http://sunsite.berkeley. edu/~ucalhist/archives_exhibits/masterplan/.

3. Other research focused universities funded by wealthy industrialists include Vanderbilt University, Tufts University, and Johns Hopkins University.

4. Bush's report can be retrieved from the National Science Foundation's website. http:// www.nsf.gov/od/lpa/nsf50/vbush1945.htm.

5. For more information on the Thiel Fellowships and the recipients visit the Thiel Foundation website, http://www.thielfoundation.org/.

6. More information on the University of Texas 1 Semester Startup can be found at http://www.1semesterstartup.com/. More information on Harvard Business School's Minimum Viable Product Fun can be found at http://www.hbs.edu/entrepreneurship/ resources/services.html.

7. For more information on the National Science Foundation's I-Corps visit http://www. nsf.gov/news/special_reports/i-corps/index.jsp.

8. Groupon Inc.'s S1 Filing with the Securities and Exchange Commission can be accessed via http://www.sec.gov/Archives/edgar/data/1490281/000104746911005613/a2203913zs-1. htm accessed 24 June 2011.

9. See New Venture Challenge Official Rules and Regulations: http://research.chicago-booth.edu/nvc/resources.aspx.

REFERENCES

Allen, P. (2010), 'Idea man: a memoir by the cofounder of Microsoft', New York: Penguin Group USA.

Altbach P., Gumport P., Johnstone, D. (2001), *In Defense of American Higher Education*, Baltimore: The Johns Hopkins University Press.

Association of University Technology Managers (2010), 'Universities report startup creation, licensing activity and income strong despite recession', *AUTM*. 17 December 2010.

Audretsch, D. (2007), *The Entrepreneurial Society*, Oxford: Oxford University Press.

Bell, D. (1999), *The Coming of Post-industrial Society: a Venture in Social Forecasting*, New York: Basic Books.

Bercovitz, J., and Feldmann, M. (2006), 'Entrepreneurial universities and technology transfer: a conceptual framework for understanding knowledge-based economic development', *Journal of Technology Transfer*, **31**, 175–88.

Blank, S. (2005), *The Four Steps to the Epiphany: Successful Strategies for Products That Win*, California: K & S Ranch Press.

Bush, V. (1945), *Science the Endless Frontier*, Washington DC: United States Government Printing Office.

Cadenhead, G. (2002), *No Longer Moot: The History of the Moot Corp Competition*, USA: Renoir.

Carlsson, B., Acs, Z., Audretsch, D., and Braunerhjelm, P. (2007), 'Knowledge creation, entrepreneurship, and economic growth: a historical review', *Industrial and Corporate Change*, **18** (6), 1193–229.

Cole, J. (2009), *The Great American University*, New York: Public Affairs.

Crow, M. (2008), 'Building an entrepreneurial university', in Kauffman Foundation, *The Future of the Research University: Meeting the Global Challenges of the 21st Century*, Kansas City, MO: Kauffman Foundation, pp. 11–30.

Curti, M. and Carstensen, V. (1949), *The University of Wisconsin: 1848–1925*, Madison, WI: University of Wisconsin Press.
De Toqueville, A. (2006), Democracy in America, vol 1. Project Gutenberg Ebook #815. http://www.projectgutenberg.org. Accessed June 2011.
Drucker, P. (1993), *Innovation and Entrepreneurship*, New York: HarperBusiness.
Economist (1976), 'The coming entrepreneurial revolution: a survey', *Economist*, 25 December, 41–65.
Economist (2005), 'The brains business: a survey of higher education', *Economist*, 10 September.
Etzkowitz, H. (2008), *The Triple Helix*, New York: Routledge.
Etzkowitz, H., Webster, A., Gebhardt, C. and Terra, B. (2000), 'The future of the university and the university of the future: evolution of ivory tower to entrepreneurial paradigm', *Research Policy*, **29**, 313–30.
Farrell, M. (2010), 'Creating competition among business plan competitions', Forbes.com, accessed 16 August 2010 at http://blogs.forbes.com/maureen farrell/2010/08/16/creating-competition-among-business-plan-competitions/.
Flexner, A. (1994), *Universities: American, English, German*, New York: Oxford University Press.
Florida, R. (2002), *The Rise of the Creative Class*, New York: Basic Books.
Florida, R., Gates, G., Knudsen, B. and Stolarick, K. (2006), 'The university and the creative economy', CreativeClass.com, retrieved 2008 at http://www.crea tiveclass.org.
Hart, B. and Etzkowitz, H. (2000) 'The origin and evolution of the university species', *Journal for Science and Technology Policy*, **13** (3–4), 9–34.
Kamenetz, A. (2010), *DIY U: Edupunks, Edupreneurs, and the Coming Transformation of Higher Education*, White River Junction, VT: Chelsea Green Publishing Company.
Katz, J. (2008), 'Fully Mature but not fully legitimate: a different perspective on the state of entrepreneurship education', *Journal of Small Business Management*, **46** (4), 550–66.
Kerr, C. (2001), *The Uses of the University*, Cambridge MA: Harvard University Press.
Lehman-Haupt, R. (2000), 'Dorm room economy', *Business 2.0*, November, 204–12.
Link, A. and Scott, J. (2003), 'The growth of research triangle park', *Small Business Economics*, **20**, 167–75.
Litan, R. and Mitchell, L. (2010), 'A faster path from lab to market', *Harvard Business Review*, **88** (1/2), 52–3.
MacMillan, D. (2011), 'Thiel awards 24 under 20 fellowships', *Businessweek*, accessed 30 June 2011 at http://www.businessweek.com/technology/content/may2011/tc20110524_317819.htm.
Mardsen, G. (1994), *The Soul of the American University*, New York: Oxford University Press.
Markman, G., Phan, P., Balkin, D. and Gianiodis, P. (2005), 'Entrepreneurship and university-based technology transfer', *Journal of Business Venturing*, **20**, 241–63.
Morr, R. (1966), *Harpers University: The Beginnings*, Chicago: University of Chicago Press.
National Science Foundation (2011), *I-Corps Factsheet*, retrieved December 2011 from www.nsf.gov/news/newsmedia/i-corps/factsheet.pdf.

O'Shea, R., Allen, T., Morse, K., O'Gorman, C. and Roche, F. (2007), 'Delineating the anatomy of an entrepreneurial university: the Massachusetts Institute of Technology experience', *R & D Management*, **37** (1), 1–16.

Penn State University (2011), *University Makes Significant Changes to Intellectual Property Policies*, Penn State Live, accessed December 2011 at http://live.psu.edu/story/56887.

Ries, E. (2011), *The Lean Startup: How Today's Entrepreneurs Use Continuous Innovation To Create Radically Successful Businesses*, New York: Crown Business.

Roberts, E. and Eesley, C. (2009), *Entrepreneurial Impact: The Role of MIT*, Kansas City: Kauffman Foundation.

Rovell, D. (2006), *First In Thirst: How Gatorade Turned the Science of Sweat into a Cultural Phenomenon*, New York: AMACON Books.

Rudolph, F. (1990), *The American College and University: A History*, Athens: University of Georgia Press.

Saxenian, A. (1996), *Regional Advantage: Culture and Competition in Silicon Valley and Route 128*, Boston: Harvard University Press.

Steiner, C. (2010), 'Meet the fastest growing company ever', *Forbes*, accessed June 2011 at http://www.forbes.com/forbes/2010/0830/entrepreneurs-groupon-facebook-twitter-next-web-phenom.html.

Storr, R. (1966), *Harper's University: The Beginnings: A History of the University of Chicago*, Chicago: University of Chicago Press.

Tappan, H. (1961), 'University education', in R. Hofstadter and W. Smith (eds), *American Higher Education: A Documentary History, Vol. II*, Chicago: The University of Chicago Press, pp. 515–44.

Thelin, J. (2004), *A History of American Higher Education*, Baltimore: The Johns Hopkins University Press.

Thorp, H. and Goldstein, B. (2010), *Engines of Innovation: The Entrepreneurial University in the Twenty-First Century*, Chapel Hill: University of North Carolina Press.

Titus, E. (2010) 'Supreme court case is about principle, not revenue, says Etchemendy'.

Stanford Daily, 5 Nov. http://www.stanforddaily.com/2010/11/05/supreme-court-case-isabout-principle-notrevenuesays-etchemendy/. Accessed 29 June 2011.

Tsotsis, A. (2011), 'Y combinator brings on alumni to be "part time partners"', *TechCrunch*, accessed 1 July 2011 at http://techcrunch.com/2011/06/13/ycombinator-brings-on-alumni-to-be-part-time-partners/.

Turner, F. (2008), *The Frontier in American History*, Charleston: BiblioBazaar.

Veysey, L. (1965), *The Emergence of the American University*, Chicago: University of Chicago Press.

3. Knowledge spillovers and commercialization in universities and their regions

Roger R. Stough, Jonathan Aberman, Tüzin Baycan and Paul Vulto

INTRODUCTION

Recent theoretical and empirical research (Acs et al., 2009; Audretsch and Lehmann, 2005) have focused on the creation and transmission of knowledge as the front end of the technical change process and more generally the full commercialization of knowledge (Chesbrough et al., 2006). A reasonable conclusion from this work is that knowledge and its transformation into economically useful knowledge is a basic element if not the key to the origins and nature of the technical change process. Herein we explore and examine the concept of the transformation of knowledge into economically useful knowledge.[1] Critical to this examination is the idea that barriers lie between the end points of this process. We organize our analysis of such barriers around three theoretical constructs: the knowledge filter and knowledge absorption, which are reasonably well developed concepts, and a new concept that we introduce called the innovation column, which may be viewed as helping to structure the discussion on barriers to knowledge commercialization. The last part of the chapter presents a case study in an effort to illustrate how the conceptual discussion can inform policy and programmatic decisions at the university level on the one hand and contribute to an improved knowledge filter at the regional level.

Knowledge is produced in many ways. While universities, public and private research centers and large corporate (public and private) organizations are often viewed as the primary knowledge creation centers, these are not the only sources of new knowledge as it arises from all sorts of human contemplation and interaction including even the seemingly mundane musings of the fisherman, hiker, commuter and so on. The time we live in is often referred to as the knowledge age because it is a high era of knowledge creation due to recent innovations in information and communications technology (ICT) that amplify society's ability to produce, amplify and share it with others, regardless of the source. At the same time, knowledge in its pure form is nothing more than that, and without extensive amplification it usually fails to become economically useful. It is the amplification of knowledge that is critical for successful technical change and outcomes.

How does this amplification occur? Theory has it that it is via the entrepreneur (Acs et al., 2009). The role of the entrepreneur is to see opportunity in knowledge (Schumpeter, 1934) and successful entrepreneurs see opportunity where others do not (Kirzner, 1985). The role of the entrepreneur in the technical change process is a major reason why entrepreneurship has become an intense focus of research not only in the technical change, development and public policy literature but also in the field of regional science, as the impact of the entrepreneur is arguably most visible at the local regional level – the level where knowledge is created. This is one of the most important insights arising from endogenous growth theory (Romer 1986 and 1990) in that technical change is primarily a phenomenon of the local regional context. Viewing technical change as a local motivating phenomenon of economic development that is in turn driven by knowledge and its transformation into economically useful knowledge by the entrepreneur has created a new and enlightening dynamic in the study of regional economic development (Stimson et al., 2009).

BARRIERS TO CREATING ECONOMICALLY USEFUL KNOWLEDGE

The spillover theory of knowledge (Acs et al., 1994) argues that knowledge 'spills' over into society and is picked up or not by entrepreneurs and then converted into economically useful knowledge. However, not all knowledge or ideas are picked up as some lie fallow or just fade away while others may be picked up, but not developed into useful or commercial products and services due to a variety of barriers. Finally, some will be picked up and developed by entrepreneurs into economically useful knowledge. But it is not enough to recognize the leadership role of the entrepreneur in knowledge commercialization and thus the technical change process, because of the barriers to entrepreneurial engagement, and these vary from one region to another. So the context within which technical change and knowledge commercialization occurs is not homogeneous.

Acs et al. (2004) have proposed the concept of a 'knowledge filter' that offers an explanation for the variation in the rate at which knowledge and knowledge conversion can occur and thus the level of entrepreneurial success. The knowledge filter is that which facilitates or detracts from the ease at which both entrepreneurship and knowledge transformation and commercialization occur. If the filter is tight or highly restrictive, it is difficult for knowledge to be converted to that which is economically useful. A highly restrictive filter (where, for example, the regulatory environment is excessive, capital availability highly constrained, and the time to form a business long) creates formidable barriers that in turn inhibit the conversion process. At the same time, if the filter is insufficiently strong to prevent chaotic behavior or disequilibrated conditions (Baumol, 1990) the same inhibiting or inefficient outcome is expected. The concept of the knowledge filter then is similar, if not analogous, to the effect of the construct of social (or institutional) capital (Williamson, 1994): when extremely strong (or extremely weak) it creates many barriers to the process of producing economically useful knowledge and thus the support that incentivizes entrepreneurial behavior. In short, the relationship between the quality of the technical change environment and the knowledge filter is inverse U shaped. The best conditions for technical change and the entrepreneur to create economically valuable knowledge is when the knowledge filter is neither too restrictive nor so relaxed or limited that chaos prevails.

However, the knowledge filter concept does not go far enough. In addition to the filter there is also a question about the absorptive capacity of the entrepreneur and the region. The knowledge absorption concept (Qian et al., 2012) argues that recognizing and considering the knowledge filter is insufficient to learn and understand all the barriers to the creation of economically useful knowledge. This complementary concept argues that even when the knowledge filter is relatively non-constraining there may still be other important limiting factors that are entrepreneur centric, i.e., having to do with the ability of the entrepreneur to absorb knowledge and thus initiate and execute the process of transforming it into economically useful knowledge. The notion of regional absorption capacity is comparable to that of the regional knowledge filter.

THE INNOVATION COLUMN AND THE KNOWLEDGE FILTER

In an effort to link together the knowledge filter and knowledge absorption concepts for understanding and modeling the barriers to knowledge transformation we now introduce a concept called the innovation column (Vulto, 2010). This is derived by analogy from what is called a separation

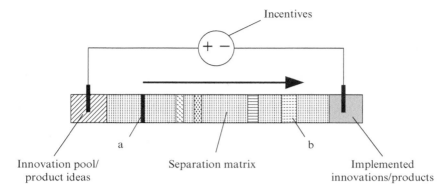

Source: Vulto, 2010.

*Figure 3.1   The innovation column: bands represent innovations of higher
(a) or lower (b) retention times*

column in (bio)analytical chemistry, such as is used in liquid or gas-chromatography or capillary electrophoresis. A separation column typically consists of a separation matrix, introducing retention of compounds by adsorption/desorption to the matrix (chromatography) or by sieving (electrophoresis). Retention times vary with the mesh density of the matrix, size of the compounds or affinity of the compounds to the matrix. Such techniques further employ a carrier liquid or gas, a sample containing the analytes of interest and a driving force, the driving force in chromatography being a pressure and in electrophoresis an electric potential.

This concept may be transformed by analogy into a model of knowledge conversion, the most obvious example being a scientific innovation and its transformation into a marketable product. This example needs an incentive (driving or motivational pressure) for scientists, entrepreneurs or others to start this process, typically money, but possibly recognition, social justice, career perspectives, honor, or perhaps even influence and power. Here we call this *commercialization pressure*. The innovation column also contains a separation matrix that introduces retention into the system. Without the separation matrix every idea will be directly, without delay, transformed into an implemented innovation (product). A representation of the innovation column is presented in Figure 3.1.

This implementation pathway is often cumbersome and time consuming, leading to some ideas reaching implementation (market) rather fast and others much more slowly. Yet others may never get there as they are too complicated, regulations are too strict or incentives too low. In other words some ideas migrate faster than others, thus a separation in time occurs, similar to the spatial separation in time of biomolecules in an electrophoresis experiment.

The innovation column concept provides a full analog model for examining the barriers to the transformation of knowledge into economically useful knowledge. It also adds an additional element in the concept of a 'driving force', which is an incentive (money or market pull, recognition, social justice, career development, power) to commercialize an idea. Beyond this there are a number of factors that determine the migration speed, or mobility of the knowledge (idea or innovation). These are determined by both external and inherent factors. The separation matrix represents external influences from the 'regional ecosystem' and includes aspects such as regional or university policy regulations, availability of entrepreneurship facilities, and availability of pre-seed, seed and venture capital. However, mobility of an innovation also depends on inherent properties of an idea, including its complexity, the business proposition and the quality of the invention. The driving potential may be determined by market demand or potential profit. The innovation column therefore models both 'technology push' and 'technology pull' cases. The commercialization pressure may represent both a market demand (technology pull) and the expectation of inventors that a technology will create a new market (technology push). The knowledge filter and knowledge absorption concepts are thus subsumed by ecosystem and separation matrix elements of the innovation column framework (Table 3.1).

To illustrate the various aspects of the innovation column, we consider a highly mobile innovation, i.e. an ICT innovation, such as an iPhone app, and an innovation of low mobility, i.e. a novel medicine. The first requires modest infrastructure, little investment and short development

Table 3.1   Influence of selected parameters on the 'mobility of knowledge'

Parameter	Influence on knowledge mobility
Idea complexity	negative
Concentration of ideas in the field	negative
Investment capital	positive
Suppliers	positive
Scientific climate	positive
Entrepreneurship facilities	positive
Role models	positive
Talent	positive

Source: Vulto, 2010.

times to reach the market. Moreover, regulations for such products are loose. The innovation will take little or no time to be implemented in the market and is rarely affected by the regional ecosystem. The introduction of a new medicine on the other hand faces a particularly restrictive separation matrix including a lengthy clinical trial procedure and FDA administration. For that reason, such an innovation requires huge investments, the nearby service organizations and a clear market demand. The slow mobility of such innovations can lead to retention times of over 12 years.

Table 3.1 presents knowledge filter and knowledge absorption aspects of the process whereby knowledge becomes economically useful. We now turn to a case study to illustrate the applicability of this conceptual and interpretive analysis.

A CASE STUDY: THE MASON ENTREPRENEURSHIP INITIATIVE

This case study focuses on technology transfer at George Mason University and its transformation from an internally focused to an externally focused program. By moving the program towards engagement with the surrounding entrepreneurial community, the program placed university-derived knowledge directly in the path of the knowledge filter.

Mason's historical viewpoints on knowledge creation and dissemination were very much shaped by its location. Mason is based in Northern Virginia, in a metropolitan region that includes Northern Virginia, Washington, DC and parts of Maryland. This region, often referred to as the National Capital Region or 'NCR,' is one of the wealthiest and most economically stable regions in the United States. The region has a population of more than 5 million, a large and highly educated labor force, and a level of per capita income at the high end of the United States cohort (see http://www.greaterwashington.org for more information). Much of the region's wealth creation and stability result from its proximity to the seat of the federal government and patterns of procurement of services, particularly in the areas of information technology, knowledge creation and sharing, and management. This co-dependence has created stability, and in times of expanding government expenditures, significant growth opportunities for commercial activities that were integrated with government procurement requirements. As a result, the NCR has exhibited exceptionally strong growth dynamics with unemployment rates among the lowest in the US.

As a result of the dominance of government spending to the local economy, the knowledge filter in the NCR and Northern Virginia has tended to channel entrepreneurial behavior into business opportunities that benefitted most directly from the available funding. For example, government programs that favor minority and women owned technology service companies have resulted in a large number of successful closely held businesses owned by underrepresented groups. As another example, the strong bias in the Department of Defense to acquire technology and products built from scratch, rather than off the shelf, has provided a bias for large vertically integrated service companies that can oversee the conception, creation and delivery of a product or service. Finally, government contracting rules and the dynamics of program manager oversight tend to drive business activity into contractual relationships which favor companies with scale, that can manage subcontracts and integrate services into a cogent delivery system. It also created a bias in favor of larger companies that could manage complex procurement programs and products.

These factors, and others, have shaped entrepreneurial activity, and have driven significant wealth creation for their owners, and also liquidity for smaller business owners through a healthy merger and acquisition market as the larger service and product integrators seek to enhance their own offerings.

Although the relationship between government spending and entrepreneurship has created many economic benefits for individual entrepreneurs and the NCR, it has also created a number of factors which make the region particularly vulnerable to changes in government spending and purchasing behavior. The largest risk is that government spending on services and products provided by the NCR declines. In addition to its structural co-dependence, the region also suffers from a unique, almost ironic challenge. Its success has created a high bar for entrepreneurial activity outside of the core. For example, the high quality human capital attracted to the regional economy has received salaries far above the national average. As a result, several counties in the region have median family incomes among the top 10 counties in the US. As another example, stability in commercial opportunities in this ecosystem has discouraged business model innovation, as business competition success was determined more by ability to deliver products and services effectively, than to modify a business model to differentiate or capture additional profits. In short, traditional models to explain commercial growth and success – changes in market behavior and positioning or consumer desires – are largely irrelevant. These factors, and others, have resulted in a region that is overly reliant on federal government spending, and comparatively inflexible. Ironically, the challenge for the NCR may be that its entrepreneur community has been too successful at converting government derived opportunities.

Notwithstanding the dominance of government derived entrepreneurial activities, the NCR has benefitted from the emergence of a smaller, and disconnected, entrepreneurial ecosystem in software and to a lesser extent life sciences that is less tightly engaged with providing products and services to the federal government. This ecosystem more closely resembles the company startup infrastructure of the Silicon Valley, and revolves around high growth technology startups focused on consumer and enterprise consumption of technology products rather than services. There have been two cycles of prominence of these activities in the NCR, a period from 1997 to 2001 which produced technology companies such as AOL, Webmethods and Medimmune, and a more recent trend commencing in 2009 and generating current technology companies such as Living Social and OPower. This entrepreneurial activity exists and operates independently of the core entrepreneurial ecosystem of the region, and is more tightly integrated with technology communities in Silicon Valley, New York and elsewhere than the NCR's dominant entrepreneurial ecosystem. This 'startup ecosystem' is challenged by the structural impediments of the NCR. For example, the high salaries and job security offered by the dominant entrepreneurial ecosystem inhibit for many the attractiveness of participating in a higher risk startup company. Notwithstanding the structural impediments, the startup ecosystem has benefitted from the concentration of wealth created by the dominant entrepreneurial ecosystem (through Angel capital and venture capital raised in the NCR) and in some instances the ability to sell products to government buyers.

Existing within these two distinct and largely disconnected entrepreneurial communities, Mason was also facing an issue of disconnection. In Mason's case it was an issue of being largely disconnected from both existing entrepreneurial ecosystems. George Mason University was founded in 1972 (see http://www.gmu.edu for more information) as a university intended to provide education for the growing population of Northern Virginia. As the Northern Virginia economy grew and the NCR developed, Mason's opportunities to acquire resources and support also grew. The university's research budget and opportunities for engagement in the larger community grew significantly, with a particular acceleration in Mason's development occurring since 2000. Today it is recognized as one of the most entrepreneurial and innovative universities in the country.

As Mason's focus changed from education to a broader mission of education, research and economic development, opportunities for knowledge creation and capture within the university increased. Its initial response to increased internal knowledge creation was to create a process to identify and protect commercially valuable knowledge through the establishment of a technology transfer office (TTO). The initial structure

and operation of the TTO was designed to encourage university employees to identify and protect technologies that they believed were commercially useful, and to base protection and commercialization efforts
largely on these beliefs. The resulting structure caused Mason to protect a
significant amount of knowledge without a consistent knowledge transfer
screen. Where questions of commercialization were analyzed the utilization of outside resources or engagement with the region's entrepreneurial
community was episodic and anecdotal. In 2010 the leadership of Mason
evaluated the university's positioning in the Northern Virginia regional
economy and determined that: (i) likely changes in federal government spending would result in significant changes in regional economic
development, (ii) the University's mission of research and knowledge
dissemination would be enhanced by increasing interaction with the
local entrepreneurial community, and (iii) the university was in a unique
market position, where it could connect the two existing entrepreneurial
communities in the region, and accentuate its own knowledge sharing
activities, by providing mechanisms to foster greater connection. The
mechanism that the university leadership chose was to embark on a
significant change in the university's process of knowledge protection
and transfer. The baseline concept was that the process of creating new
technology businesses – the combination of Mason derived knowledge,
with capital and entrepreneurial insight and commercial and market
orientation – would attract the interest of the broader community and
have the following benefits to the university: (i) enhanced conversion of
derived knowledge to commercially and socially beneficial activities, (ii)
tighter integration with the regional entrepreneurial community, creating
opportunities for sponsored research and business donations and (iii)
leadership of regional economic development.

To effect the change in its positioning and process, Mason dramatically
restructured its knowledge protection, evaluation and transfer capabilities.
The mission of Mason's technology transfer office was expressly modified
to include commercial potential as one of its criteria for the protection of
internally-generated knowledge. Secondarily, a bias was created in favor
of converting protected knowledge into opportunities to engage entrepreneurs in new business formation, rather than licensing knowledge to larger
established enterprises. This change to a 'company centric' development
model required a significant change in Mason. The primary motivation
behind this approach was to create for the NCR a path for the region's
technology community to be leveraged, and to create a process to integrate this entrepreneurial activity more closely with the broader regional
entrepreneurial infrastructure.

Given that the TTO culture had previously been inward-focused, an immediate goal of the reorientation of approach was to bring entrepreneurs, particularly technology entrepreneurs, into the knowledge review and transfer process. There were several reasons for adopting this strategy. First, for the culture to change to company centricity it was critical to involve entrepreneurs in the redesign and implementation of the transformation. Second, external entrepreneurs would be the agents who would have the experience and knowledge needed to convert Mason's knowledge into commercial products and socially relevant activities. Third, for the new approach to be successful Mason would need to have strong and deep relationships with the entrepreneur community to effectively assess the knowledge created by its faculty. Fourth, experienced entrepreneurs were the most likely filter for evaluating the suitability of knowledge as a basis for a commercial or social enterprise

To effect the required changes, Mason adopted a holistic business plan, which it referred to as the Mason Entrepreneurship Initiative or MEI. The MEI combined significant changes to Mason's approach to knowledge creation, protection and transfer, with changes in staffing and a revised process of knowledge review. The ultimate result of the MEI will be to transform Mason's knowledge creation from an isolated activity, driven by research, to an integrated process of knowledge creation, transfer and commercial relevance.

Internally, the university undertook a number of changes to effect the MEI. The first was a change in the composition of the TTO staff, bringing in professional management with experience in commercialization, technology enforcement and business creation. Additionally, the university leadership communicated with deans and academic unit leaders of changes in approach. The use of outside counsel with specific industry expertise was increased (because of their industry knowledge and contacts) and internal prosecution of intellectual property rights was deemphasized. These changes resulted in the university achieving greater cost efficiency on its knowledge protection activities.

To enhance interaction and involvement of the broader entrepreneurial activity, Mason first focused on the portion of the regional economy more likely to be open to interaction and the creation of new commercial opportunities. The MEI created a technology vetting group ('Vetting Group') composed of experienced serial technology entrepreneurs. The Vetting Group was tasked with reviewing Mason-derived knowledge with a commercial viewpoint, as well as to subsequently assist companies formed with Mason-knowledge.

A further level of entrepreneurial engagement was undertaken through the restructuring of the oversight of the TTO's commercialization. As is the case for all Virginia state universities, Mason's knowledge protection and commercialization activities are overseen by George Mason Intellectual Properties ('GMIP'), an independent not for profit entity that supports the university's knowledge conversion mission. The Board of Directors of GMIP were modified to reflect the broader entrepreneurial community; however, in the case of the GMIP Board, membership was drawn from both regional entrepreneurial communities, with the intention of helping Mason eventually broaden into both.

When the MEI was formed, an initial goal was for MEI's leadership to have sufficient prominence in the regional entrepreneurial community, to draw resources to the university, and to increase Mason's relevance to local entrepreneurs. The first Managing Director of MEI, Jonathan Aberman, is a well-known leader of the regional technology community. Through its relationship with Mr. Aberman, Mason was able to rapidly enhance its integration with the regional entrepreneurial community, and the MEI fostered the creation of new entrepreneur-driven groups that were independent of Mason but affiliated through common leadership. The most prominent example of this is FounderCorps, a regional not for profit composed of serial entrepreneurs based in the NCR. FounderCorps provides mentors and expertise to Mason TTO through the Vetting Group and sponsors entrepreneur focused educational opportunities throughout the NCR. Through FounderCorps Mason has been able to support both national (StartupAmerica) and state (the Governor's Year of the Entrepreneur) efforts to promote regional technology entrepreneurship, gain further access to entrepreneurs and build its prominence as a regional driver of entrepreneurial activity.

It is important to revisit the strategy of bringing the external entrepreneurship and business community into the operations of the Mason technology transfer program and by association more directly into its entrepreneurship incentive programs. Above we described the implementation of this strategy in terms of how we brought new external resources to patent evaluation issues, vetting of opportunities, negotiating modification of agreements, building appropriate pathways for development of intellectual property and disclosures and participating in finding and selecting appropriate entrepreneurs for partnering with inventors to commercialize their ideas. As a consequence of these efforts, a network among entrepreneurs is evolving and is resulting in a strong mutual supporting network of partners between members of these groups and Mason's technology transfer and entrepreneurial efforts.

Expanding on the initial success of MEI in integrating Mason into the technology entrepreneurship community, the second phase of the MEI has begun. This phase is designed to increase Mason's visibility and importance to the larger entrepreneurial community relating to government spending. To enhance this goal, Mason has acted to increase its attractiveness as a partner for federally funded research, in order to increase knowledge creation in areas that would be of relevance to the broader government related entrepreneurial community. University staffing has been modified to add professional leadership with direct experience in obtaining federally funded research opportunities and conversion into commercial opportunities.

Having created a revised process of knowledge protection, evaluation and commercialization, Mason's leadership anticipates that the coming dislocation in federal spending will disrupt local entrepreneurship patterns and 'free up' people and resources currently deployed in government related entrepreneurship. Plans to scale up the MEI include (i) increasing the knowledge created by the university through a significant growth in research, particularly federally funded research, (ii) forming a not for profit funding source to provide non dilutive grants to finance prototype development and business plan analysis and (iii) fostering the creation of a Mason-affiliated venture capital fund focused on technology commercialization and company formation.

The MEI, which has been operating since early 2011, has resulted in a significant improvement in the quality of startups being fostered by Mason, and a higher level of support being offered by Mason to its companies. Moreover, because these companies are often formed around technology developed through Federal research dollars, these companies are configured to bridge the technology entrepreneurship community with the broader entrepreneurial community of the NCR. For example, Invincea, a venture-backed Mason-derived spinout, is developing a secure web browser technology that has applicability for both consumer and government use, the initial development of which was financed by federal research. Another example is Percanthera, a personalized molecular medicine diagnostic company, based upon technology developed in material part through federal research grants.

This rather detailed discussion of specific aspects of the transformation of Mason's technology transfer program is presented to illustrate one organization impacted by the changing nature of the knowledge filter in the NCR and more specifically in the Northern Virginia part of the NCR. But it is helpful to illustrate this in terms of the innovation column model. While the example of the Mason Entrepreneurship Initiative is only one element of the economic ecosystem of the NCR the changes being made in that program can be illustrated in the changes in the parameters that define the knowledge filter and knowledge absorption factors and the direction of those changes. Table 3.2 illustrates where the contributions of the program changes contribute to improving knowledge

*Table 3.2   Influence of parameters on the 'mobility of knowledge': impact
of changes in the Mason OTT program on the NCR knowledge
filter and economic ecosystem*

Parameter	Influence on mobility
Idea complexity	negative
Concentration of ideas in the field	negative
Investment capital	positive+
Suppliers	positive+ (indirect)
Scientific climate	positive+
Entrepreneurship facilities	positive+
Role models	positive+
Talent	positive+

Note: The symbol '+' represents improved positive effect.

Source: Vulto, 2010.

filters. The transformation of the Mason program to a company centric philosophy and operation improves entrepreneurship facilities (institutional and infrastructural) directly, and by association creates improved role models, talent and in turn via feedback enhances the scientific climate of the university. It has also improved the capital availability by stimulating the early stage part of the existing venture capital industry and indirectly by stimulating an effort to establish a fund for Mason startup initiatives.

SUMMARY AND CONCLUSIONS

The chapter has achieved several goals. First, it has explicated the concept of the conversion of knowledge to economically useful ends. In that context it has explained the concepts of knowledge filter and knowledge absorption as they relate to the commercialization process. Then it introduces for the first time the innovation column model to provide a full synthesis of these concepts as they relate to knowledge commercialization. The innovation column model is an analog to separation columns used in bio(analytical) chemistry (Vulto, 2010). A case study of the transformation of the George Mason University technology transfer office from a patent centric design to a company centric orientation is then introduced. The specifics of the conversion process are examined and explained in terms of their contribution to a more facilitating knowledge filter and knowledge absorption conditions in Mason's region, the US National Capital Region. The innovation column model framework is used to illustrate the ways in which the move to a company centric approach has contributed a reduction in the barriers to knowledge commercialization in the region. Further research should focus on more case studies to inform policy and programmatic development at the region level, supporting knowledge commercialization as a key element of regional economic development.

NOTE

1. Throughout the chapter the reader should understand that the phrase economically useful knowledge is considered to be analogous to commercialized or marketable products and services.

REFERENCES

Acs, Z., D.B. Audretsch and M.P. Feldman (1994), 'R&D spillovers and recipient firm size', *Review of Economics and Statistics*, **76**, 336–40.

Acs, Z., D. Audretsch, P. Braunerhjelm and B. Carlsson (2004), 'The missing link: the knowledge filter and entrepreneurship in endogenous growth', Discussion Paper no. 4783, London, UK: Center for Economic Policy Research.

Acs, Z., P. Braunerhjelm, D. Audretsch and B. Carlsson (2009), 'The knowledge spillover theory of entrepreneurship', *Small Business Economics*, **32**, 15–30.

Audretsch, D. and E. Lehmann (2005), 'Does the knowledge spillover theory of entrepreneurship hold for regions?', *Research Policy*, **34**, 1191–1202.

Baumol, W.J. (1990), 'Entrepreneurship: productivity, unproductive, and destructive', *Journal of Political Economy*, **98** (5).

Chesbrough, H., W. Vanhaverbeke and J. West (eds) (2006), *Open Innovation: Researching a New Paradigm*, Oxford: Oxford University Press.

Kirzner, J. (1985), 'The entrepreneur in economic theory', in E. Dahmen, L. Hannah and I.M. Kirzner (eds) (1994), *The Dynamics of Entrepreneurship*, Lund: Lund University Press.

Qian, H., Zoltan J. Acs and Roger R. Stough (2012), 'Regional systems of entrepreneurship: the nexus of human capital, knowledge and new firm formation', *Journal of Economic Geography*, DOI: 10.1093/jeg/lbs009. Published online 23 April 2012.

Romer, P. (1986), 'Increasing returns and long run growth', *Journal of Political Economy*, **94**, 1002–37.

Romer, P.M. (1990), 'Endogenous technological change', *Journal of Political Economy*, **98**, S71–S102.

Schumpeter, J.A. (1934), *The Theory of Economic Development*, New York.

Solow, R.M. (1956), 'A contribution to the theory of economic growth', *Quarterly Journal of Economics*, **70**, 65–94.

Stimson, R., R. Stough and M. Salazar (2009), *Leadership and Institutions in*

Regional Endogenous Development, Cheltenham, UK and Northampton, MA, USA: Edward Elgar.

Vulto, P. (2010), 'The Innovation Column: separating the fast from the slow', unpublished manuscript, The Hague, Netherlands.

Williamson, O.E. (1994), *Institutions and Economic Organization – The Governance Perspective*, Washington, DC: World Bank.

4. University engagement and knowledge commercialization: an analysis of faculty attitudes

Harvey Goldstein and Alexander Rehbogen

1. INTRODUCTION

The 'entrepreneurial turn' of universities has a number of faces. Research universities are widely perceived to be important assets and actors in helping states and regions become and remain competitive in the globalized, knowledge-based economy. Indeed, the well-known, traditional tripartite mission of public research universities, of teaching, research, and public service, has now become a four-part mission with the addition of economic development. While state legislatures may use a subtle set of sticks and carrots for universities to become engaged in activities to promote economic development, there is also a sense of social responsibility by university officials and research faculty to be engaged in economic development, in exchange for the privileges and benefits they receive as both organizations and as individual researchers. At the same time, almost all research universities in the US, both public and private, have been motivated to become more involved in the commercialization of knowledge in order to diversify research funding sources, to more generally improve their revenue picture and endowments, and to retain and attract entrepreneurially inclined faculty and graduate students.

While university engagement in assisting economic development, on the one hand, and universities' commercialization of knowledge, on the other, might be seen as a continuum of highly overlapping activities, we hypothesize that these activities may be quite distinct in terms of the institutional and individual norms that guide attitudes and behavior within universities, and their perceived appropriateness. Specifically, we suggest that the Mertonian norms of open science (Merton 1973), still widely upheld by individual faculty, are perceived by faculty as in conflict with commercialization, but not in conflict with engagement in regional economic development. Using a web-based attitudinal survey of university faculty in the US, we explore the structure of attitudes towards these two faces of academic entrepreneurship. The results will shed light on the prospects of universities being able to act entrepreneurially and at the same time preserve a set of norms that are valuable, if not necessary, for universities to be able to continue the important fiduciary role given to them by society.

The next section provides a brief review of the relevant literature, followed in section 3 by a description of the study population and data. Section 4 provides a descriptive analysis of the survey responses. In section 5 we present our hypotheses and report on the results of a factor analysis performed on the data. The last section summarizes the main conclusions from our research and draws several implications of these results for universities continuing on the entrepreneurial path after making the 'turn'.

2.   LITERATURE REVIEW

There is by now a large extant literature on academic entrepreneurship. A comprehensive literature review is found in Rothaermel et al. (2007). This literature spans both positive and normative dimensions of universities engaging in patenting and other forms of commercialization, including the opportunities and threats posed by the 'entrepreneurial turn' (e.g. Etzkowitz et al. 2000; Bok 2003), the impacts of intellectual property laws and regulations on university technology transfer activities (e.g., Mowery et al. 2001; Murray 2006; Litan et al. 2007), the productivity and effectiveness of university technology transfer offices (Thursby and Kemp 2002; Siegel et al. 2004), and motivations for, and explanations of, entrepreneurial behavior within the academy (e.g, Owen-Smith and Powell 2001; Stuart and Ding 2006).

There is also a fairly large literature on the emergence and growth of an entrepreneurial culture within universities, with implications for norms that govern or guide behavior as well as institutional policies and priorities. Etzkowitz et al. (2000) have argued that the traditional norms governing or guiding behavior within universities will (and should) change to adapt to the entrepreneurial turn. Clark (1998, 2001) and Davies (2001) use a broader concept of academic entrepreneurship and suggest the behavior of some universities to adapt and adjust to an altered set of external demands and even to take advantage of new opportunities such as greater autonomy does not necessarily imply erosion of the hallmark of institutions of higher education as places of open and free inquiry. Yet one of the most oft-discussed potential impacts of the entrepreneurial turn is whether it has led to an erosion of the norms of open science. Analyzing survey data of about 700 natural scientists in Japan, Shibayama (2010) concluded that the norm of making 'practical' contributions, and the norms of open science are determined independently. In other words, they are not perceived to be inherently conflictual, leaving open the possibility that academic entrepreneurship can be promoted by universities without compromising the norms of open science. Ambos et al. (2008) consider the institutional, organizational, and individual attributes that allow university researchers to reconcile the conflicting demands (and norms) of academic research and commercialization and thus behave 'ambidextrously'.

While the attitudes of faculty and other university-based researchers actively involved in knowledge commercialization have been studied (e.g. Blumenthal et al. 1996; Louis et al. 2001), there have been relatively few attempts to systematically gauge the attitudes of a broad range of university faculty towards the university's 'entrepreneurial turn', whether they are actually engaged in commercialization activities or not, with the exception of Lee (1996).

Lee surveyed faculty in 115 research universities in the US from nine different disciplinary groupings in the natural sciences, engineering, and the social sciences. They were asked questions about whether they approved of changes in evaluative standards of faculty performance with respect to weighing user-oriented research and patentable inventions, and whether they were in agreement with a variety of university roles involving industry collaboration. The results of Lee's study were that:

(1) a large majority of faculty respondents were in favor of changes in the criteria for evaluating faculty performance by giving weight to 'user-oriented research' and patentable inventions and this represented an increase from the 1980s;
(2) a majority of respondents said they agreed with their universities actively participating in local and regional development, facilitating commercialization of university-based research, and encouraging faculty to engage in consulting for private firms; but
(3) a majority did not support their universities providing start-up assistance or making equity investments in private firms.

Lee's 1996 study suggests that while there is broad (and growing) acceptance of some aspects of the 'entrepreneurial turn', there are other activities or roles – those that pose the greatest perceived threats to the 'core values of the research university' (Lee 1996, p. 860) – that are opposed by a significant portion of faculty members.

In part as an alternative response to some of the same pressures that have driven universities to become actively involved in knowledge commercialization, many universities in the US have rededicated themselves to the ideal of 'public engagement'. With a long tradition rooted in the land-grant colleges' and universities' activity of cooperative extension, perhaps best exemplified in the 'Wisconsin idea' (Ward 1992), the engaged university represents:

> ... the partnership of university knowledge and resources with those of the public and private sectors to enrich scholarship, research, and creative activity; enhance curriculum, teaching, and learning; prepare educated, engaged citizens; strengthen democratic values and civic responsibility; address critical societal issues; and contribute to the public good. (CIC Committee on Engagement 2005)

Even within the domain of university-industry collaboration, there are activities that fall within the sphere of engagement rather than commercialization. These include consulting, joint research, and training, in contrast to patenting and licensing and spin-off activities (D'Este and Patel 2007).

As university involvement in academic entrepreneurship has clearly increased over the last twenty years, so have the attitudes, for and against, changed. These attitudes, we suspect, are more complex, because there are a number of different impacts generated by academic entrepreneurship, and their valuations vary among actors. For example, many faculty may believe that technology-based start-ups by university staff are appropriate because they can enhance the innovativeness and hence the competitiveness of the regional economy. On the other hand, faculty may perceive that the same activities can also lead to thorny conflicts of interest or dilute the quality of more basic, scholarly research.

In this chapter we analyze the relationships among attitudes towards different dimensions of academic entrepreneurship, including public engagement, by university faculty in the US. Using factor analysis, we address what is the underlying structure of faculty attitudes towards two forms of academic entrepreneurship, engagement and commercialization, and to what degree attitudes towards knowledge commercialization and belief in open science are compatible.

3.   STUDY POPULATION AND DATA

The study population for the survey consists of faculty from eight selected disciplines from all research universities in the US. A random sample of 71 universities stratified by public land-grant, public non land-grant, and private, was drawn from the population of research universities in the US in the 'Very high' and 'High' research intensive categories.[1] The resulting sample is shown in Table 4.1.

Table 4.1   Sample of research universities: US

Research intensity*	Public land-grant	Public non land-grant	Private	Total
Very high	13	13	16	42
High	7	14	8	29
Total	20	27	24	71

Note: *Based upon Carnegie Foundation for the Advancement of Teaching (2006), Classification of Institutions of Higher Education.

The eight disciplines are biological sciences, physics, computer science, chemical engineering, economics, political science, history, and English. They were selected based upon their: ubiquity among research universities, variation in the approaches and styles of inquiry and knowledge production using the Stokes (1997) typology, and variation in the likelihood of opportunities for faculty to produce research that has potential for commercialization.[2] For each of the eight academic departments in the 71 research universities, one tenured or tenure-track faculty member was randomly selected from each academic rank: assistant, associate, and full professor, plus the department chairperson. The web page of each department was used to provide the full listing of tenured and tenure-track faculty from which the particular faculty members were drawn for the final sample. A total of 2148 faculty members were sent web-based questionnaires in January 2007, of which 112 were returned as undeliverable. After several follow-ups to non-respondents, we ended up with 547 usable responses for an effective response rate of 25.5 percent.

A set of attitudinal questions were included in the survey questionnaire. Faculty were asked to indicate on a five point Likert-scale if they: strongly agree (coded 5), agree (4), neither agree nor disagree (3), disagree (2), or strongly disagree (1) with each statement.

The questions are intended to either directly reveal attitudes towards at least two different faces of academic entrepreneurship – university engagement and knowledge commercialization – or underlying belief structures that are considered to affect attitudes. The belief structures include degree of commitment to the norms of open science, and the degree of commitment to the separation of personal financial interest from the roles of faculty members as researchers and teachers. We discuss each question, in terms of how we interpret the responses as measures of the conceptual categories of academic entrepreneurship and the underlying norms.

Q1   My university, in addition to its basic functions of teaching and research, should be actively and directly involved in assisting state and regional economic development   This provides a direct way to measure acceptance of the idea that universities have a larger societal obligation beyond the traditional missions of teaching and advancement of knowledge, and specifically to help improve regional economic conditions by bringing to bear knowledge and expertise. This role does not necessarily exclude knowledge commercialization as a means to improve regional economic development, but it is broader and implies an institutional commitment to social responsibility in return for receiving public resources.

Q2   My university should encourage and reward faculty for providing technical and/or managerial assistance to existing business organizations located in the region or state   Providing technical or managerial assistance to existing regional businesses is a more specific means of universities assisting regional economic development, but compared to the broader role in question 1, the 'public good' dimension of this role is given up since the beneficiaries are individual businesses.

Q3   My university should be actively involved in the commercialization of university-based academic research   This question very directly probes the respondent's views that a legitimate mission of the modern research university is to pro-actively assist and encourage university researchers to commercialize their research when there is a potential market.

Q4   My university should provide start-up assistance for technology-oriented firms that grow out of university-based research   Providing assistance to start-ups that grew out of university research is a direct form of knowledge commercialization and with the university possibly having a financial interest in helping such start-ups.

Q5   My university should make equity investments in technology-oriented start-up businesses that grow out of university-based research   This activity explicitly includes a university financial interest in the generation of technology-based start-up businesses as a form of knowledge commercialization. It places the university in the role of a venture capitalist typically where the university's investments are high risks.

Q6   My university should encourage and reward faculty to engage in user-oriented, proprietary research with industry funding   This university policy is aimed at increasing research funding from private industry sources. Seeking new and under-exploited sources of research funding helps universities to move up in the National Science Foundation rankings and incidentally to enhance their prestige. The policy described focuses on conducting applied research, which can be construed as a form of engagement, but it is also proprietary, which can mean restrictions on the dissemination of research results.

Q7   My university should reward faculty who produce a patentable invention at least the same amount of credit as a peer-reviewed article when making tenure and promotion decisions   This is another policy aimed at giving 'weight' to a form of knowledge commercialization – patentable inventions – as part of the reward structure for faculty performance and productivity. The policy enlarges the scope of what has been understood to be scholarly achievement in most research universities, so as to create incentives for junior faculty to engage in commercialization.

Q8   Knowledge creation is best measured by scholarly, peer-review publications   This statement is intended to indicate the respondent's views on one of the norms of open science, peer review. It also identifies distinctions in views about the concept of knowledge: restricted to traditional, basic, scholarly knowledge, on the one hand, or inclusive of user-oriented knowledge.

Q9   Unfettered inquiry and the free exchange of ideas are important in my work   This statement also focuses on the degree of commitment to the central norms of open science. It counterposes any restrictions being placed on *what* is researched and on the dissemination of results.

Q10   The increasing emphasis within many universities for commercializing university research threatens the quality of basic, scholarly research   This expresses a perception that one of the major harms of commercialization within universities is a substitution of effort and resources from basic, 'scientific' research, to user-oriented research, leading to a long-term loss in the production of cutting-edge scholarship.

Q11   A full-time faculty member on average spends more than one day per week consulting   This scenario poses a situation where the respondent may feel there is a conflict of interest introduced between personal financial interest – expressed as spending more than the 'customary' time for consulting – and meeting the teaching, research, service, and other obligations of a faculty member and university employee.

Q12   It is legitimate for scholarly findings to be delayed for circulation and peer review for six months in order to benefit the private industry funding source   This statement is specifically about restrictions on dissemination of research results, and generally about the respondent's degree of commitment to the norms of open science.

Q13   A faculty member supervises a graduate student's dissertation research when the research is funded by a private company and the faculty member has a financial interest in that company   The scenario poses another possible conflict-of-interest situation, between the financial interest of the faculty member and the role of mentor and supervisor for the training of future scholars.

Q14   A faculty member has a research contract with a company in which the faculty member has a financial interest   This is a variant of the scenario in Q13. Since it does not involve the role of supervising graduate students, however, it focuses just on the potential harm of the faculty member slanting, and/or restricting dissemination, of his/her own research results when there is a financial interest involved.

4.   DESCRIPTIVE RESULTS

The percentages of respondents who disagree or strongly disagree with selected questions/statements above are shown in Table 4.2, disaggregated by discipline. First, looking at the total, all disciplines combined, the results show distinctions in the attitudes towards the various faces of academic entrepreneurship. Universities taking an active engagement role in assisting regional economic development has strong acceptance by faculty – only 14.9 percent disagree or strongly disagree – while there is substantial higher incidence of disapproval of knowledge commercialization (32.5 percent). More than 60 percent of respondents disapprove of delaying the dissemination of scholarly findings in order to benefit a private industry funding source.

There is also substantial variation in the attitudes towards knowledge commercialization among disciplines. Generally, faculty from economics, political science, history (the North disciplines) plus English are less approving of academic entrepreneurship, and faculty from computer science (a Pasteur discipline) are more approving. On the other hand, there are consistently high levels of approval of universities assisting regional economic development across all disciplines.

The degree of disapproval of academic entrepreneurship by faculty respondents who have previously received private industry research funding within the last five years should serve as a type of 'benchmark', since this subset of respondents would be expected to be most approving of various forms of academic entrepreneurship relative to virtually all other

Table 4.2 Faculty attitudes by academic discipline

	Percent respondents who disagree or strongly disagree								
	Bio (N=70)	CS (62)	Econ (65)	ChEngr (54)	Engl (84)	Hist (82)	Phys (63)	PolSci (68)	ALL (N=548)
My university should:									
Assist in state and regional economic development**	15.8	8.0	20.0	14.8	15.5	13.4	12.7	19.1	14.9
Be actively involved in commercialization of research**	22.9	14.5	23.4	20.4	53.0	57.4	15.9	36.5	32.5
Assist in starting up businesses from university research**	41.4	27.5	44.6	32.0	61.2	61.0	30.2	43.5	44.2
Make equity investments in start-ups from university research**	35.7	30.7	44.6	42.6	45.9	56.1	29.0	48.4	42.1
Reward faculty for engaging in user-oriented, proprietary research**	35.7	25.8	33.8	37.0	51.7	61.0	42.9	32.3	41.2
Reward faculty for patentable inventions in tenure decisions	21.4	24.2	27.7	22.3	19.0	10.9	19.1	19.3	20.3
'Dissemination of scholarly findings are delayed to benefit private industry funding source' **	70.1	58.6	49.2	37.7	67.1	61.6	66.7	67.2	60.3

Note: ** Chi-square significant @ 0.01.

Table 4.3   Faculty attitudes by previous industry funding

	Percent respondents who disagree or strongly disagree	
	Industry funding (N= 103)	No industry funding (427)
My university should:		
Assist in state and regional economic development	14.6	15.0
Be actively involved in commercialization of research**	17.5	35.7
Assist in starting up businesses from university research**	32.4	46.9
Make equity investments in start-ups from university research**	34.3	43.6
Reward faculty for conducting proprietary research**	34.0	43.6
Reward faculty for patentable inventions in tenure decisions**	16.7	21.9
'Dissemination of scholarly findings are delayed to benefit private industry funding source'**	50.5	63.0

Note: ** Chi-square significant at 0.001.

categories. In Table 4.3 we see that while recipients of private industry funding have clearly more favorable attitudes towards academic entrepreneurship generally, there remain a significant percentage of such faculty members who do not agree with many of the faces of entrepreneurship.

When we look at differences in faculty attitudes by type of university in Table 4.4, there is a generally higher level of disapproval of both engagement and commercialization by faculty from private universities, and only minor differences between faculty in land-grant universities and non land-grant public universities. What is perhaps most striking is the difference in approval for the university engagement role in regional economic development: only about 11 percent of faculty from public universities disapprove, while the percentage of disapproval from private universities is doubled to 22 percent. For faculty in public universities, their institutions' engagement in regional economic development can be regarded as close to consensual and non-controversial.

Finally, it is reasonable to expect that faculty attitudes towards both engagement and commercialization may be affected by regional economic

Table 4.4   Faculty attitudes by type of university

	Percent who disagree or strongly disagree		
	Public non LG (N = 172)	Public LG (202)	Private (173)
My university should . . .			
Assist state and regional economic development**	10.3	12.2	22.1
Be actively involved in commercialization	30.5	33.2	32.4
Provide assistance to start-ups from university research	44.4	44.1	42.1
Make equity investments in start-ups from university research	40.8	46.5	37.7
Reward faculty for engaging in proprietary research**	35.1	40.5	48.0
Reward faculty for patentable inventions in tenure decisions	16.7	16.2	28.5
'Dissemination of scholarly findings is delayed to benefit private industry funding source'	61.0	57.9	62.6

Notes:
LG: land-grant institution.
** t significant @ 0.001.

conditions. Classifying faculty respondents by whether the annual unemployment rate of their respective region was low, medium or high relative to the national unemployment (UE) rate (4.6 percent in 2006), we display in Table 4.5 the percentage who disagreed or strongly disagreed with selected dimensions of academic entrepreneurship. Respondents in regions with high unemployment rates were much more likely to approve their university assisting regional economic development compared to respondents coming from regions with mid-level unemployment rates. Curiously, respondents from regions with the lowest unemployment rates were more likely to approve university assistance in regional economic development compared to their counterparts in the mid-level UE regions. This is perhaps because they perceive the need to be pro-active in sustaining regional economic vitality, or have witnessed the positive economic development effects of previous university assistance.

A similar pattern is revealed when we look at the percentage of faculty respondents who oppose or strongly oppose knowledge commercialization, though the differences across levels of unemployment are not as

Table 4.5   Faculty attitudes by regional economic condition

	Percent who disagree or strongly disagree		
	Low UE (N = 221)	Medium UE (264)	High UE (66)
My university should . . .			
Assist state and regional economic development**	10.9	20.1	6.1
Be actively involved in commercialization	29.9	36.0	25.8
Provide assistance to start-ups from university research	42.5	45.0	46.2
Make equity investments in start-ups from university research	39.9	44.7	37.9
Reward faculty for engaging in proprietary research**	38.6	46.9	27.7
Reward faculty for patentable inventions in tenure decisions	20.2	21.4	16.7
'Dissemination of scholarly findings is delayed to benefit private industry funding source'	61.1	61.6	52.4

Note: ** t significant @ 0.001.

dramatic. Respondents in regions with the highest levels of unemployment are less likely to disapprove commercialization activities compared to those in other regions, but respondents in the lowest UE regions are less likely to disapprove than their counterparts in mid-level UE regions.

Overall, the descriptive analysis results indicate that the condition of the regional economy is related to faculty attitudes towards university involvement in regional economic development and in knowledge commercialization, though the relationship is neither a simple one nor necessarily significant when controlling for other factors that may be more important in helping form attitudes.

5.   FACTOR ANALYSIS OF ATTITUDES TOWARDS THE MULTIPLE FACES OF ACADEMIC ENTREPRENEURSHIP

To examine the relationships among attitudes towards the different dimensions of academic entrepreneurship we employ factor analysis. Factor analysis allows us to view the underlying multivariate structure of correlations among the variables by conveying the variation from the original set of variables into a more parsimonious set of new variables, or factors. The original variables entered in the analysis are the responses to the 14 questions listed above. We specifically are interested in what the relationship is between faculty attitudes towards university engagement, on the one hand, and knowledge commercialization, on the other. But we also are able to investigate to what extent the norms of open science and perception of ethical conflicts of interest are associated with commercialization.

The questions that reveal attitudes towards university engagement are Q1 and Q2; questions that reveal attitudes towards knowledge commercialization are Q3, Q4, Q5, Q7 and Q10; questions that reveal attitudes towards the norms of open science are Q6, Q8, Q9 and Q12; and questions that reveal attitudes towards potential conflicts of interest are Q11, Q13, and Q14. Our working hypotheses are that (i) attitudes towards university engagement and knowledge commercialization are largely independent; (ii) adherence to the norms of open science will be inconsistent with positive attitudes towards knowledge commercialization; (iii) negative attitudes towards knowledge commercialization are associated with disapproval of behavior that potentially poses conflicts of interest among roles for faculty members.

The factor loadings after using a varimax rotation are shown in Table 4.6 (the full correlation matrix is shown in Appendix Table 4A.1).[3] There are four distinct factors that have eigenvalues above the threshold of 1.0, and which collectively explain 60.4 percent of the total variance in the data.

Factor 1, accounting for 26.3 percent of the total variance, has high positive loadings on Q1–Q7 and a negative loading on Q10. Q1–Q7 include all dimensions of academic entrepreneurship activities, including engagement in addition to knowledge commercialization. A negative loading on Q10 means that those who believe that all the activities are appropriate tend also to believe that commercialization does not threaten scholarly research quality.

Factor 2, accounting for 14.7 percent of the total variance, has high positive loadings on Q12, Q13, and Q14. It is interpreted as attitudes regarding conflicts between faculty acting in the interests of private industry in which faculty have a financial interest and/or from which they receive research funding, and their responsibilities and obligations to their students and colleagues.

Factor 3, which adds 9.7 percent of the total variance explained, has high positive loadings on Q8 and Q9, but also a moderate positive loading on Q10, belief that knowledge commercialization threatens the quality of

Table 4.6   Rotated component matrix[a]

	Component			
	1	2	3	4
Q1-RED	.606	.041	.183	.419
Q2-TA	.668	.059	.038	.476
Q3-Comm	.772	.270	−.043	−.100
Q4-Startup	.778	.192	.011	−.019
Q5-Equity	.725	.140	−.006	−.034
Q6-ProprR	.669	.184	−.161	.181
Q7-Patent	.477	−.138	−.302	.382
Q8-PeerR	.009	.118	.742	−.363
Q9-FreeEx	−.068	−.282	.721	.166
Q10-Threat	−.592	−.306	.348	.196
Q11-Consult	−.051	.277	−.076	.687
Q12-Delay	.138	.577	−.086	.295
Q13-StdCOI	.188	.815	−.048	.044
Q14-FacCOI	.231	.783	−.029	.023

Notes:
Extraction method: Principal component analysis.
Rotation method: Varimax with Kaiser normalization.
[a] The rotation converged in 9 iterations.

basic research. This factor is interpreted as beliefs in the importance of the norms of open science.

Finally, factor 4, accounting for another 9.7 percent of the total variance, has high positive loadings on Q11, Q1, and Q2. It has somewhat lower loadings on Q7, approval of rewarding faculty for patentable inventions in tenure and promotion decisions, and Q8, belief (negative) in the importance of peer review in publication outlets. This factor is interpreted as attitudes towards engagement, albeit offering greater discretion to faculty in how and how much they are engaged outside of their university responsibilities, since consulting for more than the 'standard' one day per week has such a high (positive) loading.

Factor scores are the normalized values for the new variables (factors) for each observation.[4] The mean factor scores for particular categories of faculty respondents are shown in Tables 4.7 to 4.9 and allow us to identify those likely to hold maximal approving or disapproving views on each of the four factors.

Categories of faculty most likely to have favorable attitudes towards academic entrepreneurship overall (factor 1) are those in computer science, and to a lesser extent biology, while those in English and history

Table 4.7   Factor scores by academic discipline

Discipline		Factor Score 1***	Factor Score 2***	Factor Score 3**	Factor Score 4**
Biology	Mean	.3390	−.0689	.1980	−.3296
	N	66	66	66	66
	Std. Deviation	1.074	.9385	.8782	.8365
Computer	Mean	.5610	.3223	−.1935	−.0503
Science	N	57	57	57	57
	Std. Deviation	.8827	1.096	1.045	1.059
Economics	Mean	−.1857	.3577	−.3389	−.0954
	N	62	62	62	62
	Std. Deviation	.9146	.8993	1.212	1.228
Engineering	Mean	.1970	.5106	−.0018	−.0834
	N	51	51	51	51
	Std. Deviation	1.128	1.034	.9754	.9344
English	Mean	−.4089	−.4531	.0886	.2725
	N	77	77	77	77
	Std. Deviation	.9608	.8676	1.001	1.015
History	Mean	−.4827	−.3544	.2504	.2294
	N	76	76	76	76
	Std. Deviation	.8316	.8730	.9074	.7964
Physics	Mean	.2746	.1961	.1016	−.1572
	N	57	57	57	57
	Std. Deviation	.7833	.8570	.9768	1.027
Political	Mean	−.0144	−.2613	−.2419	.1408
Science	N	57	57	57	57
	Std. Deviation	.8955	1.013	.8671	.9557
Total	Mean	.0000	.0000	.0000	.0000
	N	508	508	508	508
	Std. Deviation	1.000	1.000	1.000	1.000

Notes:
*** Significant at 0.001.
** Significant at 0.01.

are most likely to be disapproving of academic entrepreneurship as a whole. Those in public universities (both land-grant and non land-grant) are more favourable to academic entrepreneurship than those in private universities, as are those located in regions with mid levels of economic distress, vis á vis low or high levels.

Those most sensitive to potential conflicts of interest posed by academic entrepreneurship (factor 2) are those in biology, English, and history, while those in chemical engineering, economics, and computer science are least troubled by potential conflicts of interest. There are no significant

Table 4.8   Factor scores by type of university

University Type		Factor score 1*	Factor score 2	Factor score 3	Factor score 4***
Public	Mean	.1452	.0091	−.0183	.1333
Non-LG	N	161	161	161	161
	Std. Deviation	1.014	1.038	.9803	.8762
Public L-G	Mean	.0101	−.0183	.0419	.1709
	N	186	186	186	186
	Std. Deviation	1.023	1.047	.9445	1.033
Private	Mean	−.1569	.0119	−.0301	−.3308
	N	161	161	161	161
	Std. Deviation	.9388	.9059	1.082	1.002
Total	Mean	.0000	.0000	.0000	.0000
	N	508	508	508	508
	Std. Deviation	1.000	1.000	1.000	1.000

Notes:
*   Significant at 0.05.
***   Significant at 0.01.

Table 4.9   Factor scores by regional economic condition

UE category		Factor Score 1**	Factor Score 2	Factor Score 3	Factor Score 4**
High UE	Mean	.1159	.0534	−.0291	.3488
	N	60	60	60	60
	Std. deviation	.8249	1.038	.9105	.8540
Low UE	Mean	−.5289	−.1111	.0149	.0108
	N	202	202	202	202
	Std. deviation	1.051	1.042	1.079	1.062
Med UE	Mean	−.1538	.0782	−.0052	−.0940
	N	246	246	246	246
	Std. deviation	.9759	.9495	.9554	.636
Total	Mean	.0000	.0000	.0000	.0000
	N	508	508	508	508
	Std. deviation	1.000	1.000	1.000	1.000

Note:
**   Significant at 0.01.

differences in the scores on this factor across types of university and regional economic conditions.

Faculty in economics, and to a lesser extent those in political science and computer science, are less likely to be concerned with the affect of knowledge commercialization on the norms of open science, while faculty in history and biology are the most concerned about this threat. There are no statistically significant differences on this factor across types of universities or across regional economic conditions.

Finally, faculty in history and English have the most supportive views of university engagement (factor 4), while those in biology are the least supportive of this role, and to a lesser extent those in physics. Faculty members in private universities have a significantly less favorable view on this role than colleagues in public universities, while faculty located in regions with relatively high levels of economic distress indicate considerably more favorable approval of this role compared to faculty in universities located in other types of regions.

The results reveal several interesting aspects of the relationships among the attitudes towards the dimensions of academic entrepreneurship. First, and consistent with the hypothesis posed earlier, faculty do perceive a distinction between the university activities of knowledge commercialization and engagement. That distinction, however, has some caveats and some additional complexity. The largest factor combines in the same direction, rather than separates, knowledge commercialization and engagement. It is only in the fourth factor that there is an uncoupling of engagement from academic entrepreneurship generally. The notion of engagement from our interpretation of the fourth factor is perhaps broader than serving the 'public interest' or working for the public good, since faculty serving as consultants in lieu of some of their university responsibilities is highly and positively loaded. Receiving credit for patentable inventions represents a change and broadening of the university's traditional reward system and seems to be perceived as a mechanism that allows faculty to become more engaged, not as an activity motivated primarily by personal financial gain.

Second, the results indicate that many faculty members believe that academic entrepreneurship generally, and commercialization specifically, can be compatible with strong and positive views on the norms of open science. This conclusion is based on the pattern of respective loadings of variables on factors 1 and 3. Moreover, positive attitudes towards academic entrepreneurship and negative attitudes towards situations of conflicts of interest between university responsibilities and private financial gain that comes with knowledge commercialization appear to be held simultaneously (factors 1 and 2)

Attitudes towards the norms of open science are independent of commercialization variables as well as of potential conflicts of interest.

Third, there are notable differences in views across disciplines, across types of universities, and across regional economic conditions between academic entrepreneurship generally (factor 1) and university engagement (factor 4). While faculty in the humanities, and to a lesser extent political science, are less likely to approve academic entrepreneurship in general but approve of university engagement, faculty from biology, physics, computer science and chemical engineering are more likely to approve academic entrepreneurship and either disapprove or be neutral about engagement, while faculty in economics are more likely to disapprove both academic entrepreneurship and university engagement. The differences in views across disciplines are consistent with the likelihood of opportunities for commercialization or engagement, so we cannot separate this from commitment to certain values or norms except in the case of economics, where there seems to be an ideological commitment of respondents away from active public sector or university institutional intervention in markets.

Faculty in private universities are less approving than their colleagues in public universities on both academic entrepreneurship and engagement. There is less of a social contract binding private universities to engagement on the one hand, and to commercialization activities for the sake of commitment to economic development on the other.

That faculty at universities in regions at the extremes on levels of economic distress are more likely to approve both academic entrepreneurship and engagement is understood as an attitude of 'continuing what has brought us success' on the one hand, and the perception of the need for universities to bring to bear their knowledge assets in high distress regions, on the other.

Figure 4.1 shows the relationship between factor scores on the dimensions of academic entrepreneurship and university engagement graphically for various categories of faculty respondents.

6.   CONCLUSIONS

We have analyzed the relationships among attitudes towards multiple dimensions of academic entrepreneurship held by faculty in US research universities. Both knowledge commercialization and engagement are 'on the rise'; they each represent ways that universities can demonstrate their responsiveness to external demands, as well as ways that the institutions can enhance their revenue (in the case of commercialization) and their attractiveness to entrepreneurially-minded faculty and graduate students

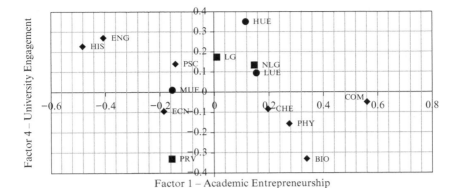

Factor 1 – Academic Entrepreneurship

Notes: ENG – english; HIS – history; PSC – political science; ECN – economics; CHE – chemical engineering; COM – computer science; PHY – physics; BIO – biological sciences; HUE – high unemployment regions; MUE – medium unemployment regions; LUE – low unemployment regions; LG – public, land-grant universities; NLG – public, non land-grant universities; PRV – private universities.

Figure 4.1   Factor scores: academic entrepreneurship and university engagement

who seek non-academic outlets for their scholarly and professional work. But still there are important differences. While university engagement has a long and generally noble tradition in the US, going back to the Morrill Act of 1865 which initiated the establishment of land-grant universities, knowledge commercialization is relatively new. It poses (to many) a putative threat to the widely-held norms of open science and involves situations rife with conflicts of interest.

Our factor analytic results indicate that, on the one hand, faculty in general perceive engagement and knowledge commercialization as activities on the same continuum of academic entrepreneurship, albeit with different levels of perceived conflicts or threats. But on the other hand, the respondents also indicate favorable or unfavorable attitudes towards university engagement – of faculty connecting with other actors and organizations outside of academia – that are largely independent of commercialization. This is seen most vividly when we examine the relationship between scores on factor 1, interpreted as academic entrepreneurship in general, and on factor 4, interpreted as university engagement. Somewhat surprising to us is that the attitude towards university engagement appears *not* to be motivated primarily as commitment to work for the common or public good, but rather to engage for engagement's sake, to extend the beneficiaries of their knowledge transmission and expertise beyond the ivory tower. In terms of threats posed by academic entrepreneurship, faculty separate erosion of the norms of open science from conflicts of interest between the faculty member fulfilling university and collegial responsibilities, and faculty member as entrepreneur with financial interests.

The results shed some new light on why faculty may approve or disapprove of different dimensions of academic entrepreneurship. Attitudes towards knowledge commercialization are bound up with one's degree of commitment to the norms of open science and to the risks one perceives of conflicts of interest. These results reinforce the importance of universities being able to safeguard long-cherished norms of open science and taking steps to enforce conflict of interest policies, not relaxing them, as they proceed further on the path of entrepreneurialism.

NOTES

1. Public, land-grant universities are a subset of public universities originally created by legislation of the US Congress (Morill Acts of 1862 and 1890). They historically had the special mission of teaching the practical subjects of agriculture, applied science, and engineering, and specializing in research related to the needs of the states' agricultural and industrial sectors. In general there is designated one land-grant university per state.
   The Carnegie Foundation for the Advancement of Teaching has a widely used classification system of all institutions of higher education in the US. Their latest classification has three categories of doctoral-granting universities. Doctoral-granting are those that awarded a minimum of 20 doctorate degrees in 2003–04. Within 'Doctoral granting' are three sub-categories: Research university/Very high intensity (RU/VH); Research university/High intensity (RU/H); and doctoral granting (DRU). Assignment of an institution to one of these sub-categories is based upon a set of multiple indicators of the amount of research activity that occurs within the institution. Based upon the Carnegie classification in 2006, there were 96 RU/VH institutions, 103 RU/H institutions, and 87 DRU institutions.
2. Biology and physics fit within Stokes's 'Bohr disciplines', and computer science and chemical engineering are 'Pasteur disciplines'. Extending Stokes's typology, economics and political science can be considered 'North disciplines', as they provide the theoretical and conceptual backing for institutional arrangements (Bergman 2009). English and history are not considered scientific disciplines.
3. We conducted factor analyses using equamax and quartimax rotations to test the robustness of the results to the choice of rotation algorithms. The differences in results were negligible. We also conducted the analysis with data from only the Pasteur and Bohr disciplines, and the results were substantially different.
4. Because factors are linear combinations of original variables with different scales, factor scores are normalized with means = 0.0 and the standard deviations = 1.0.

REFERENCES

Ambos, T.C., K. Mäkelä, J. Birkinshaw and P. D'Este (2008), 'When does university research get commercialized? Creating ambidexterity in research institutions', *Journal of Management Studies*, **45**, 1424–47.

Bergman, E.M. (2009), 'Marshall's dilemma: intangible assets and European universities', IAREG Working Paper 1.3.e, p. 29.

Blumenthal, D., E.G. Campbell, N. Causino and K.S. Louis (1996), 'Participation of life-science faculty in research relationships with industry', *New England Journal of Medicine*, **335**, 1734–9.

Bok, D. (2003), *Universities in the Marketplace: The Commercialization of Higher Education*, Princeton, US: Princeton University Press.

Carnegie Foundation for the Advancement of Teaching (2006), www.carnegie foundation.org/classification.

CIC Committee on Engagement (2005), *Resource Guide and Recommendations for Defining and Benchmarking Engagement*, Champaign, US: Committee on Institutional Cooperation.

Clark, B. (1998), 'The entrepreneurial university: demand and response', *Tertiary Education and Management*, **4** (1), 5–16.

Clark, B. (2001), 'The entrepreneurial university: new foundations for collegiality, autonomy, and achievement', *Higher Education Management*, **13** (2), 9–24.

D'Este, P. and P. Patel (2007), 'University-industry linkages in the UK: what are the factors underlying the variety of interactions with industry?', *Research Policy*, **36**, 1295–313.

Davies, J.L. (2001), 'The emergence of entrepreneurial cultures in European universities', *Higher Education Management*, **13** (2), 25–43.

Etzkowitz, H., A. Webster, C. Gebhardt and B.R.C. Terra (2000), 'The future of the university and the university of the future: evolution of ivory tower to entrepreneurial paradigm', *Research Policy*, **29**, 313–30.

Lee, Y.S. (1996), 'Technology transfer and the research university: a search for the boundaries of university-industry collaboration', *Research Policy*, **25**, 843–63.

Litan, R.E., L. Mitchell, and E.J. Reedy (2007), 'Commercializing university innovations: a better way', NBER Working Paper (April), Cambridge, US: National Bureau of Economic Research.

Louis, K.S., L.M. Jones, M.S. Anderson, D. Blumenthal, and E.G. Campbell (2001), 'Entrepreneurship, secrecy, and productivity: a comparison of clinical and non-clinical life sciences faculty', *Journal of Technology Transfer*, **26**, 233–45.

Merton, R.K. (1973), *The Sociology of Science*, Chicago, US: University of Chicago Press.

Mowery, D., R. Nelson, B. Sampat and A. Ziedonis (2001), 'The growth of patenting and licensing by U.S. universities: an assessment of the effects of the Bayh-Dole Act of 1980', *Research Policy*, **30**, 99–119.

Murray, F. (2006), 'The oncomouse that roared: resistance and accommodation to patenting in academic science', unpublished manuscript, MIT Sloan School of Management, February.

Owen-Smith, J. and W.W. Powell (2001), 'Careers and contradictions: faculty responses to the transformation of knowledge and its uses in the life sciences', *Research in the Sociology of Work*, **10**, 109–40.

Rothaermel, F.T., S.D. Agung and L. Jiang (2007), 'University entrepreneurship: a taxonomy of the literature', *Industrial and Corporate Change*, **16** (4), 691–791.

Shibayama, S. (2012), 'Conflict between entrepreneurship and open science, and the transition of scientific norms', *Journal of Technology Transfer*, **37**, 508–31.

Siegel, D.S., D.A. Waldman, L.E. Atwater and A.N. Link (2004), 'Toward a model of the effective transfer of scientific knowledge from academicians to practitioners: qualitative evidence from the commercialization of university technologies', *Journal of Engineering & Technology Management*, **21** (1–2), 115–42.

Stokes, D.E. (1997), *Pasteur's Quadrant: Basic Science and Technological Innovation*, Washington, DC: Brookings Institution Press.

Stuart, T. and W.W. Ding (2006), 'When do scientists become entrepreneurs? The social structural antecedents of commercial activity in the academic life sciences', *American Journal of Sociology*, **112** (1), 97–144.

Thursby, J.G. and S. Kemp (2002), 'Growth and productive efficiency of university intellectual property licensing', *Research Policy*, **31**, 109–24.

Ward, D. (1992), 'Serving the state: the Wisconsin idea revisited', *Educational Record* (Spring), 12–17.

APPENDIX

Table 4A.1 Bivariate correlations

	Q1 RED	Q2 TA	Q3 Com	Q4 Start	Q5 Equity	Q6 ProprR	Q7 Patent	Q8 PeerR	Q9 FreeEx	Q10 Threat	Q11 Consult	Q12 Delay	Q13 StCOI	Q14 FacCOI
Q1 RED	1.000													
Pr														
Q2 TA	.616**	1.000												
Pr	0													
Q3 Comm	.385**	.424**	1.000											
Pr	0	0												
Q4 Startup	.374**	.467**	.599**	1.000										
Pr	0	0	0											
Q5 Equity	.288**	.370**	.520**	.677**	1.000									
Pr	0	0	0	0										
Q6 ProprR	.358**	.511**	.500**	.412**	.422**	1.000								
Pr	0	0	0	0	0									
Q7 Patent	.290**	.376**	.292**	.234**	.241**	.357**	1.000							
Pr	0	0	0	0	0	0								
Q8 PeerR	-0.04	-.099*	.044	.025	-.011	-.086*	-.212**	1.000						
Pr	0.348	0.021	0.302	0.566	0.806	0.044	0							

83

Table 4A.1   (continued)

	Q1 RED	Q2 TA	Q3 Com	Q4 Start	Q5 Equity	Q6 ProprR	Q7 Patent	Q8 PeerR	Q9 FreeEx	Q10 Threat	Q11 Consult	Q12 Delay	Q13 StCOI	Q14 FacCOI
Q9 Free Exch	.031	−0.06	−.140**	−.148**	−.091*	−.145**	−.085*	.229**	1.000					
Pr	0.477	0.166	0.001	0.001	0.035	0.001	0.048	0						
Q10 Threat	−.281**	−.313**	−.539**	−.413**	−.384**	−.419**	−.225**	.137**	.230**	1.000				
Pr	0	0	0	0	0	0	0	.001	0					
Q11 Consult	.074	.166**	.066	.121**	.160**	.128**	.104*	−.173**	−.054	−.027	1.000			
Pr	0.091	0	0.128	0.005	0	0.003	0.017	0	0.216	0.531				
Q12 Delay	.194**	.206**	.254**	.231**	.151**	.285**	.127**	−.04	−.220**	−.191**	.221**	1.000		
Pr	0	0	0	0	0.001	0	0.004	0.362	0	0.531	0			
Q13 StdCOI	.189**	.233**	.310**	.221**	.180**	.295**	.108*	−.039	−.193**	−.328**	.113**	.352**	1.000	
Pr	0	0	0	0	0	0	0.013	0.379	0	0	0.009	0		
Q14 FacCOI	.215**	.242**	.320**	.294**	.271**	.274**	.124**	−.033	−.163**	−.348**	.129**	.282**	.636**	1.000
Pr	0	0	0	0	0	0	0.004	0.45	0	0	0.003	0	0	

Notes:
** Correlation is significant at the 0.01 level (2-tailed).
* Correlation is significant at the 0.05 level (2-tailed).

84

5. Professors' attitude to collaboration and central infrastructure for collaboration: an analysis of social capital establishment within higher education institutions

Maria Ljunggren and Hans Westlund

1. INTRODUCTION

Collaboration between higher education institutions (HEI) and industry is of significant importance in the development of economic and educational policy. The European Union's Lisbon strategy 2000 and the Bologna process highlight the aim of modernizing the higher education system; one of the important factors is the issue of establishing sustainable partnerships between HEI and the business community (Commission of the European Communities 2006). This was already emphasized in the EU research and framework programmes with a general aim to strengthen the scientific and technological bases of European industry and make it more competitive at the international level (Luukkonen 1998).

Clark (1983, 1998) analysed organizational change within HEI and identified different typologies for governing HEI with an emphasis on the differences between institutional capacities to engage in collaboration with the surrounding community. HEIs have got the role of knowledge generator where academic knowledge generation is a significant foundation for career progress. Within the academic community attitudes to, and traditions of, collaboration differ between faculties, as do the incentives for researchers to participate in collaboration projects (Lee 2000; Balconi and Laboranti 2006; Foray and Steinmueller 2003; Castro et al. 2008; van Hemert and van Nijkamp et al. 2009).

There is an emerging scientific field of innovation studies that also highlight collaboration involving HEI (Fagerberg and Verspagen 2009). Still, there is a gap in research on collaboration between the HEI and the public and private sector, as well as the interfaculty variation to relate collaboration to education and take advantage of HEI's developed infrastructure for collaboration.

The type of infrastructure for collaboration can vary between types of academic institutions but in this study it indicates a unit for exchange of knowledge and technology, attached to the central level of the HEI, covering all faculties with an ambition to increase collaboration with the private and public sectors, and to increase commercialization of research. The definition of collaboration may also vary between focusing on commercialization, on collaboration with the private sector or public sector, or collaboration between academics or academic institutions. In our case, collaboration refers to the actual exchange of knowledge within networks between the public sector, private sector, and civil society and academics within the HEI. Hence, all types of such networks imply active collaboration, either formal through established structures, or informal through personal connections. When using social capital we refer to social networks and the social attributes being distributed in the networks, such as norms and attitudes (Westlund 2006), these being the social infrastructure for collaboration.

The aim of this study is to add further to the understanding of collaboration and the potential differences in attitude and ambition to participate in collaboration activities within the academic community. Using a web-based questionnaire and interviews we explore attitudes to external collaboration, and participation in collaboration activities among professors in the faculties of humanities, social sciences, and technology. The findings are analysed using social capital theory, which here is interpreted as a theory of the social infrastructure and norms that govern the exchange of knowledge and technology between HEIs and external actors. The professors' ability and ambition to collaborate reveal their ambition to use their own networks or build social capital to new external actors by using the HEI's central infrastructure.

The next section provides a brief review of previous research on collaboration, followed in section 3 by a description of the conceptual framework. Thereafter, the data, method and results are presented. Section 5 provides a discussion of the findings in the light of social capital theory. This is followed by a conclusion and an outlook for future implications for HEI collaboration related to policy initiatives for collaboration.

2. PREVIOUS RESEARCH ON COLLABORATION

Collaboration was initially based on reliance on the personal relationship between academic researchers and the industry, when a single scientist could come up with a single invention that quickly transformed into a successful product and establish a company from a prototype or method. Such contacts were not established at a central level but were initiated and established by individual professors and people within industry. The scientists developed a network of interactions through acting as both problem solvers and advisers (Geuna and Muscio 2008).

Developments since the 1990s have moved industry collaborations from being purely focused on firms' research agreements to seeing knowledge transfer as mainly connected to technology transfer and intellectual property, with HEIs as one significant source of knowledge for firms attempting to develop innovation activity (Aruendel and Geuna 2004). Suggestively, the dualism that has been apparent in research and industry relations is no longer an accepted description of reality. Basic research does not counteract applied research nor does a high level of publishing rule out a high level of patents (Magnusson et al. 2008).

Etzkowitz (1998) discusses HEIs' progression towards being more entrepreneurial and how researchers view research, their scientific role and interaction with colleagues, companies and universities. He describes the entrepreneurial researcher as someone who in addition to securing research funds also actively collaborates with industry through allowing access to students' research results before publishing and securing future funding through two-way communication. He suggests that researchers with a traditional view of research prevent the development towards the entrepreneurial university or an establishment of collaboration on a central level, since such development requires interaction between the different agendas of intervention and research, but he further argues that an increasing number of faculties have assimilated to the capitalization of knowledge and pursue basic research in parallel with applied research.

Etzkowitz (2004) argues that the entrepreneurial university integrates society's interests of economic growth as a mission within the HEI, alongside research and education. Little research has further analysed how HEIs' undergraduate and postgraduate education are affected by collaboration. Jenkins (2004) and Zubrik et al. (2001) added to the research through analysing undergraduate students' involvement in research activities off campus in co-operation with regional industry and applied research projects, and found that researchers from more specialized research centres tended to be less interested in relating their research to education. Bodas-Freitas and Verspagen (2009) found students writing a master thesis in collaboration with the industry to be a much stronger instrument for promoting collaboration than policy makers had previously believed. Ljunggren (2009) found collaboration to enhance research and teaching links within collaboration environments situated outside the HEI.

As a response to the ongoing development, governmental policies have supported HEIs' development of infrastructure for technology and knowledge transfer. This refers to a central support unit at the HEI that supports researchers with commercialization of research and network building. The infrastructure varies greatly between types of academic institutions, from purely commercial technology transfer offices (TTO) to knowledge interchange organizations focusing on entrepreneurial activities and learning (Magnusson et al. 2008; Mowery et al. 2001; Siegel et al. 2004). Siegel et al. (2004) found in their study on a selection of North American universities that personal relationship was more important for scientists in technology transfer than contractual relationships. They further suggested that TTO offices in most cases were either too narrowly focused on a small set of technical areas, or too focused on the legal aspects of licensing. However, the central infrastructure should, for example, also accommodate different faculties' varying needs for collaboration and attitudes to collaboration, since the differences between faculties and between faculty staff are more significant than other factors, such as type of institutional organization (Lee 1996).

The humanities and social sciences are not as prone to tailor collaboration towards commercialization as engineering and the natural sciences (McKelvey et al. 2008; van Hemert et al. 2009). Additionally, the traditional view of research as purely indicating basic research without any application value is more strongly expressed within the social sciences and humanities (McKelvey et al. 2008). Conventional wisdom suggests that such findings would imply that researchers from the humanities and social sciences would be passive in terms of participating in actual collaboration activities. Social sciences and humanities are as important for innovation processes but are not as visible in the process as production development. However, there are concrete examples of active collaboration within the humanities and social sciences. One example is 'Knowledge Transfer Partnerships' (www.ktponline.org.uk). The partnership is a relationship between a company and an academic institution, facilitating the transfer of knowledge, technology and skills from the institution to the company partner. The humanities and social sciences are both active in this type of collaboration. A Danish policy evaluation (2005) building on results from eight HEIs indicates that the majority of the departments within both humanities and social sciences indeed have significant collaboration with the private, public and civil sectors.

It is complex to establish policies for collaboration suited for all faculties within one specific HEI. However the majority of Swedish HEIs have developed central infrastructure for collaboration (see, for example, the key actor programme, www.vinnova.se). Additional governmental initiatives that enhance collaboration and commercialization have also been established outside the HEIs (Etzkowitz 2005). As a result, collaboration is often financed through different types of EU projects or governmental agency-financed programmes not integrated on a central level within the HEI. One problem with these top-down processes is the concentration on short term results instead of the creation of a sustainable structure for collaboration and innovation (Johansson and Westlund 2008).

3. CONCEPTUAL FRAMEWORK

The governmental intention to support and increase collaboration between HEIs and the surrounding community is visible through developed policies but may not necessarily serve as an initiator of collaboration activities. Collaboration occurs through actively using one's networks; and when we attempt to analyse policy changes, social capital serves as a useful framework as it deals with social infrastructure that enables other policies to be effective (Schuller 2001).

Social capital is suggestively an individual benefit (Bourdieu 1986; Burt 1997) but with an emphasis on individuals' sharing of social ties to advance the creation of effective norms (Burt 2001). A norm, in terms of social capital building, functions as an investment. Norms and information sharing are significant foundations for individuals when being admitted into a group's social capital (Coleman 1990). Social capital functions as a club good with varying levels of selection (Westlund 2006). Buchanan (1965) discusses club good in terms of small groups having lower decision-making costs, which is an outcome facilitated by homogeneity of members' interests. The ability to secure benefits is purely the entitlement of members of the group since private networks are available only to their members. This suggests that established social capital would be fixed to the group. However, individual members of the groups possess social characteristics that form the development, which also may make social capital individual and close to human capital (Glaser et al. 2001).

Putnam (1993, 2000) focuses on social capital in civil society and suggests that some groups have fully closed networks, whereas others have more fluid networks that relate more to public good. Importantly, Westlund (2006) emphasized that norms and values, and the social networks they are being distributed in, are not restricted to civil society but exist in all parts of society.

When discussing HEIs' social capital it is relevant to include both internal and external social capital. Table 5.1 demonstrates social capital in the

Table 5.1　Universities' social capital broken down into different component parts

Internal social capital	External social capital		
	Related to education and research	Related to the environment	Related to the market
Links/relations charged with attitudes, norms, traditions etc. that are expressed in the form of: • 'Spirit' • Climate for cooperation • Methods for renewal and development, conflict resolution etc. • Incentive structures	Links/relations to research and education financiers, users of research, external researchers and other cooperation and development partners	Links/relations to the local/ regional environment, to decision makers in the public sector etc. (Lobbying capacity, etc.)	Universities as brands and trademarks and other general relations to stakeholders with whom there is no direct contact

Source:　Application of Westlund (2009).

HEI sector. The internal social capital consists of individuals' networks, norms and attitudes, whereas the external social capital consists of three types, of which the education and research related social capital usually is mostly associated with collaboration. To form a base for a climate of collaboration, the structure of internal incentives and traditions should interrelate with the building of external social capital. Changes in internal social capital can only come about if it is to the advantage of teachers and researchers. If collaboration with other parts of society were to mean, for example, better salaries, more research funds, and academic qualifications, it is probable that changed attitudes would lead to a greater interest in building links to stakeholders outside HEIs. So far, only a few studies on attitudes and relations in Swedish HEIs and their importance for building external links and relations have been made (Wahlbin and Wigren 2007; Johansson and Westlund 2008). In this respect research on companies is much more advanced than research on HEIs.

As described in Table 5.1, the social capital of universities is also related to their environments (i.e. the environment that is not directly linked to education and research) and includes the participation of the personnel and the students in formal bodies and networks of a less formal nature. It also includes the role of the universities as creators of attractive urban environments with a wide selection of culture and recreation facilities. The market-related social capital of the universities demonstrates how the universities participate in a market place where they compete for students, personnel and financial resources. In principle, the universities act in these areas like companies and invest in various types of marketing activities with a focus on establishing external social capital through networks to external financiers, and regional surroundings and industry.

When studying professors' attitudes towards collaboration, it is relevant to analyse whether the external social capital benefits from or is disadvantaged by components of the internal social capital. In other words, both the external and internal social capital consists of networks with varied intensity and structure that stem from norms and attitudes. For a behavioural change there should be a balance between the two.

In this chapter we use social capital theory as a framework for analysing interfaculty differences in attitude to collaboration and professors' use of the central infrastructure when collaborating with the public or private sector. Our first hypothesis is that the attitude to collaboration and taking advantage of the developed central infrastructure is related and differs between faculties. The second hypothesis is that professors' level of collaboration activity influences their willingness to share their networks with the HEI's central infrastructure for collaboration.

4. DATA, METHOD AND RESULTS

The study is based on a web-based questionnaire and 21 interviews developed from the results of the web-based questionnaire.

4.1 The Web-Based Questionnaire

The questionnaire was a web-based survey of all faculty members and researchers, i.e. teachers and PhD students, at Stockholm University, totalling approximately 3200 respondents. This includes researchers and teachers from the humanities, social sciences, natural sciences, and faculty of law. Only employees working no less than 40 per cent were asked to complete the survey. At the closure of the survey there were 1469 replies ($N = 1469$), corresponding to a reply frequency of 48 per cent, failed addresses excluded. The response rate was slightly higher in natural

Table 5.2   Characteristics of the respondents in the sample

Position	Humanities	Law	Social sciences	Natural science	Total replies	Total reply frequency
Professors	58 (53.7%)	13 (48.2%)	99 (70.2%)	120 (62.2%)	290	61.7%
Lecturers, Docents, Fellows	139 (39.6%)	5 (22.7%)	199 (37.8%)	112 (46.3%)	455	39.9%
PhD students	105 (55.6%)	14 (48.3%)	157 (70.4%)	241 (58.5%)	517	60.1%
Research assistants, Assistants	52 (41.6%)	4 (26.6%)	66 (27.7%)	85 (34.1%)	207	29.6%
Total	354 (45.9%)	36 (30.8%)	521 (45.6%)	558 (49.6%)	1469	45.9%

Note: Within each category, the number of replies is followed by reply frequency in percentage.

sciences (50 per cent) than in the humanities and social sciences (46 per cent), and the response rate among professors and PhD students was significantly higher than among the other groups. There were no significant differences in the response rate between men and women or between the different age groups of the subjects. Stockholm University has a fairly modest central infrastructure for collaboration, with a turnover of 3.6 million SEK in 2009. The questionnaire provided an extensive background of the attitudes towards collaboration and participation level in collaboration projects. Table 5.2 describes the characteristics of the respondents in the sample.

We used multiple regressions to analyse the questionnaire data with dummy variables. The control groups for each test were not given any dummy whereas the other groups had dummy variable 1. The questionnaire contained the following independent variables: gender, age, faculty (natural science, social science, humanities, faculty of law), position (PhD students and assistants, lecturer, research assistants, associate professors, professors, adjunct professors), academic credentials (doctorate, licentiate, first degree), number of popular scientific publications (0 publications, 1–3 publications, 4–6 publications, more than 7 publications), and number of scientific publications (0 publications, 1–3 publications, 4–6 publications, more than 7 publications). Sex: female was given the value 0, male the value 1; Age: younger than 45 years old = 0 and older than 45 = 1. Dependent variable was the mean on questions 1–3 and the proportion of yes on questions 4–9. The full questions are presented in Tables 5.3 and 5.4.

Table 5.3   *Compilation of questions and replies regarding attitude to collaboration*

Questions regarding attitude to collaboration	Significant positive attitude (5–7)	Significant negative attitude (1–3)
Q1. I consider that increased collaboration by Stockholm University would: 1 (substantially restrict academic freedom) – 7 (substantially increase academic freedom)	Professors (0.110, 0.055)	Faculty of humanities (0.066, 0.038)
Q2. At my place of work/institution within Stockholm University there is: 1 (no support for collaboration) – 7 (keen support for collaboration that can offer greater resources)	Faculty of natural science (0.145, 0.040)	
Q3. Where I work within Stockholm University, commitment to collaboration has: 1 (a highly negative impact on one's academic career) – 7 (a highly favourable impact on one's academic career)	Faculty of natural science (0.145, 0.040)	

Note: The level of significance is $P < 0.05$. Numbers in brackets are coefficients and standard errors, respectively.

4.1.1   Questionnaire results

The quantitative data for the university (without the faculty of technology) is presented to provide an extensive background to the subjects and their level of participation in collaboration activities.

As shown in Table 5.3, it is clear that researchers from the humanities experience less support for collaboration, and also find that collaboration would have an effect on academic freedom, whereas researchers from the faculty of natural science express a more positive view of collaboration, and have experienced more support. This challenges the mission of the developed central infrastructure which is aimed to serve as a support for a broad type of knowledge transfer other than production development and patents that are more common for the natural scientists. However it does relate to the previous research describing researchers from the humanities as more negative towards collaboration than natural scientists.

Table 5.4   Compilation of questions and replies regarding participation in numerous joint activities

Questions regarding participation in numerous joint activities	Significant positive relationship	Significant negative relationship
Q4. Have you participated in research projects during 2008 where the organization funding the research has promoted participation with an organization (such as a company or local authority) other than the University or another institute of education?	Associate professors (0.109, 0.042) Professors (0.130, 0.041) Research assistants (0.114, 0.035)	Faculty of humanities (−0.126, 0.030) Faculty of law (−0.204, 0.073) PhD students (−0.087, 0.040) Assistants (−0.214, 0.103)
Q5. Have you published a scientific publication during 2008 that was co-authored with someone not employed by the University or another institute of higher education?	Faculty of natural science (0.055, 0.022) Associate professors (0.096, 0.034) Adjunct professor (0.293, 0.113) Research assistants (0.048, 0.034)	
Q6. Have you worked as an advisor/consultant for an organization other than the University or another institute of higher education during 2008?	Faculty of social science (0.070, 0.027) Faculty of law (0.359, 0.075) Associate professors (0.179, 0.043) Adjunct professors (0.294, 0.140) Professors (0.235,0.041)	
Q7. Have you held a directorship on a board apart from the University or another institute of higher education during 2008 (other than local associations, tenant-owner associations or similar)?	Faculty of law (0.326, 0.059) Associate professors (0.085, 0.034) Professors (0.185, 0.033)	
Q8. Have you arranged assignments for and/or supervised students who have resolved problems for companies or public sector organizations during 2008 – in the form of projects, papers, theses, etc?	Faculty of law (0.275, 0.061) Lecturers (0.082, 0.030) Professors (0.159, 0.037)	Faculty of humanities (−0.056, 0.025) Faculty of natural science (−0.086, 0.022)

Table 5.4   (continued)

Questions regarding participation in numerous joint activities	Significant positive relationship	Significant negative relationship
Q9. Have you participated as a teacher/lecturer in a commissioned education assignment during 2008?	Faculty of law (0.275, 0.061) Lecturers (0.082, 0.030) Professors (0.159, 0.037) Associate professors (0.101, 0.038) Research assistants (0.065, 0.032)	Faculty of humanities (−0.056, 0.025) Faculty of natural science (−0.086, 0.022)

Note: The level of significance chosen is P < 0.05. Numbers in brackets are coefficients and standard errors, respectively.

The first question in Table 5.4 (Q4) indicates that faculty engaged in research, except PhD students, have been active in research funded by an organization other than the HEI. Surprisingly, the faculty of law demonstrates a negative relationship whereas the humanities also have a negative correlation as expected. The following question indicates that the faculty staff other than professors significantly more often published in collaboration with someone outside the HEI as well as researchers from the natural sciences. Question 6 demonstrates that faculty engaged in research also serve significantly more as consultants, as well as the faculty of law and the faculty of social science. Furthermore, professors and associate professors and the faculty of law to a larger extent hold directorships on a board outside the HEI. The two last questions (Q8 and Q9) concerning the arrangement of assignments and supervision of students and commissioned education reveal that the faculty of law engages significantly more in these, in contrast to the faculties of humanities and natural sciences, which have a negative relationship. Professors are more prone to engage students in collaboration activities whereas lecturers and associate professors are active in commissioned education.

The questionnaire results shown in Tables 5.3 and 5.4 illustrate that in the majority of the questions, employment as a professor but also as an associate professor has a significant effect on experience of and attitude towards collaboration. The results indicate that position has a significant impact on level of participation in collaboration activities. A position as a professor facilitates more opportunities for external activities than those afforded to a full-time PhD student. Surprisingly the results also indicate that despite expressing a positive attitude towards collaboration (Table

5.2) researchers in natural sciences do not indicate any positive relationship for participating in collaboration activities and in fact demonstrate a negative relationship when it comes to enrolling students in collaboration projects and commissioned education.

4.2 The Interviews

The interviews were carried out during the autumn of 2010. All interviews were semi-structured, allowing for open ended replies in order to enable a full exploration of the individuals' attitude to and experience of collaboration, the central infrastructure for collaboration, and to hear their reflections on research development and undergraduate education. The informants were a group consisting of 21 professors, six from the faculty of humanities, eight from the faculty of social science, and seven from the faculty of technology. Ten professors declined to participate, of which five were from the humanities and five were from the social sciences. All contacted professors from the faculty of technology agreed to be interviewed.

The interviewees from the humanities and the social sciences were all chosen because they belonged to the group that had indicated in the questionnaire that they had been active in some type of collaboration activity and also expressed an interest in information regarding collaboration opportunities. This indicated that they possessed the relevant experience of collaboration and were able to discuss and relate to the concept as well as providing an interesting base for further discussion. However, a general conclusion can not be drawn from the sample since the interviewed professors, as previously mentioned, already represent a group with experience of collaboration and an interest in the issue.

A group of professors from a technical university was also included as interviewees to provide a more comprehensive analysis of attitudes towards and experience of collaboration research and the central infrastructure. The technical university was the Royal Institute for Technology, with a developed central infrastructure (with a turnover of 25–30 million SEK in 2009) for collaboration and a more profound tradition of collaboration with industry and the public sector. The chosen professors were all from either one of the two departments consisting of only social scientists, and all professors from the departments were asked to participate in the study. The choice to include a group of social scientists from a technical faculty was made to provide a more valid sample for the interviews and an interesting base for smaller comparisons between the institutions as well as an invitation to expand the study further in future research. When referring to this group, we use the term professors from the technical faculty.

Due to the relatively small sample no general conclusions should be drawn from the sample.

4.2.1   Interview data

The interviews allowed for a more thorough evaluation of attitudes to collaboration and a central infrastructure for collaboration, and the ability to link collaboration with undergraduate education.

4.2.1.1   Professors' attitudes to collaboration enhancing undergraduate education   Professors from all faculties were positive towards collaboration in terms of its ability to enhance undergraduate education, provide possibilities for external funding, and provide valuable feedback on research questions. Participation in collaboration activities was seen to add value to the undergraduate programmes as well as the master programmes through direct feedback on the educational programme's value in the surrounding society, in terms of both companies and the public sector. This was considered important for the quality control of the educational value of the course and students' employability.

The majority of the professors from the faculty of technology and some professors from the faculty of social sciences updated course plans as a result of their experience from collaboration projects. They had a continuing dialogue with their representatives from the industry and the public sector to make their courses more applicable to their partners' needs, which they also argued helped when attracting new students to their courses. The interview data illustrated the professors' belief that collaboration provided students with more opportunities to write master theses in collaboration with a company. A number of professors also stated that research and teaching links became stronger when students were involved in collaboration since that kept them more focused on defining and keeping to the research question.

Professors within the humanities were less frequently engaged in collaboration projects. Within the humanities and to a large extent the social sciences, a number of professors discussed collaboration and the value of utilizing experience from the surrounding society, as well as involving their students in their collaboration projects. However, the professors articulated a need for an incentive in order to participate in anything other than traditional research and education since there are no earmarked resources for engaging in collaboration activities. The majority of the professors in humanities and social sciences also believed that their PhD students should focus on their doctoral dissertations instead of losing research time to participation in collaboration work. This type of attitude towards collaboration was not expressed in the faculty of technology.

4.2.1.2   Professors attitude to collaboration activities   The results of the interviews suggest that ambition to engage in collaboration differs between the faculties. Within the humanities external collaboration projects were few. Professors expressed an interest in collaboration but still lacked the real ambition to participate in collaboration activities. The time spent on collaboration must bring some type of additional value to their work since there were no formalized incentives for researchers to collaborate. The two most active professors emphasized that all contacts were created on an individual informal basis, including former PhD students who had moved outside academia. Their experience from industry was varied, with low levels of trust but an acknowledgement of the valuable knowledge gained from the collaboration.

Within the social sciences, some of the professors lacked real ambition to participate in collaboration activities. Only three professors strongly expressed their ambition to work closely with their departments and form a strong internal social capital that aimed at developing social capital with external actors. In collaboration projects, the development of networks through the informal alliances that they had was believed to be significant, and PhD students and research assistants were invited to join them. The most sustainable networks were the informal academic networks with former colleagues and students, as well as those formed with new colleagues met through conferences. Still, there was no structured system for developing collaboration. One procedure was to allow external parties to bring in new partners resulting in new contacts for the research project. Only one professor expressed a different opinion from the others: he had a very strong internal and external network and enrolled the members of the department in the activities in an attempt to formalize network building.

There were three professors who expressed a tendency to be affected by the HEI's actual culture for collaboration and had developed more external networks while active at other HEIs. Presently they collaborate at an individual level but to a less significant extent and in a less formalized manner. They all agreed that the networks were often open only to selected individuals and that they only collaborated in terms of being an expert within a specific field, which was why they were contacted by external parties.

The professors from the technical faculty were more likely to collaborate and had more substantive individual external networks, but also informal networks at a departmental level. They expressed an ambition to establish the process, and PhD students or other research assistants were involved from the department. However, the majority of the professors defined their collaboration work as reactive and informal. External contacts were built through collaboration that occurred through the networks that they became connected to during their academic career. A large part of the contacts were, as with the other faculties, through former students and former academic colleagues. Former students were considered by some as the best source for spreading informal channels and for creating a strong link with industry and the public sector. Several professors made sure they involved their current PhD students so that they were provided with an opportunity to inherit the network. The professors informed their PhD students mostly of how to collaborate through projects and the potential impacts such networks could have on their future careers.

One professor did attempt to establish a formalized network on a departmental level, but it was still too dependent on the individual professor and did not function without the professor's attendance. A professor from the same department emphasized that there was not necessarily any need for formal arrangements with industry during collaboration due to the high level of trust between the professor and the external partner. Commissioned education for the industry had, for example, been arranged without any contracts.

4.2.1.3 Professors' attitudes to the central infrastructure for collaboration Within the humanities, it emerged that professors were more positive about using the central infrastructure than within the other faculties. However, in contrast to professors from other faculties, they had very little experience of collaboration. Their experience of using the functions was also limited to a few projects; but they had no ambition to use the function for future projects. One professor stated that the function might be useful for an external party that intended to get in contact with academia. Another professor was supportive of the principle of having competent people at hand but still had no intention of participating in collaboration projects since his primary focus was on traditional research. Furthermore, two professors expressed positive feelings towards the principle of a central infrastructure but had no intention of using it and considered a structure for collaboration to be more useful on a departmental level indicating that the central infrastructure should be decentralized to the departments. It was also stated that the use of a structure for collaboration in terms of commercialization of research was helpful and one professor had used it since he lacked networks within the commercial world, and did not intend to build any networks with the industry for future purposes.

As in the humanities, the professors within social science expressed a more positive attitude to the central infrastructure for collaboration when they themselves had very little experience of collaboration. Despite the positive attitude towards a professional administrator performing collaboration, no one had actually used the infrastructure provided. Three social science researchers with experience of collaboration expressed the view that a central infrastructure was theoretically useful, but as with the professors from the humanities they still did not intend to use the infrastructure for improving their networks or for increasing opportunities for collaboration projects. A few had used it for commercialization but not for network building.

Within the technical faculty, professors were already well established in collaboration activities and projects and had developed sustainable networks that were often shared with departmental colleagues and PhD students, but there was no incentive for the researchers or interest in sharing one's network with the central infrastructure at the HEI. Instead the attitude towards the central infrastructure was competitive and the function regarded as inefficient. One professor even used an external organization outside the HEI for commissioned education when needing expertise and help with matters such as contract writing.

The central infrastructure as a fixed organization within the HEI's larger organization appeared as an inefficient source for building of external social capital or influence internal social capital. Instead, a significant number of the professors expressed an ability to build external networks with the industry, while participating in EU projects that enhanced commitment to both external collaborative partners and academic colleagues. This means that the projects were not purely research collaborations but always involved partners from the industry. It was also emphasized that industry representatives successfully searched for an expert in a specific research field through EU projects, suggesting that such a structure could be more efficient for enhancing collaboration than a fixed organization such as the central infrastructure.

Professors from both social sciences and the humanities preferred the EU projects as an active involvement in collaboration but only one professor from the technical faculty expressed the same opinion. Within the social sciences it was more strongly expressed that using the central infrastructure was less useful than actively engaging in EU projects, which a majority of the professors were also doing.

5.   DISCUSSION

The subsequent analysis focuses on social capital as a social infrastructure including external networks and internal norms, attitudes and values, both on the individual level and in relation to the department and the central infrastructure for collaboration.

5.1   Conflict Between Network Building and Attitudes to Collaboration

The overall data illustrates that the majority of the professors who were active in collaboration projects preferred to use their own networks and paid little attention to the central infrastructure developed for this purpose. They possess a strong internal social capital with clear traditions for collaboration and a strong individualism. Their identity was first and foremost connected to their research area, and collaboration often occurred as a result of attending research conferences relating to the research field. The creation and growth of social capital was complex to control by all involved. The individual level of building external networks and adding to the external social capital through better links and relations to external partners frequently occurred, but there was no attempt to formalize the network building on a departmental level, indicating that the internal social capital remained unchanged. Each department possessed individual professors who accumulated networks at an individual level but the technical faculty differed slightly since they showed a more positive attitude to collaboration with attempts to establish external networks through actively influencing colleagues and sharing.

For HEIs' external collaboration, it would be an advantage if the developed policies that attempt to increase participation in collaboration projects also created a stable relation between internal and external social capital at departmental and central level. However, when analysing the process of social capital building and the strong incentivesfor keeping one's individual networks, as well as the lack of incentives for collaborating when focusing on traditional research, it appears to be somewhat unrealistic to expect collaboration projects to develop towards a change in internal social capital and increasing external social capital. For the professors, building internal and external social capital concerned how they perceived their influence on the actors within the network and whether there was any 'leakage' in the network inviting others to join. External networks could possibly be better established among the departmental members if collaboration projects were prevented from being a single professor's informal business.

5.2   Central Infrastructure for Collaboration Rarely Established Social Capital

When analysing the data it seems very complicated to actually establish a central unit for collaboration since it would need to change the internal social capital in order to function. Due to strong internal social capital which is both path dependent and individualistic it also becomes complicated to initiate and build external social capital from a central unit. Professors from all faculties expressed that informal networks and the need for specific expertise were the key components for successful building of external social capital. All informants agreed that such expertise could be possessed only by the individual professor, which provides an example of strong internal social capital conflicting with the building of external social capital on a central level.

The external networks were developed and established from bottom-up level through informal channels and no one believed that a representative on a central level possessed the skills, knowledge or the right connections to either build relevant external networks or encourage external social capital building. This was illustrated in the common argument among all professors active in collaboration, emphasizing that no representative on a central function would know how to communicate with informal contacts, and that the need for expertise was essential when arranging collaboration projects. This expertise could not be possessed by administrators working at the central level.

Figure 5.1 illustrates how internal and external networks flows within and outside HEI in relation to external collaboration partners. The dotted arrows indicate a positive attitude and potential for building a positive internal social capital, and the full arrows show external social capital that has been formed. The full lines not leading to a circle below each faculty illustrate that there are several research groups within each faculty. The P represents a professor and the smaller circles connected to the Ps are PhD students, other researchers and research assistants.

Figure 5.1 illustrates that professors from the humanities and the social sciences have a positive attitude to a central infrastructure, whereas only professors from the humanities have used the central infrastructure for collaboration without developing any internal social capital, due to the modest frequency of interactions. The use of the infrastructure for commercialization is not included in the figure. The professors from the technical faculty have strong external social capital with their collaboration partners outside the HEI and the professors from social sciences and humanities have some contact but have not established external social capital. There is a stronger belief in the departmental tradition for collaboration within the technical faculties.

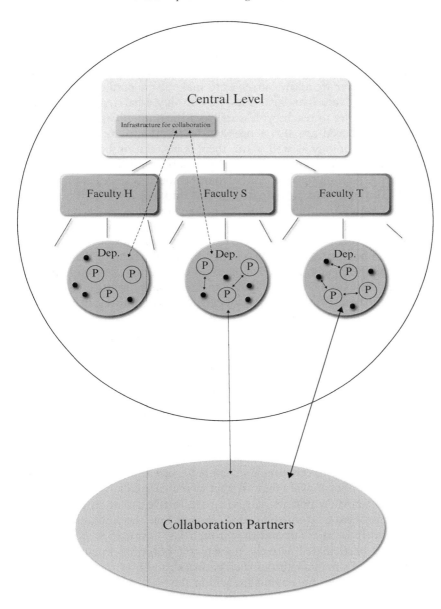

Figure 5.1   Social capital establishment within the HEI

6.   CONCLUSION AND FUTURE OUTLOOK

Naturally our study has its limitations in terms of the limited number of professors for the interviews and including only two different HEIs in the sample. However we allow ourselves to make some predictions from the results. Firstly, values and attitudes are not only a barrier for the central unit when aiming to reach professors from the humanities and the social sciences but indeed are also a problem when attempting to involve the faculty of technology as well. Also, there is no relation between positive attitude to a central infrastructure for collaboration and actual use of this facility. Among the professors from the social sciences and the technical faculty that had participated in and initiated collaboration activities, the common attitude was to keep the external network building to oneself or within the research group, illustrating a path dependent and bottom-up process. Consequently, it becomes complex to network due to the common attitudes to such activities. There seems to be a conflict within two different components of social capital: network building that enhances the external social capital, and the common attitudes that are proof of the type of internal capital being the current norm. For a change in the internal social capital there must be advantage to the researchers. With the lack of incentives for collaboration and sharing one's network, there is little possibility for this to occur.

HEIs are permeated with researchers' strong tradition of individualism and independence, which complicates building of external social capital. Our analysis has demonstrated that network building is inhibited by individuals' attitudes, resulting in a conflict that prevents external social capital from being sustainable. To avoid collaboration projects within the HEI from being short period initiatives or individual professors' 'property', policy makers need to include the complex nature of building and sustaining networks as well as creating a structure for incentives for collaboration.

Secondly, policy makers that attempt to increase collaboration need to contemplate how the policies may be most effective. An additional finding was that professors from the social sciences and the humanities had a positive attitude to collaboration through EU framework programmes and indeed participated actively in such collaboration. Further research should analyse what constitutes such networks and how they are different from networks that are established within the HEI. Is it likely that such networks are less affected by internal social capital when not fixed to a specific institution?

This chapter has highlighted the tensions between HEIs and the individual professors and researchers that control human and social capital. Such tensions exist in many other industries and activities, but because of the public mission of HEIs and the lack of market forces at play, the institutions and the human capital (which holds the social capital) do not appear equipped to solve this disconnect. If the public policies that aim to promote university-industry-public sector collaboration continue to pretend that these problems do not exist, projects will come and go, but the potential for improving collaboration will remain unredeemed.

ACKNOWLEDGEMENTS

We are grateful to the LE Lundberg foundation for being interested in this research topic and generously financing this study. We are also grateful to the two anonymous reviewers for their insightful and constructive comments on the earlier version of this chapter.

REFERENCES

Aruendel, A., and Geuna, A. (2004), 'Proximity and the use of public science by innovative European firms', *Economics of Innovation and New Technology*, **13** (6), 559–80.

Balconi, M., and Laboranti, A. (2006), 'University-industry interactions in applied research: the case of microelectronics', *Research Policy*, **35**, 1616–30.

Bodas-Freitas, I.M., and Verspagen, B. (2009), 'The motivations, organisation and outcomes of university-industry interaction in the Netherlands', United Nations University: Working paper series, 2009–011.

Bourdieu, P. (1986), 'The forms of capital', in J.G. Richardson (ed), *Handbook of Theory and Research for the Sociology of Education*, New York: Greenwood Press.

Buchanan, J.M. (1965), 'An economic theory of clubs', *Economica*, **32**, 1–14.

Burt, R.S. (1997), 'The contingent value of social capital', *Administrative Science Quarterly*, **42**, 339–65.

Burt, R.S. (2001), 'Structural holes versus network closure as a social capital', in N. Lin, K. Cook, and R.S. Burt (eds), *Social Capital: Theory and Research*, New York: Aldine de Gruyter.

Castro Martínez, E., Molas Gallart, J., and Fernández de Lucio, I. (2008), 'Knowledge transfer in the human and social sciences: the importance of informal relationships and its organizational consequences', The Prime-Latin America Conference, Mexico City, 24–6 September.

Clark, B.R. (1983), *The Higher Education System*, Berkeley: University of California Press.

Clark, B.R. (1998), *Creating Entrepreneurial Universities: Organizational Pathways of Transformation*, Oxford: Pergamon Issues in Higher Education.

Coleman, J. (1990), *Foundations of Social Theory*, Cambridge: Harvard University Press.

Commission of the European Communities (2006), 'Delivering on the modernisation agenda for universities: education, research and innovation',

Communication from the Commission to the Council and the European Parliament, Brussels, 10.5.2006 COM(2006) 208 final.

Etzkowitz, H. (1998), 'The norms of entrepreneurial science: cognitive effects of the new university-industry linkages', *Research Policy*, **27**, 823–33.

Etzkowitz, H. (2004), 'The evolution of the entrepreneurial university', *International Journal of Technology and Globalisation*, **1**, 64–77.

Etzkowitz, H. (2005), *Triple Helix: A New Model of Innovation*, Stockholm: SNS Press.

Fagerberg, J., and Verspagen, B. (2009), 'Innovation studies – the emerging structure of a new scientific field', *Research Policy*, **38**, 218–33.

Foray, D., and Steinmueller, W.E. (2003), 'The economics of knowledge reproduction by inscription', *Industrial and Corporate Change*, Oxford University Press, **12** (2), 299–319.

Geuna, A., and Muscio, A. (2008), 'The governance of university knowledge transfer', SPRU Electronic Working Paper Series 173, University of Sussex, SPRU – Science and Technology Policy Research.

Glaser, E., Laibson, D., and Sacerdote, B. (2001), 'The economic approach to social capital', Harvard Institute of Economic Research, Discussion Paper Number 1916.

Jenkins, A. (2004), 'A guide to the research evidence on teaching-research relations', The Higher Education Academy.

Johansson, M., and Westlund, H. (2008), 'Social capital enhancement through regional co-operation: a study of a Swedish policy program', *Romanian Journal of Regional Science*, **2** (1), 35–53.

Lee, Y.S. (1996), 'Technology transfer and the research university: a search for the boundaries of university-industry collaboration', *Research Policy*, **23**, 843–63.

Lee, Y.S. (2000), 'The sustainability of university-industry research collaboration: an empirical assessment' *Journal of Technology Transfer*, **25**, 111–33.

Ljunggren, M. (2009), 'Interaction between research and education – can industry cooperation improve the link?', *The Journal of Tertiary Education and Management*, **15** (2), 97–112.

Luukkonen, T. (1998), 'The difficulties in assessing the impact of EU-framework programmes', *Research Policy*, **27**, 599–610.

Magnusson, M., McKelvey, M., and Versiglioni, M. (2008), 'The forgotten individuals in the commercialization of science: attitudes and skills in relation to commercialization in Sweden', in M. McKelvey and M. Holmén (eds), *Learning to Compete in European Universities: From Social Institutions to Knowledge Business*, Cheltenham UK and Northampton, MA, USA: Edward Elgar.

McKelvey, M., Magnusson, M., Wallin, M., and Ljungberg, D. (2008), 'Forskning och kommersialisering vad är problemet?' (Research and commercialization – what is the problem?), in S. Sörlin and M. Benner (eds) *Forska lagom och vara världsbäst. Sverige inför forskningens globala strukturomvandling (Research just enough and still be at the international top – Sweden and the global change in research)*, Stockholm: SNS Förlag.

Mowery, D., Nelson, R., Sampat, B., and Ziedonis, A. (2001), 'The growth of patenting and licensing by U.S. universities: an assessment of the effects of the Bayh-Dole Act of 1980', *Research Policy*, **30**, 99–119.

Putnam, R.D. (1993), *Making Democracy Work: Civic Traditions in Modern Italy*, Princeton NJ: Princeton University Press.

Putnam, R.D. (2000), *Bowling Alone. The Collapse and Revival of American Community*, New York: Simon & Schuster.

Schuller, T. (2001), 'The complementary roles of human and social capital', in *The Contribution of Human and Social Capital to Sustained Economic Growth and Well-Being*, International Symposium Report edited by the OECD and HRDC.

Siegel, D., Waldman, D., Atwater, L., and Link, A. (2004), 'Toward a model of the effective transfer of scientific knowledge from academicians to practitioners: qualitative evidence from the commercialization of university technologies', *Journal of Engineering & Technology Management*, **21** (1–2), 115–42.

van Hemert, P., Nijkamp, P., and Verbraak, J. (2009), 'Evaluating social science and humanities knowledge production: an exploratory analysis of dynamics in science systems', paper provided by VU University Amsterdam, Faculty of Economics, Business Administration and Econometrics, Serie Research Memoranda number 0013.

Wahlbin, C., and Wigren, C. (2007), 'Samverkan i det akademiska vardagslivet' (Collaboration in the academic every day life), *NUTEK infonr*, 060-2007.

Westlund, H. (2006), *Social Capital in the Knowledge Economy: Theory and Empirics*, Berlin, Heidelberg, New York: Springer.

Westlund, H. (2009), 'The social capital of regional dynamics: a policy perspective', in C. Karlsson, Å.E. Andersson, P.C. Cheshire, and R.R. Stough (eds), *New Directions in Regional Economic Development*, Berlin, Heidelberg, New York: Springer, pp. 121–42.

Zubrik, A., Reid, I., and Rossiter, P. (2001), 'Strengthening the nexus between teaching and research', Evaluations and Investigations Programme Higher Education Division, 01/2 April.

APPENDIX

Interview questions

Name, Title, How long have you been at the institution?

Part 1 – Research and academic environment

- How would you define research? How is the relation between your research group and the departmental board, and the faculty board?
- Can you provide an overall description of your research, seminars at the department, and the research group's position at the HEI?
- What identity do you have? Do you belong to: the department, the discipline, the HEI or something else? What are you planning for the near future? What are the opportunities, difficulties? What do you think you will be doing in ten years?
- If you have collaborated with industry, how did this affect your own research? Possible advantages, disadvantages? Is there support for industry collaboration at your department, faculty, and HEI? Have you used the central infrastructure for collaboration? How?

Part 2 – Collaboration projects

- Have you participated in any collaboration projects in the last five years, with the public, private sector or civil society? If not, why? Would you have liked to participate? How would you have done this? Develop your answer.
- If yes, how did the project start? Who initiated the idea? Were there previous experiences of collaboration between the actors? What actors did collaborate in the project? Why did these actors participate? Where there any informal contacts between the actors?
- How do you keep the collaboration process sustainable?
- Have individuals within the HEI (other than project participants) showed an interest for the collaboration project? Have any additional networks been established internally or externally (have organizational structures been established that function regardless of the people being active in the collaboration work today)? What actors have been engaged in the continuing activities?
- How is the relationship between the collaboration partners? Do you trust each other? Has it changed during the cause of the project?

- Has the collaboration resulted in any innovations, business ideas, companies, patents, new research, commissioned education, new financing?
- What was your expectation on the collaboration? Did you want to achieve anything specifically with the collaboration? What expectations were put on you from the collaboration partners?

Part 3 – Collaborations' effect on education

- If you have been active in any type of collaboration work, has it had any effect on you as a teacher? How?
- If not, how do you think collaboration could influence undergraduate, master and PhD education? Develop your answer.
- Has collaboration influenced the curricula? On what level? Has it increased the number of internships, increased the number of guest teachers?
- Have you been active in commissioned education? Has it influenced you as a researcher, teacher?
- Do you use cases from commissioned education in your undergraduate teaching? On what level? Are there any other examples of collaboration projects that influence the education in any other level?
- Do you discuss collaboration with your PhD students? When, why and how?
- Do you relate collaboration to the Bologna processes and employability? Why or why not?
- Do you believe that collaboration can affect the research and teaching links in undergraduate education? How?

6. Entrepreneurship education in the research-intensive entrepreneurial university

Edward Feser

1. INTRODUCTION

The notion of the entrepreneurial university is the subject of a rapidly expanding literature, with scholarly work accelerating beginning in the 1990s (Henrekson and Rosenberg 2001; Rothaermel, Agung et al. 2007). According to Jacob et al. (2003, p.1556) an entrepreneurial university is one that has "developed a comprehensive internal system for the commercialization and commodification of its knowledge". The commercialization of university knowledge includes the delivery of custom courses such as executive education, consultancy services, fee-based extension services, contract research, and even new degree programmes designed to capture non-traditional student markets using new teaching approaches, technologies or delivery models (i.e., online education, blended online and traditional teaching, offsite programmes, etc.). Commodification is the effort to catalyse the development of wholly new goods and services from knowledge, innovation and technologies generated from university basic and applied research. Universities promote commodification through knowledge transfer programmes, cooperative research agreements with industry, patenting, licensing, marketing, and the cultivation of faculty or student start-ups and spin-outs, often in incubators and research parks. Commercialization and commodification activities are important mechanisms through which universities directly influence national and regional economic development (Etzkowitz, Webster et al. 2000; Nelles and Vorley 2010). They are elements of universities' broader "Third Mission", the idea that universities have a general socio-economic and public engagement role to play, specifically in their home regions and with local stakeholders (Arbo and Benneworth 2007; Jongbloed, Enders et al. 2008).

The design and delivery of entrepreneurship education is also attracting much attention from scholars and policy makers (Rizza and Varum ND). In Europe, entrepreneurship education is reinforced as a priority in the European Union's recent Europe 2020 strategy, which calls on member states to "ensure a supply of science, maths, and engineering graduates and to focus school curricula on creativity, innovation, and entrepreneurship" (European Commission 2010, p. 13). Entrepreneurship education seeks to equip learners with "the knowledge, skills and competencies to exploit opportunities" in an increasingly knowledge-intensive economy (Hynes and Richardson 2007, p. 734).[1] The basic training needed to start a new business is the core of many such programmes, but approaches to risk taking, factors influencing entrepreneurial attitudes, and skills needed to pursue entrepreneurship from within existing businesses—the practice of intrapreneurship or corporate venturing—are also common subjects. Much of the research literature on entrepreneurship education focuses on the impact of different pedagogies on student entrepreneurial outcomes, ways of involving internal and external stakeholders, and alternative institutional homes for teaching programmes (e.g., business schools, schools of social science, university-wide centres, etc.). That is not to argue that traditional students are the sole target of entrepreneurship education programmes. Some are geared to providing training to would-be entrepreneurs in the universities' immediate regions as well as academic staff inside the university (Lawton Smith and Bagchi-Sen 2011).

With just a few exceptions, there is almost no overlap in the entrepreneurial university and entrepreneurship education literatures. The topic of entrepreneurship education does not receive a single mention in Rothaermel et al.'s (2007) 101-page taxonomy of the university entrepreneurship literature, a review that examines papers published in leading journals between 1980 and 2005. Although there are several contributions that post-date 2005 (noted below), it is safe to claim that the question of what role entrepreneurship education can play in supporting technology transfer and commercialization has received very little scholarly attention. Likewise, universities' aims in the commercialization and commodification of knowledge—in essence, the commercial engagement component of their "Third Mission"—have been only rarely identified by scholars as creating opportunities to leverage or strengthen the delivery of entrepreneurship education.

Scholarship aside, it is doubtless the case that there is a high degree of networking and collaboration among staff implementing the entrepreneurship education and commercial engagement agendas at various institutions. The "entrepreneurial turn" being taken by many universities is a work in progress in which experimentation and learning by doing are the order of the day. That suggests that researchers are lagging practitioners in exploring the interface between commercial engagement and entrepreneurship education.

It is that interface that is the focus of this chapter. The method is a case study, specifically the examination of the evolution of the entrepreneurship education initiative of a single research-intensive institution—the University of Manchester in the United Kingdom—and the ways in which that initiative has or has not contributed to the broader entrepreneurial and commercial engagement objectives of the university.[2] The Manchester case suggests that research-intensive universities wishing to bring entrepreneurship education and knowledge commercialization and commodification into effective and beneficial alignment—that is, in a broader model of the "entrepreneurial university" than characterizes conventional thinking today—face significant challenges that require determined strategies to overcome. At the same time, the potential benefits of mutually leveraging entrepreneurship education and commercial engagement are considerable. Since little can be generalized to other university situations from a single case, the challenges and opportunities identified in this chapter should be viewed as hypotheses requiring subsequent research.

The next section summarizes the work of the comparatively few scholars who have sought to conceptualize the link between entrepreneurial education and the entrepreneurial university. The section is followed by the case study, a discussion that draws implications for universities' efforts to link entrepreneurship education and commercial engagement and for scholars conducting research in this arena, and a brief conclusion.

2.   ANTECEDENTS

While research on the intersection of entrepreneurship education and the commercial engagement activities of universities' Third Mission is limited, there are several perspectives in the extant literature that merit discussion as background to the case study. Laukkanen (2000) argues universities should be understood as business "evolutionary machines" within their regions. As such, university officials may take different views of their institutions' appropriate engagement roles. For example, universities electing to take a *laissez-faire* approach would simply let their research and teaching activities drive any regional economic connections and impacts indirectly and randomly, implying no explicit commercial engagement strategy. Alternatively, a university adopting a *facilitative* model would encourage commercial linkages to university research activities and other assets in order support external economic activity but it would leave new venture creation to external actors and businesses. Finally, a university taking a *generative* approach would seek to directly foster university spin-outs and university-industry linkages for the express purpose of supporting regional venture creation or expansion.

For those many universities wishing to pursue a generative role, finding ways to influence the factors that drive new venture formation—things like environmental push and pull conditions, financial and technological resources, entrepreneurial actors and entrepreneurial teams, and business and product ideas and concepts—is essential. In turn, argues Laukkanen, any effort in the area of entrepreneurship education needs to be designed to contribute to this "business-generative strategy". In practice, that means much greater attention on tying students into real business contexts (e.g., via internships, project work, guest lectures by business owners, and site visits); orienting programmes around fostering business embryos or concepts; developing business teams and networks; and nurturing problem-solving skills whilst working on real problems with company partners. In essence, entrepreneurship education would entail building entrepreneurship skills and knowledge in the course of directly influencing regional economic development.

Laukkanen (2000) argues that universities often taken an overly individualistic approach to entrepreneurship education. The individualistic mind-set can be traced to the many theories of new venture creation which tend to emphasize the pivotal role of the lone and courageous entrepreneur, coupled with a predominance of empirical research that attempts to isolate the personal characteristics, traits, and family and professional backgrounds of entrepreneurs. Those theoretical and empirical traditions have strongly influenced many universities to design entrepreneurship education programmes with a mission to produce individual entrepreneurs, that is, "entrepreneurial individuals with high-level action tendencies and learning capabilities" along with appropriate levels of know-what, know-how, know-who (e.g., contacts and networks), and know-why (e.g., entrepreneurial values and goals) (Laukkanen, 2000, p. 29). Consistent with general business education, the programmes tend to prioritize the teaching of generalist skills, concepts, and theories over exposing students to highly specific existing and emerging business contexts, perhaps under the assumption that students will bring knowledge of business, technology, and market contexts with them to campus upon matriculation, especially at the postgraduate level where prior experience may be a nominal pre-requisite for admission. Laukkanen claims this model of entrepreneurship education actually aligns most closely with a laissez-faire view of the university's commercial engagement role in the sense that, although it is hoped the university will make contributions to job growth and economic development, it is "unusual to include such elements in the operative expectations, targets, and practices" of the entrepreneurship education programmes themselves (2000, p. 31). Thus the most common model of entrepreneurship education is inconsistent with a vision of the university as an actively generative agent in regional economic development.

Laukkanen claims there are several additional inadvertent effects of an individualistic, entrepreneur-as-business-hero, approach. First, it drives away analytically inclined students who are sceptical of their own abilities to arrive at a viable business idea, technology or product but who could be an important part of an entrepreneurial team, or who may have the capability to contribute to corporate entrepreneurship in an existing firm. Second, it places undue emphasis on cultivating the presumed traits of bold and entrepreneurial individuals and neglects the development of basic but perhaps more mundane managerial and technical skills. Third, it assumes too readily that students are capable of translating context-free knowledge and ideas to specific business and market situations. Finally, it over-emphasizes fostering business start-ups whilst neglecting to teach students how to detect opportunities in existing businesses, to build networks and teams, and to grow existing ventures. Growing companies, as opposed to founding them, typically requires teams of individuals with widely varying skill sets and interests, many of whom would not necessarily consider themselves entrepreneurial *per se*.

Context-specific training as advocated by Laukkanen is also endorsed by Hynes and Richardson (2007), who argue that entrepreneurship education programmes represent an opportunity to build valuable networks between faculty, students, and small business owners and local entrepreneurs. The premise is that an effective way for universities to deliver entrepreneurship training is by involving business owners and managers in course design and delivery, which serves to promote a broader internal culture of entrepreneurship among staff, which is then passed on to students through classroom work and hands-on projects. In principle, the benefits of such a model flow in two directions. Educators are able to tap the expertise of local business people and entrepreneurs while also creating a stock of real world business challenges for students to tackle through project or laboratory components of the training curriculum. Regular exposure to local entrepreneurs increases the likelihood of positive demonstration effects, found in some studies to be a key influence on students' choices to pursue their own entrepreneurial opportunities. In addition, by engaging regularly with students and faculty in entrepreneurship education programmes, business owners, managers, and entrepreneurs learn new concepts and skills themselves. In effect, entrepreneurship education serves a kind of double duty as skills training for students and an institutional mechanism for lifelong learning for local business people. In essence, it is one mode of commercial engagement.

Guenther and Wagner (2008) identify entrepreneurship education as an indirect mechanism for commercializing university knowledge, arguing that universities should develop ways to maximize internal synergies between entrepreneurship education and technology transfer activity. They investigate the entrepreneurship education and direct technology transfer activities of 49 German universities, focusing on the activities of entrepreneurship professorships. They find evidence of active cooperation between such professors and the technology transfer offices of many of the campuses in their sample, with the professor providing advisory services, offering consultation to would-be faculty entrepreneurs, serving in a partial staff role in the technology transfer office, or holding positions in local associations organized to support entrepreneurial activities. They conclude that the position of professor of entrepreneurship, whose numbers are growing across universities in Europe and the United States, is an important binding agent or node in a network that links technology transfer and the entrepreneurship education sides of the university. Unfortunately, Guenther and Wagner offer no specifics on the prescriptive question of how best to structure the professorships. One would expect that the details of the official duties, departmental home, resources, intellectual backgrounds, and research agendas of such professors would significantly influence their likelihood of advancing both the entrepreneurship education and commercial engagement missions of their campuses.

Each of the above contributions adds valuable insights but what is needed is an appropriate conceptual framework for characterizing and subsequently evaluating competing claims about how best to link entrepreneurship education and the commercial engagement component of the Third Mission, from Laukkanen's (2000) emphasis on real world business application, to Hynes and Richardson's (2007) argument for heavy reliance on external networks, to Guenther and Wagner's (2008) endorsement of entrepreneurship professorships. One option that has some promise is Burns's (2008) notion of the entrepreneurial architecture of a firm as applied to the higher education context by Nelles and Vorley (2010). Nelles and Vorley do not discuss entrepreneurship education. Rather, their concern is to find a way to bridge a divided literature on university commercial engagement that consists of macro studies of the entrepreneurial university and micro studies of university entrepreneurship but little overlap between the two. Following Burns, they posit that a university's entrepreneurial architecture consists of five institutional building blocks: *structures*, like technology transfer offices, incubators, and technology parks; *systems*, like formal linkages and networks of communication between structures and departmental units; *strategies*, namely institutional goals as codified in documents and plans as well as formally adopted incentives structures and policies; *leadership* as characterized by leaders' qualifications and their orientation toward the Third Mission; and culture, specifically institutional and departmental norms and attitudes toward enterprise and the concept of the entrepreneurial university.

Although Nelles and Vorley do not discuss the place of entrepreneurship education in this scheme, it is not hard to see where it might fit, such as in the systems element as a networking mechanism (à la Hynes and Richardson) or the cultural element through the shaping of norms and practices. For the purposes of this chapter, the validity of the specific elements of the entrepreneurial architecture is less important than the concept of architecture as a problem framing device. Nelles and Vorley's approach is an advance in the literature on university-business engagement in that it looks to construct a general framework for describing and comparing different university models and approaches. Still, there is much work to do to actually carry out those comparisons. At present, existing research mostly provides just a sketch of some of the ways entrepreneurship education may interface with university commercial engagement and the entrepreneurial university very generally. The aim of the case study reported in the next section is to use one research-intensive university's experience with entrepreneurship education to specify areas of existing and potential alignment between entrepreneurship education and commercial engagement in greater detail and to identify challenges that need to be overcome to leverage the two areas jointly.

The focus is the Manchester Enterprise Centre, now in its thirteenth year of operation in a large research university—the University of Manchester—situated in a region of England with a long history of academic science in service of industrialization. In Laukkanen's (2000) framework, it could be argued that the University of Manchester has evolved from a de facto laissez-faire approach to a generative approach to its commercial engagement and entrepreneurial activities, although the implementation of its engagement and entrepreneurial aspirations has at times been somewhat haphazard. The mission and programmes of the Manchester Enterprise Centre have both evolved alongside the university's Third Mission agenda whilst also helping to shape that agenda.

3.   THE CASE

The Manchester Enterprise Centre (MEC) was established as a joint effort of the University of Manchester Institute of Science and Technology

(UMIST) and the Victoria University of Manchester (VUM) in March 2000, with the Manchester Metropolitan University and University of Salford participating loosely as collaborating institutions.[3] Together, VUM and UMIST were arguably among the UK's most "entrepreneurial" universities at the time of MEC's founding. A review prepared in 2003 identified some 40 spin-off companies between the two campuses (the 40 firms collectively raising over £100 million in start-up funding) and 30 licences or sales of intellectual property. Both VUM and UMIST had well-established and effective commercialization offices, a diverse mix of externally facing centres of excellence, and solid record of networking and business engagement (VUM and UMIST 2003).[4] A bibliometric study of university-industry co-publishing ranked the Victoria University of Manchester among the top five co-publishing universities in the UK over the 1995–2000 period, with 120 industrial partners identified, including Astrazeneca, Glaxo Wellcome, SmithKline Beecham, ICI, AEA Technology, and Unilever (Calvert and Patel 2003).

A £3 million Science Enterprise Challenge (SEC) grant provided the start-up support for MEC, originally named the Manchester Science and Enterprise Centre (MSEC), reflecting its initial mandate to establish an entrepreneurship education agenda targeted on the science and engineering disciplines. The UK Department for Business Innovation and Skills states that the purpose of the Science Enterprise Challenge was to establish "a network of centres in UK universities, specializing in the teaching and practice of commercialization and entrepreneurialism in the field of science and technology".[5] MEC was one of twelve centres created with the first round of SEC spending; a second round of funding added a thirteenth centre in 2001, bringing the total number of universities involved in the programme to 39, given collaborative efforts among institutions. After 2001, the SEC programme was absorbed as an initiative of the Higher Education Innovation Fund (HEIF). SEC and related HEIF-supported initiatives in entrepreneurship education are part of the broader effort to promote an "enterprise culture" in the UK, an agenda developed by the Thatcher government in the 1980s as a solution to high unemployment arising from a campaign to tackle a running deficit and accumulating national debt by eliminating significant public spending, deregulating selected sectors, curbing union power, and encouraging private investment by cutting taxes and reducing regulatory red tape (Della-Giusta and King 2006). Enterprise has been advanced in various ways by subsequent governments ever since (Hannon 2007).

MEC moved quickly to develop a set of internally accredited undergraduate and graduate courses aimed at assisting students to refine their own ideas for new marketable technologies or services and to develop the beginnings of related new ventures, a kind of "how to" approach to entrepreneurship education. From the very beginning, the core of MEC's programme has been a one-year university-wide Master of Enterprise (MEnt), which students pursue from a specific disciplinary home under the teaching and guidance of MEC staff. The MEnt admitted its first cohort in fall 2001 and currently educates around fifteen students per year. Despite its nominally small size, MEC considers the MEnt as central to its mission because the degree's design and content embodies MEC's philosophy of enterprise teaching as cultivating the nascent entrepreneur from business idea to business creation. MEC describes its mission as "taking students from undergraduate level to entrepreneurial proficiency" (MSEC 2000b, p. 6).[6] MEC routinely carves off or modifies MEnt modules to serve audiences with different interests and foci, whether at the undergraduate, graduate, or executive education levels.

While no undergraduate enterprise degree programmes are currently offered at Manchester, undergraduates may take up to 20 MEC-delivered enterprise-related credits per year under the guidelines of their individual schools or departments, either as required or optional study units. Many of MEC's undergraduate offerings are designed to help the physical and life sciences, computer science, and engineering disciplines meet a need for entrepreneurship content demanded by their own external accrediting bodies. Those disciplines thus represent a reasonably stable source of demand for MEC's programmes, although there is nothing to prevent individual disciplines and schools from meeting their accreditation requirements through in-house teaching. Another source of demand for MEC is the significant number of non-business students who value access to courses on entrepreneurship themes, especially if they are tailored in ways that align with their chosen fields, something MEC emphasizes in its course design and teaching model.

MEC also contributes electives to a Master of Science (MSc) in Innovation, Management and Entrepreneurship, which is intended for students who have no immediate desire to start a business but who wish to know more about entrepreneurship, often as part of plans to pursue a PhD in innovation management. Other MEC programmes include a postgraduate Diploma in Enterprise Management as a mandatory element of the Engineering Doctorate and as a part-time executive education option; an enterprise pathway for an MSc in International Fashion Retailing; and an MSc in Biotechnology and Enterprise offered in the Faculty of Life Sciences. The mix of MEC's teaching is broad but it is the approximately 1,000 University of Manchester undergraduates taking MEC courses each year who are particularly important: they provide the fee transfer income that forms the largest share of the Centre's financial support.

In fall 2004, UMIST and the Victoria University of Manchester merged to form the current University of Manchester (UM). MEC was situated in the new university's Faculty of Engineering and Physical Sciences until early 2008, when its home shifted to the Manchester Business School (MBS) by mutual agreement of the University, MBS and MEC. Administratively, MEC now resides in one of MBS's four academic divisions—the Division of Innovation, Management and Policy (IMP)—and MEC's governance is aided by an advisory board consisting of the director of MBS (the chair of the board), the Head of the IMP Division, representatives of the university's four faculties, UM's Vice President for Economic Development and Innovation, and UM's Vice President for Research and Engagement (in an ex officio capacity). Therefore, MEC is line managed at the sub-school level but the advisory board provides a mechanism for addressing its historically university-wide remit.

MEC currently has a staff of twelve, including a non-academic executive director, five professional and administrative staff (two of whom also teach), six lecturers with teaching-focused appointments, one lecturer with a research and teaching appointment, and several very loosely affiliated research-focused faculty members.[7] Although its teaching-focused faculty are expected to conduct some research or knowledge transfer as part of their duties and for their own professional advancement, MEC does not have a significant academic research programme. Its non-teaching activities mainly consist of holding yearly on-campus venture competitions, hosting an annual conference on entrepreneurship designed for graduate students in all fields, and undertaking a variety of informal networking and partnering activities with stakeholders on and off campus.

3.1 Evolution

MEC has transitioned from its inception as grant-funded entity without an on-going revenue stream and facing the need to develop programmes from the ground up to a successful teaching centre fuelled by a stable source of student fee income, a share of HEIF funding, and occasional project grants and contracts. MEC has put considerable effort into developing its suite of course offerings, which are tailored to deliver a logical sequence of entrepreneurship education content. Unlike some university entrepreneurship centres, MEC is not simply an umbrella and broker for entrepreneurship-related courses around the campus. MEC contributes to the mission of its parent entity—the Manchester Business School—by providing a vehicle for the extension of business and management teaching into non-business fields in the university, at least with respect to entrepreneurship-related content, and by spearheading MBS' teaching contribution to the larger university's strategic goal of enhancing enterprise. Organizationally, MEC stands as an entrepreneurship education partner alongside the university's technology commercialization infrastructure and portfolio of scholarly research in entrepreneurship conducted by individual faculty members. What such partnerships mean in practice remains a work in progress, however.

The evolution of entrepreneurship education at Manchester diverged somewhat from the plans and rhetoric expressed by the university partners at MEC's founding, when a vision of MEC with a broad remit that extended tangibly into the commercialization arena was laid out. At its launch event, UMIST Chancellor Professor Sir Roland Smith declared that the centre would be "an enabling body—promoting the learning and practice of enterprise and the exploitation of our intellectual property" and that the aim was "to create an internationally renowned centre of excellence [in] Manchester, to study and understand enterprise and to stimulate entrepreneurial activity so that the region will be known throughout the world as a centre for technology transfer at the forefront of knowledge" (MSEC 2000a, p. 1–2). The centre's first business plan called for it to establish entrepreneurship education programmes for both students and would-be academic entrepreneurs (professors and staff researchers, particularly bench scientists with the greatest potential to generate innovations and technologies with commercial potential), professional training programmes for aspiring entrepreneurs in the area business community, and a scholarly research agenda around enterprise (MSEC 2000b). The latter would be led by a professor of entrepreneurship based in the centre. In fact, an entrepreneurship professor appointment that brought an internationally renowned entrepreneurship scholar to the university was made shortly before launch. MEC was off to a fast start.

Operationalizing specific connections between MEC and the commercialization activities of the university proved easier said than done, however, as did developing a corpus of entrepreneurship research. Certainly MEC was loosely affiliated with the separate technology commercialization offices of Victoria University of Manchester and UMIST before the universities merged and is now so affiliated with the University of Manchester Innovation Group, UMI³, the I-cubed moniker referencing the university's goals to inspire, invent, and innovate. UMI³ is a consortium and centralized professional support services provider to the merged university's incubator organization (University Manchester Incubator Centre, or UMIC) and intellectual property commercialization office (University of Manchester Intellectual Property, or UMIP). UMI³ was established in late 2011 to better integrate the efforts of UMIC and UMIP around the broader agenda of commercialization and technology transfer.

UMI[3]'s major integrative strategy is an Enterprise Forum, which aims to "unite the external community, whose interests lie in entrepreneurship and innovation, with the University's academic/research community through a series of workshops, seminars and events".[8] The Enterprise Forum sounds much like an activity MEC might have been expected to undertake as it was conceived in 2000. At present, MEC does not have a significant commercial engagement effort, in part because of uncertainty about what role it is best suited to play in the Business School and broader campus.

In the area of research, MEC has articulated a set of broad themes it sees as important to advancing its work. However, because there is no longer a professor of entrepreneurship appointed in MEC, and because the majority of MEC staff hold teaching-focused appointments, the Centre does not have the resources and expertise currently to pursue a goal of becoming an internationally renowned centre in the study of entrepreneurship.

3.2 A Shift in Focus

There are several reasons why MEC's focus shifted ever more heavily into on-campus undergraduate and post-graduate teaching and away from the kinds of commercial engagement activities epitomized by UMI[3]'s Enterprise Forum or research in entrepreneurship as conceived in its original business plan. Those reasons provide insights into why entrepreneurship education, entrepreneurship research, and "entrepreneurial university" functions (commercialization and commodification activities) remain as silos on many university campuses despite the calls of scholars and policy makers for greater integration (e.g., Guenther and Wagner 2008; PACEC 2009). In turn, they suggest ways those silos might be broken down if universities committed themselves to doing so.

Among the most important reasons is that MEC has been shaped profoundly by an overriding objective to secure a base level of funding to sustain its activities. Universities and business schools sometimes develop entrepreneurship education programmes as one among several strategic responses to a shifting fiscal and political environment (Laukkanen 2000). Universities are being called upon to demonstrate their contributions to job creation while at the same time facing a need to broaden their revenue sources. Cultivating entrepreneurs is one way to meet both needs, along with efforts in the areas of commercialization and commodification (Jacob, Lundqvist et al. 2003). Although that may be part of the story behind the decisions of UMIST and Victoria University to create MEC, initially the two partner universities relied heavily on a national government initiative because it promised substantial external resources. That obviated the need to dedicate significant initial internal funding; they needed only provide indirect support in facilities and services. The national government's intention was that universities receiving SEC support would find a way to achieve financial sustainability for enterprise programmes. The universities, in turn, viewed achieving financial sustainability as one of MEC's chief concerns.

MEC set out to achieve resource sustainability in two ways: by remaining flexible and responsive to other national enterprise-related initiatives that presented opportunities to win more grants and by prioritizing on-campus accredited undergraduate and post-graduate courses and modules that would generate stable tuition fee or fee-transfer income. That had two important implications. On the one hand, MEC sometimes involved itself in initiatives that were not well-aligned with the entrepreneurship agenda laid out in its founding, in part to tap grant revenue and in part to maintain its involvement in general university efforts around entrepreneurship and commercial engagement. On the other hand, MEC was anxious to protect the quality of its educational programmes since they drove the most secure revenue source. That inevitably meant that it could not always commit fully to special projects. For a small organization, pursuing special projects grant by grant and building new education programmes do not always dovetail with one another; new grant-funded initiatives often require the devotion of staff effort to meeting implementation and performance monitoring requirements that detract from, rather than leverage or enrich, teaching programmes.

Initially, from the perspective of survival, it made some sense for the organization to couple opportunism in grantsmanship with a focus on establishing and protecting a flow of tuition revenue. However, as the number of students on its teaching programmes expanded, MEC naturally shifted its resources and energy toward satisfying and growing that student demand. In turn, that reduced the organization's incentive to develop a more comprehensive strategy for linking entrepreneurship education, entrepreneurship research, and commercial engagement. Gradually concerns over such linkages receded into the background, especially as other university entities such as UMIP and UMIC formalized and expanded their functions. A general approach to entrepreneurship education and the entrepreneurial university as a division of labour among organizations focused in different spheres—the seeds of a silo approach, in essence— found its origins in the default financial model the partner universities chose to adopt for MEC from the start.

Yet, in some sense, the financial considerations around the formation of an entrepreneurship education agenda at Manchester are only an indicator of a more fundamental issue. When UMIST and Victoria University joined forces to pursue SEC funding to establish an enterprise centre, certainly they embraced the view that building entrepreneurship education into their missions had inherent value. However, the imperative of responding to the SEC programme also effectively substituted for a need to develop an independent university-level entrepreneurship education strategy from first principles. For reasons noted above, in subsequent years, MEC, along with a shifting mix of university partners, applied for and received a series of grants to implement selected initiatives driven by the UK government's enterprise agenda. Under those circumstances, MEC's strategic perspective was naturally oriented toward meeting the goals of national funding agencies rather than any explicit internal university strategy. In fact, it would be fair to say that there really has been no explicit university strategy for entrepreneurship education at Manchester beyond MEC, and MEC itself is ultimately a creature of a very general central government vision of the role and importance of enterprise in higher education. It is notable that in the University of Manchester's 2011/12 strategic planning document, entrepreneurship and enterprise skills training is mentioned very briefly, but it is in reference to the Manchester Leadership Programme rather than MEC (UM 2011, p. 10).

After the merger, the new university had to bring together two sets of technology commercialization and technology transfer functions, first in UMIP and UMIC, and then in UMI[3] as a consortium of those two entities. It was recognized that clarifying MEC's position and role within the university's broader Third Mission agenda could have considerable value. MEC's relocation to within Manchester Business School (MBS) reflected MBS's general aspirations in entrepreneurship and business engagement, and was certainly consistent with the prevailing trend in Europe and the United States to situate entrepreneurship education in business schools. MBS inherited MEC's well-established teaching programmes but also its sense of uncertainty about how best to contribute in the areas of entrepreneurship research and commercial engagement. Since the new business school itself had not yet developed a specific strategy for how it wished to incorporate entrepreneurship education into its existing curricula or how enterprise might form part of its own external engagement and research missions, it has looked to MEC to help shape that strategy. That appears to make sense on the face of it, since entrepreneurship constitutes MEC's expertise. Yet MEC's evolution in terms of mission, structure and staffing means that it is not in a strong position to shape a wider business school agenda.

To some members of faculty in Manchester Business School, which aspires to be a world leader in research and also aggressively engage with entrepreneurs and corporate leaders, especially in greater Manchester and northern England, MEC's central mission of on-campus interdisciplinary teaching is perceived as somewhat pedestrian, a version of "business-light" or "mini-MBA" education. For its part, MEC believes it is satisfying, on behalf of the business school, an important university-level strategic goal of embedding entrepreneurship in the Manchester student experience. The result is a kind of impasse; each organization's view of how best to strengthen and expand the school's entrepreneurship and engagement activities differs significantly. It is easiest to see this by considering how MEC's activities have evolved with respect to the two traditional missions of the modern research university: teaching and research.

3.3   MEC and Enterprise Teaching

MEC's original teaching mission was to strengthen an understanding of entrepreneurship, and to encourage entrepreneurial behaviour, among students in the science and engineering disciplines. Much as Hynes and Richardson (2007) suggest, initially it sought to do that by identifying and recruiting mentors from among entrepreneurs in the region and tapping professors and lecturers from among its partner universities (MSEC 2000b). Opportunities to teach courses, workshops, and seminars were also seen as a potential means of drawing in external stakeholders like small business owners and specialist real-world experts in technology transfer, finance, and business strategy. The Centre's professor of entrepreneurship was also expected to deliver entrepreneurship teaching.

MEC struggled with the model early on. Although area entrepreneurs and external stakeholders were often willing to offer workshops or individual lectures on a one-off basis, few were interested in the kind of sustained relationship necessary to effectively staff repeated teaching offerings in a broad but carefully sequenced curriculum. The quality of the teaching of the externals was also mixed; students often reviewed the course deliveries poorly. Here MEC's imperative to establish stable tuition fee income via accredited courses came heavily into play. The organization had to assure the delivery of reasonably fixed, high quality content on a routine basis if partnering disciplines were to trust it as an "outsourcing" option for their entrepreneurship training needs. The value of relying more heavily on internal instructors whose deliveries would strengthen with repeated offerings of the same material, an approach that also minimized the transactions costs of delivering sequences of courses within the academic calendar, became evident. However, many university faculty members with research expertise in entrepreneurship are most comfortable teaching *about* entrepreneurship in historical, theoretical, and conceptual terms and are not particularly well suited to delivering courses in the "how to" of vetting ideas and creating new ventures. Moreover, those faculty members conducting research about entrepreneurship are typically based in the business and social sciences disciplines. Only a few possess the cases, examples, and practical experiences to readily connect with students in engineering, physical sciences, and life sciences whose interests in entrepreneurship fundamentally are instrumental rather than substantive.

MEC's response was to cultivate its own corps of instructors. It set up an Enterprise Fellowship Programme that provided funding for graduate students to attend classes in the Master of Enterprise programme; take university-offered short courses in teaching skills, pedagogy, technologies; and generally participate in the activities of the Centre. Upon completion of the programme, participants were given the opportunity to apply for lectureships in MEC. In fact, several former and current MEC staff members were Enterprise Fellows. In this way, MEC was able to build stable teaching capacity tailored to its particular model of entrepreneurship education. That worked well in the context of its teaching-focused mission and financial model, but it also distanced the organization from both research and commercial engagement as traditionally conceived in the university. It meant also that the majority of its members of staff do not have a strong academic research background or orientation, that there are only loose ties between researchers elsewhere in the university and MEC, and that external stakeholders like small firm owners or entrepreneurs are not core to the bulk of MEC's teaching. On the other hand, permanent lecturers with a teaching focus often draw in external experts as guests and small firms as project cases, creating scope for the kinds of synergistic learning advocated by many entrepreneurship education scholars (Smith, Collins et al. 2006).

3.4   MEC and Entrepreneurship Research

As noted above, MEC's founding mission called for it to be a centre of excellence in the study of entrepreneurship. This dimension of its activities was expected to be shaped and led by its appointed professor of entrepreneurship, who was a noted scholar in the characteristics and behaviours of entrepreneurs. Yet efforts to build a research programme never materialized in a significant way, in large measure because the scholarly agenda of the entrepreneurship professor did not align with the practical teaching mission of the Centre. The source of the problem might be traced to differences in perspectives and personalities among the individuals involved. Certainly that was part of the issue. However, building a scholarly research agenda that draws advantage from the undertaking of practical entrepreneurship teaching is not an obvious task. Shane and Venkataraman (2000, p. 218) define entrepreneurship research as "the scholarly examination of how, by whom, and with what effects opportunities to create future goods and services are discovered, evaluated, and exploited". They stress that entrepreneurship as an area of enquiry is neither simply a research setting—the study of small firms, new firms, or new firm founders—nor a teaching application. This notion of entrepreneurship research is quite distinct from the kind of scholarship that would seem to align with an entrepreneurship education organization, namely research on approaches to, and impacts of, entrepreneurship teaching (e.g., Lee, Chang et al. 2005; Matlay 2005; Fayolle, Gailly et al. 2006; Matlay 2006b; Oosterbeek, van Praag et al. 2010; von Graevenitz, Harhoff et al. 2010). On the other hand, one could envision ways that the teaching of entrepreneurship might serve as a laboratory for scholars inclined to study entrepreneurial behaviour, entrepreneurial opportunity capture, and other foci of traditional entrepreneurship research.

3.5 A Crossroads

As of this writing, MEC and MBS have reached a strategic crossroads. There is clearly a need to reconsider from first principles the role of entrepreneurship in the school, alongside the larger question of where the business school can best contribute to the university's commercial engagement agenda. Laying out an entrepreneurship strategy for the school that firmly embeds entrepreneurship education—which is effectively what MEC currently represents—would not seem an impossible task. Indeed, there would appear to be many opportunities to align entrepreneurship education in ways that both draw on and leverage the school's activities in traditional management teaching, business research, and external engagement. However, the experience at Manchester suggests that the challenge may be greater than it first appears. The expertise and background of MEC's enterprise teaching staff are, in many ways, considerably different than those of traditional business school faculty; the research activities that MEC might best undertake are not self-evident and attempts to chart a course in scholarship have stalled once already; and the best ways MEC might link to the university's commercial engagement and technology transfer missions remain to be worked out. The picture is one of considerable strength on which to build, but much building remains to be done.

4. DISCUSSION

What are the major lessons one can draw from the Manchester case regarding the prospect of fruitfully aligning entrepreneurship education and the commercial engagement component of universities' Third Mission? In posing this question, the presumption is that the Manchester experience is at least somewhat emblematic of the evolution of enterprise and Third Mission initiatives at other universities.

First, one unintended legacy of the Science Enterprise Challenge initiative and follow-on programmes that supported the development of entrepreneurship education in the UK may have been to slow the development of tangible, self-driven university-level strategies for entrepreneurship. Rumelt (2011) defines the "kernel" of good strategy as consisting of a diagnosis that characterizes a challenge or opportunity, a guiding policy that frames general principles for selecting actions to address the challenge or capture the opportunity, and a set of consistent and coordinated actions. A strategy does not necessarily require a strategic plan as conventionally understood, but it should be articulated in clear and explicit terms if it is both to serve as a guide to policy and action, and to be subjected to evaluation, reconsideration, and adjustment. By this standard, there was some strategic thinking that guided the development of MEC (in its original business plan, annual report updates, and strategic plans) but there was very little strategy for how MEC was to be situated in the larger Third Mission agenda of the university. In other words, there was a plan that facilitated the winning of SEC grant funds and provided criteria for performance and evaluation of MEC as an organization, but that plan was shaped by government in large measure. Likewise, within the Manchester Business School, a school-level strategy for the field of entrepreneurship remains to be defined. For example, entrepreneurship teaching of the kind MEC delivers does not figure explicitly in MBS's current strategic plan. Thus, the Manchester case may be an example of the challenge of firmly embedding an initiative catalysed with external resources into a broader institutional strategy. Certainly the pattern of research and other kinds of centres languishing or disappearing after external funding is exhausted is common in academia. MEC has avoided that fate, a testimony to its resourcefulness and the general campus and business school commitments to its programmes. However, MEC also needs to nest itself in strategies for entrepreneurship and engagement that are specified at levels beyond its control, namely MBS and the university. Those strategies are still under development.

Second, the question of the sustainability of entrepreneurship education programmes on university campuses is itself complicated. MEC regards itself as self-sustaining; in essence, a success story when juxtaposed against several other similar centres established around the UK with SEC funds which are now defunct. However, from the perspective of the University of Manchester, the bulk of MEC's revenue is a transfer. Students mostly in sciences and engineering disciplines take MEC courses and a portion of their fees accrue back to MEC. The kinds of programmes that might draw external fees into the campus, things like executive education or fundraising to solicit corporate donations or contributions, are a very small part of MEC's activities, in large measure because MEC must concentrate on generating fee income transfers. In some sense, then, MEC's focus on general entrepreneurship teaching in traditional classroom settings *is* the university's entrepreneurship education strategy. A different model for MEC, one that involved greater involvement in research and engagement, would necessitate either the university or business school providing the necessary funding to justify the diversion of MEC staff effort from mainline on-campus teaching. Again, the issue comes back to how the entrepreneurship and commercial engagement missions are defined above the level of MEC itself.

Third, calls in the scholarly literature for the involvement of high level local entrepreneurs and business people as teachers in entrepreneurship education courses ignore the challenge such a model poses for operating comprehensive entrepreneurship education curricula in a cost-effective way on a routine basis. Likewise, the notion that entrepreneurship education programmes can draw mostly on traditional university faculty members across multiple disciplines to offer courses is overly optimistic. Establishing long-term relationships with external instructors can be very difficult, especially when those instructors are working in highly fluid and unstable industries, as entrepreneurs tend to be. Traditional university faculty often lack the experience and background to deliver the heavily practice-based teaching common to entrepreneurship education. Manchester's cultivation of its own teaching staff is one solution. It is a model that needs to be compared to those of other universities to determine if it is the best solution.

Fourth, the proper role of scholarly research in entrepreneurship education remains unclear. The problem can be traced to issues of expertise and substantive focus. Regarding expertise, the best entrepreneurship education teachers may not be those with the disciplinary training and professional interest to develop and maintain a scholarly research agenda around entrepreneurship. Regarding substance, the kinds of insights that the practice of entrepreneurship education might yield for the understanding of entrepreneurship are not self-evident. The solution may be to assume that the research agenda of entrepreneurship educators should be focused on the pedagogies and technologies of entrepreneurship teaching. On the other hand, there may be more significant opportunities to align entrepreneurship teaching, entrepreneurship research, and research *about* the entrepreneurial university than initially appears. For example, entrepreneurship educators work very closely with students and sometimes faculty who are would-be entrepreneurs. Viewing the undertaking of entrepreneurship teaching itself as a unique laboratory setting for understanding entrepreneurship would grant organizations like MEC an important role in contributing observational data to support research on the behaviour, inclinations, and approaches of specific classes of entrepreneurs, namely students and university staff. Organizations like MEC would have the potential to make specific kinds of research contributions on the substance of entrepreneurship and the Third Mission, a vision that broadens the research scope of specialized entrepreneurship educators modestly beyond the study of alternative learning models and pedagogy. Clearly, more thinking is needed on the potential synergies among different areas of entrepreneurship and entrepreneurship education research, but there may be more opportunities to mutually leverage the entrepreneurship teaching and research agendas of entrepreneurial universities than first meets the eye.

5.   CONCLUSION

Many research-intensive universities are seeking to develop proactive commercialization, commodification, and commercial engagement strategies to replace ad hoc efforts driven by the individual initiatives of researchers and their networks. Together, commercialization and commodification may be seen as selected components of universities' broader "Third Mission" to contribute to the development of their home regions by strengthening their engagement with the public, private, and third sectors. Entrepreneurship education programmes have tended to develop in parallel to such "entrepreneurial university" initiatives, rather than in intentional alignment with them. This is reflected in the research literature as well, where the analysis of the *entrepreneurial university* and studies of *entrepreneurship education* have almost no overlap. Drawing on a case study of the University of Manchester, this chapter identifies several issues related to resources, research emphasis and expertise, and pedagogical approach that must be addressed to properly integrate entrepreneurship education and entrepreneurial university strategies. Since findings are based on a single case, the issues identified constitute hypotheses worthy of further study.

NOTES

1. Although *enterprise education* and *entrepreneurship education* are terms that are often used synonymously in the international literature, they have specific meanings in the context of the UK education system (Gibb 1993). *Enterprise education* refers to efforts

to impart "enterprising" attributes and behaviours (e.g., self-confidence, creativity, resourcefulness) without a particular focus on encouraging the exploitation of for-profit opportunities or new venture formation. A central educational objective of *entrepreneurship education* is to develop in individuals both the skills and inclination to create a new enterprise or establish a new line of business in an existing firm. The focus of this chapter primarily is on entrepreneurship education activities of universities, although the lines between entrepreneurship and enterprise education tend to be blurred in practice. The subject of the case study—the Manchester Enterprise Centre—delivers a mix of entrepreneurship and enterprise education programmes.

2. The clarification of the type of university is important. Ways in which entrepreneurship education and commercial engagement can be joined up and mutually leveraged are different for research-intensive versus teaching focused institutions. For example, whether or not staff in entrepreneurship education programmes should engage in significant research as part of a larger entrepreneurship research agenda is likely to be a greater concern in research-intensives than in other kinds of institutions. Likewise, teaching focused institutions will engage with the business sector differently than research-intensive universities with significant capacity to conduct contract research, spin-out companies, and enter into licensing agreements. I thank an anonymous reviewer for pointing this out.

3. The information and data reported in the case study is based on extensive interviews with staff of the Manchester Enterprise Centre and Manchester Business School as well as a review of the organization's original business plan, annual reports, curricula materials, and strategic planning documents. Special thanks to Lynn Sheppard for reading the manuscript with care and offering clarifications, corrections, and suggestions.

4. Victoria University of Manchester was served by Manchester Innovation Ltd. (MIL), which at the time of MEC's founding was processing about 80 disclosures per year. UMIST Ventures Ltd. (UVL) acted as UMIST's commercialization agent and support service. MIL and UVL were combined to form one intellectual property office following the merger of the two universities.

5. See http://www.bis.gov.uk/policies/science/knowledge-transfer/earlierschemes/science_enterprise_challenge.

6. An analogy to medical training is articulated in MEC's founding business plan (MSEC 2000b, p. 6): "The Centre will follow the form of the successful model of medical training, which depends upon a structured relationship between a medical school and its associated teaching hospitals. This approach encompasses the worlds of the academic and the practitioner, allowing both to fulfil their respective duties with mutual benefit. Through problem based learning and mentored experience, students will learn the facts and how to apply them. The Centre will operate in conjunction with the business incubators of its Partners and Collaborators, forming the 'teaching hospital' part of the model. The defining feature of this model is the way it amalgamates and interlocks education and training, taking students from undergraduate level to entrepreneurial proficiency."

7. Staff members in teaching-focused appointments at UM are expected to spend 20 per cent of their time in research and creative activity, as compared to 40 per cent for traditional academic appointments. In addition, it is usually assumed that the research and creative activity of teaching-focused staff will address teaching philosophy, pedagogy, and methods, and/or knowledge transfer.

8. See http://www.umi3.co.uk/enterprise.htm.

REFERENCES

Arbo, Peter and Paul Benneworth (2007), 'Understanding the regional contribution of higher education institutions', OECD Education Working Papers No. 9, Paris: OECD.

Burns, Paul (2008), *Corporate Entrepreneurship: Building the Entrepreneurial Organization*, Basingstoke, UK: Palgrave Macmillan.

Calvert, J. and P. Patel (2003), 'University-industry research collaborations in the UK: bibliometric trends', *Science and Public Policy*, 30, 85–96.

Della-Giusta, Marina and Zella King (2006), 'Enterprise culture', in M. Casson, B. Yeung, A. Basu and N. Wadeson (eds), *The Oxford Handbook of Entrepreneurship*, Oxford, UK: Oxford University Press, pp. 629–47.

Etzkowitz, Henry, Andrew Webster, Christiane Gebhardt and Branca Regina Cantisano Terra (2000), 'The future of the university and the university of the future: evolution of ivory tower to entrepreneurial paradigm', *Research Policy*, 29, 313–30.

European Commission (2010), *Europe 2010: A Strategy for Smart, Sustainable and Inclusive Growth*, Brussels: European Commission.

Fayolle, Alain, Benoît Gailly and Narjisse Lassas-Clerc (2006), 'Assessing the impact of entrepreneurship education programmes: a new methodology', *Journal of European Industrial Training*, 30, 701–20.

Gibb, Allan A. (1993), 'The enterprise culture and education: understanding enterprise education and its links with small business, entrepreneurship and wider educational goals', *International Small Business Journal*, 11, 11–34.

Guenther, Jutta and Kerstin Wagner (2008), 'Getting out of the ivory tower – new perspectives on the entrepreneurial university', *European Journal of International Management*, 2, 400–417.

Hannon, Paul (2007), 'Enterprise for all? The fragility of enterprise provision across England's HEIs', *Journal of Small Business and Enterprise Development*, 14, 183–210.

Henrekson, Magnus and Nathan Rosenberg (2001), 'Designing efficient institutions for science-based entrepreneurship: lesson from the US and Sweden', *Journal of Technology Transfer*, 26, 207–31.

Hynes, Briga and Ita Richardson (2007), 'Entrepreneurship education: a mechanism for engaging and exchanging with the small business sector', *Education + Training*, 49, 732–44.

Jacob, Merle, Mats Lundqvist and Hans Hellsmark (2003), 'Entrepreneurial transformations in the Swedish university system: the case of Chalmers University of Technology', *Research Policy*, 32, 1555–68.

Jongbloed, Ben, Jürgen Enders and Carlo Salerno (2008), 'Higher education and its communities: interconnections, interdependencies and a research agenda', *Higher Education*, 56, 303–24.

Laukkanen, Mauri (2000), 'Exploring alternative approaches in high-level entrepreneurship education: creating micro-mechanisms for endogenous regional growth', *Entrepreneurship and Regional Development*, 12, 25–47.

Lawton Smith, Helen and Sharmistha Bagchi-Sen (2011), 'The research university, entrepreneurship and regional development: research propositions and current evidence', *Entrepreneurship and Regional Development*, iFirst.

Lee, Sang M., Daesung Chang and Seong-Base Lim (2005), 'Impact of entrepreneurial education: a comparative study of the U.S. and Korea', *International Entrepreneurship and Management Journal*, 1, 27–43.

Matlay, Harry (2005), 'Researching entrepreneurship and education, Part 1: What is entrepreneurship and does it matter?', *Education + Training*, 47, 665–77.

Matlay, Harry (2006b), 'Researching entrepreneurship and education, Part 2:

What is entrepreneurship education and does it matter?', *Education + Training*, 48, 704–18.

MSEC (2000a), Launch Event Draft Speeches Amended 20.11.00. Manchester, UK, Manchester Science Enterprise Centre.

MSEC (2000b), *Manchester Science Enterprise Center: Business Plan 2000*, Manchester, UK: Manchester Science Enterprise Centre.

Nelles, Jen and Tim Vorley (2010), 'Constructing an entrepreneurial architecture: an emergent framework for studying the contemporary university beyond the entrepreneurial turn', *Innovation in Higher Education*, 35, 161–76.

Oosterbeek, Hessel, Mirjam van Praag and Auke Ijsselstein (2010), 'The impact of entrepreneurship education on entrepreneurship skills and motivation', *European Economic Review*, 54, 442–54.

PACEC (2009), *Evaluation of the Effectiveness and Role of HEFCE/OSI Third Stream Funding*, Cambridge, UK: Public and Corporate Economic Consultants.

Rizza, Caroline and Celeste Amorim Varum (ND), 'Directions in entrepreneurship education in Europe', Ispra, Italy, European Commission, Joint Research Centre, Econometrics and Applied Statistics Unit, Centre for Research on Lifelong Learning.

Rothaermel, Frank T., Shanti D. Agung and Lin Jiang (2007), 'University entrepreneurship: a taxonomy of the literature', *Industrial and Corporate Change*, 16, 691–791.

Rumelt, Richard (2011), *Good Strategy, Bad Strategy*, London: Profile Books.

Shane, Scott and S. Venkataraman (2000), 'The promise of entrepreneurship as a field of research', *Academy of Management Review*, 25, 217–26.

Smith, A.J., L.A. Collins and P.D. Hannon (2006), 'Embedding new entrepreneurship programmes in UK higher education institutions: challenges and considerations', *Education + Training*, 48, 555–67.

UM (2011), *Advancing the Manchester 2015 Agenda: The Strategic Plan of The University of Manchester*, Manchester, UK: University of Manchester.

VUM and UMIST (2003), *Delivering New University/Business Partnerships: Submission to the Lambert Review of Business-University Collaboration*, Manchester: University of Manchester and University of Manchester Institute of Science and Technology.

von Graevenitz, Georg, Dietmar Harhoff and Richard Weber (2010), 'The effects of entrepreneurship education', *Journal of Economic Behavior and Organization*, 76, 90–112.

PART III

Knowledge and technology transfer dynamics and regional economic development

7. Valorization of university knowledge: what are the barriers and can 'living labs' provide solutions?

Marina van Geenhuizen

1. KNOWLEDGE VALORIZATION IN AN OPEN INNOVATION CONTEXT

Bringing new knowledge to market is increasingly recognized as the third mission of universities today. Accordingly, universities are seen as creators of new knowledge while being involved in contract-research commissioned by the business sector, in collaborative research projects with business partners, in licensing of patents, in the creation of spin-off firms, etc. (van Geenhuizen and Nijkamp, 2007; Huggins and Johnston, 2009; McDowell, 2010; O'Shea et al., 2005; Shane, 2004). In Europe, this new role of universities started to grow in the early 1980s (Charles and Howells, 1992) and has now fully entered the research policy of modern universities (Hussler et al., 2010; van Looy et al., 2011; Rasmussen et al., 2006).

Knowledge valorization[1] is broadly defined in this study as 'the process of creation of value from knowledge, by adapting it and/or making it available for economic/societal use and transform[ing] it into competing products, services, processes and new economic activity' (Innovation Platform, 2009, p. 8). It is a complex and iterative process with interaction between knowledge institutes and the business world as key in all stages. Knowledge valorization encompasses a chain of processes (partly cycles) that starts with first thoughts about market introduction (eventually together with a firm) and about steps to be taken to reach this goal through various channels (Bekkers and Bodas Freitas, 2008; Markman et al., 2008).

The demand for a quicker market introduction and cost reduction in a globalized economy since the early 2000s has urged many universities, technology institutes and firms to adopt models of open innovation. The underlying assumption of open innovation is that actors in innovation preferably use external ideas as well as internal ideas, and internal and external paths to market, as they look to advance their technology. In the line of Chesbrough (2003) and Chesbrough et al. (2006) open innovation among firms can be defined as the systematic encouraging and exploration of a large set of internal and external sources of innovation opportunities, consciously integrating that exploration with firm capabilities and resources, and broadly exploiting those opportunities through multiple channels (West and Gallagher, 2006).

The general logic of open innovation is based on the idea of distributed knowledge. However, opening up the innovation process is not about just giving up control and hoping for the best (Boudreau and Lakhani, 2009); it is about carefully implementing mechanisms to govern, shape, direct and, if necessary, constrain external innovators. Note that certain aspects of open innovation are not new, such as co-design. In addition, one firm may adopt various types of open innovation simultaneously but also move to other types of open innovation over time. It needs also to be realized that the term open means 'relatively open', thereby positioning the learning of firms on a wide spectrum of openness with fully closed and fully open at each end (Dahlander and Gann, 2010).

An important development in open innovation is the purposeful engagement of end-users or customers in valorization processes and practices (Bogers et al., 2010; Thomke and Von Hippel, 2002). Using an active input of users as co-creators – including their feed-back in developing and testing – is generally seen as an important way of better serving the needs of users and society, thereby increasing efficiency, including speed of market introduction. In this context, 'living labs' (described in section 3.3) are a relevant and increasingly popular policy tool. However, without knowing the causes of delay and failure of knowledge valorization, many policymakers today embrace the concept of livings labs. In addition, the small experience to date with living labs suggests as many advantages as drawbacks, calling for a state-of-the-art study and evaluation of potential performance and success of this tool.

This chapter takes the Netherlands as an example. As a relatively small country in Western Europe (a population of 16.4 million) it has committed itself to the Lisbon and Barcelona objectives to improve the competitive performance of Europe. The Netherlands represents a set of European countries facing a paradox in their innovation system. The country has a relatively strong performance in scientific output, and two of its universities – Technical University of Eindhoven and Delft University of Technology – are among the world-best universities in scientific publications in collaboration with business partners (Tijssen et al., 2009), but this goes along with relatively low levels of application of innovations in manufacturing and services (NOWT, 2011). Apparently, university and industry suffer from a lack of bridging activities (or organizations) between them.

The above situation seems to be mainly concerned with cognitive distance (Nooteboom, 2009). A large cognitive distance is necessary, in order to make collaboration sufficiently interesting for two organizations in their search for complementary external knowledge. If there is, however, too much cognitive distance, the partners may face problems in understanding each other. Thus, opportunities for novel combinations of complementary knowledge need to go along with a cognitive distance that is not so large as to preclude mutual understanding to utilize these opportunities.

The aim of the current study is, first, to elucidate the extent in which new knowledge created at universities is brought to market and the circumstances that cause barriers in the processes involved, with a focus on cognitive distance between university and business. Secondly, given a number of issues concerning cognitive distance, the use of living labs will be evaluated. The chapter has the following structure. It starts with a brief exploration of innovation in the Netherlands compared with some other small economies in Europe (section 2). Theoretical perspectives are examined in section 3. This is followed by a discussion of the methodology of the empirical study and an examination of its results, focusing on market introduction, delay and failure (section 4). An analysis of barriers to knowledge valorization is presented in section 5. The concept of living labs is highlighted and an assessment of its potential role in improving valorization is given in section 6. The chapter closes with a summary and a brief outlook on future research.

2.   THE NETHERLANDS AS A CASE STUDY

The Netherlands is an interesting case study because of a paradox in its innovation system: the country experiences a relatively strong performance in scientific output, for most-cited scientific publications worldwide a score of >250, and for public–private scientific co-publications a score of 248 (Table 7.1). This, however, goes along with relatively low levels of introducing innovations among SMEs, i.e. 92 for product/process innovation and 73 for market and organizational innovation, and a low level of sales of innovations, i.e. 67 for sales of innovation that are new to market/new to firm. Business investments are also relatively low, a score of 70 for R&D expenditure, and 73 for non-R&D innovation expenditure.

Table 7.1   Scores on selected science and innovation performance indicators

	NL	Austria	Belgium	UK	Norway	Finland
Int. scientific co-publications	>250	>250	>300	>250	n.a.	>300
Worldwide scientific citations	137	108	122	118	106	101
Public–private scientific co-publications	248	156	170	171	>240	290
Public R&D expenditure	128	108	83	89	115	148
Venture capital	100	26	128	>250	95	131
Business R&D expenditure	70	155	106	93	76	226
Non-R&D innovation expenditure	73	66	80	n.a.	15	80
SMEs innovating in-house	87	113	133	n.a.	84	127
Collaboration between innovative SMEs	116	132	199	240	117	137
SMEs introducing product/process innovation	92	116	129	73	85	122
SMEs introducing market or organizational innovation	73	109	113	79	79	81
Sales of innovations new to market or to firm	67	85	72	55	25	118

Source: Pro-Inno 2011 (EU-27 Innovation Union Scoreboard), EU-27 =100.

As a result, the Netherlands is a qualified 'innovation follower' in the Innovation Union Scoreboard (Pro Inno Europe, 2011).

We may observe similar patterns in other small and some large European economies qualified as 'followers', such as Austria, Belgium, Norway and UK (Table 7.1). For example, the Netherlands compares with Norway with regard to the contrast between public–private co-publications and the relatively low level of firm investments and SMEs' innovative behaviour. In Austria, the contrast is somewhat smaller, except for the low score on venture capital. The Netherlands and UK compare with regard to modest investment levels, except for high levels of venture capital in the UK, and modest SME innovation performance, i.e. innovation introduction and sales of innovations. In order to understand some of the differences with 'innovation leaders', Finland is shown in Table 7.1. On at least six of the selected indicators Finland gains relatively high scores.

Given the relatively good performance in science and publications, but poor performance of innovation output indicators mainly connected to SMEs, we may assume that many barriers hinder university-business interaction and collaboration in the Netherlands.

In this chapter, we perceive knowledge valorization to take off in university cities/regions and perceive knowledge valorization to be partially influenced by circumstances in the region (Figure 7.1). A distinction in this study is made between two types of regions in the Netherlands: the densely populated Randstad in the western part of the country, including the three large university cities of Amsterdam, Rotterdam and Utrecht as important nodes in a service-based economy (named core region in the chapter), and less populated regions at a distance from the Randstad with important centres of high-tech manufacturing, including the university city of Eindhoven (named southeast in this chapter). This region is distinguished from others by an early adoption of open innovation models and by a relatively high level of R&D expenditure per firm (Statistics Netherlands, 2010). We take a regional perspective in the analysis of barriers to valorization (sections 3 and 5).

3.   FACTORS AFFECTING KNOWLEDGE VALORIZATION

An overview of factors affecting valorization in regions is given in Figure 7.1. We distinguish between direct and indirect (or enabling) factors. The direct factors are concerned with cognitive distance, including the question of whether the profile of university inventions is sufficiently appealing for firms to become involved in collaboration with the university and whether such collaboration can be sustained given the relatively turbulent environment of the firms. Direct factors are also concerned with value systems, needs and routines at university and a sufficient match with them in the firms. In contrast, indirect factors have their origin in the regional and national valorization system and influence to a certain extent the direct factors. We take a brief look at these factors in the next sections.

3.1   Direct Factors

The profile of the invention and the sector involved may have important consequences in gaining interest from the business world (Utterback, 1996). Radical inventions which require structural changes in manufacturing facilities and in systems of application (infrastructures) face more obstructions than inventions that are incremental and fit into existing structures (Geels, 2004). The same may hold true for inventions meant for small market segments compared with inventions providing mass-market potentials. In addition, some industry sectors are subject to heavy regulation and long time-lines, such as designing of new medicines (van Geenhuizen, 2003). Conversely, inventions without such regulation and supported by additional public investment may face an acceleration in establishing collaboration with firms, such as in clean technologies and sustainable energy.

The sector is also important regarding the type of learning in university-business collaboration. There is a basic difference between science-based learning including laws of nature such as in life sciences and nanotechnology, and engineering or problem-based learning such as in micro-electronic systems, medical instruments and sports equipment, the latter causing better chances for a quick involvement of firms (Asheim et al., 2007; Thomke and Von Hippel, 2002; Tidd and Bessant, 2009; Von Hippel, 2005). In order for firms to benefit from opportunities of complementary knowledge at university, cognitive distance should not be too large in terms of learning modes and routines.

Regarding teams at university, Etzkowitz (2003) describes an ideal model of research groups as 'quasi' firms. Such teams are led by a principal investigator and contain team members who are perfect in proposal writing to raise funds, writing and reviewing of scientific and applied articles, managing post docs, and membership of panels judging other teams or institutions, etc. These teams also tend to better understand the values, needs and routines of the business world. In reality, however, many research groups are not so skilled and dominant in the scientific world and in university-business relationships, due to, for example, a small size and negative impacts from re-organization.

An inherent tension between the value system in universities and the business world lies at the heart of many problems in valorization of university knowledge (Ambos et al., 2008). The cognitive distance between university and industry is often too large and prevents mutual understanding of each other's different values, needs and routines. First, universities and industry are likely to prioritize different research goals: industry usually focuses on less risky research with direct commercial applicability, while government-funded academic research typically undertakes projects with longer time horizons (typical of PhD research) and less predictability (Di Gregorio and Shane, 2003; Mora-Valentin et al., 2004). Also, industry faces the need to adapt quickly to changing circumstances in the market while universities can remain quite stable in their choices. Second, academia traditionally encourages knowledge dissemination and full disclosure of methods and results (in peer-reviewed journals) whereas the commercial sector often prefers to keep the new knowledge secret and seeks ownership or tight control of intellectual property. These contradictory demands create tensions at the organizational level as they make it difficult for universities to set clear priorities in terms of structures, resources and incentives.

The tensions in university-business relationships are also profound for individual researchers, leading to significant variation in entrepreneurial involvement among them (D'Este and Patel, 2007). First, academic and commercial activities tend to represent fundamentally different and potentially contradictory activity (Bercovitz and Feldman, 2008). Valuable avenues and norms for scientific research are shaped by communities of peers, and this makes it risky for a scientist to deviate from these patterns by seeking involvement in commercial activity. Second, commercial activities do not often carry weight in tenure and promotion decisions in career policies at university (Markman et al., 2004). A successful academic career requires significant investment in a specific style of research, paper-writing and network-building, leaving little time for pursuing other – commercial – activities.

Universities usually deal with these tensions as an 'ambidextrous' organization, by a dual structure that deals with conflicting situations. For example, technology transfer organizations within the universities are engaged with commercialization efforts, 'third stream' research is often concentrated in separate legal institutes within the university organization, and researchers concerned with commercialization follow different career paths compared to researchers involved in scientific research. Relatively few studies have investigated empirically these tensions and dual structures, and the nature of related inhibiting or, conversely, converging factors in university-industry relations. Attention is nevertheless quickly increasing (e.g. Bergman 2011; Bjerregaard, 2010; Bruneel et al., 2010; Kim, 2011).

Currently, the idea is that universities show a large variation in smoothing the tensions and in bridging dual structures. Technical universities are different from general universities (beta faculties) due to the former's stronger orientation on manufacturing and on applied and engineering-type research. In addition, universities established with an entrepreneurial

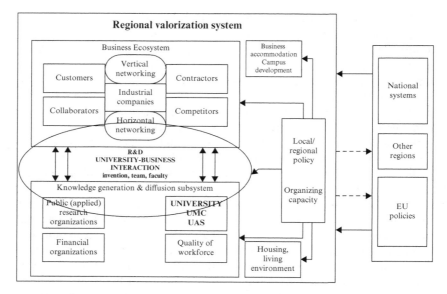

Note: UMC: University Medical Centre; UAS: University of Applied Sciences.

Source: Author's modification of Tödtling and Trippl (2005).

Figure 7.1   A simplified model of a regional valorization system

mission and role in regional economic development have usually developed stronger links with the regional business ecosystem and the generation and diffusion subsystem (Figure 7.1).

3.2   Enabling Factors

We distinguish between the regional business ecosystem, including con-tractors, competitors, and collaborators, and the knowledge creation and diffusion subsystem, including the universities themselves, universities of applied sciences, public research institutes, financial and intermediary organizations and quality of the labour market (Figure 7.1). If well devel-oped, these systems provide supportive services, subcontracting oppor-tunities, collective learning, specific financial arrangements enhancing innovation, specialized academic knowledge workers and skilled practical workers in the labour market, etc. In addition, adequate business accom-modation and land on industrial (science) parks can be seen as important enabling factors in building university-business links (Soetanto and van Geenhuizen, 2007). These circumstances have been addressed in many publications on regional innovation systems, agglomeration economies and clusters (e.g. Asheim et al., 2011; Bathelt et al., 2004; Cooke et al., 2004; Feldman, 1999; Florida, 2002; Porter, 2003; Tödtling and Trippl, 2005).

Furthermore, the 'organizing capacity' of local/regional authorities has increasingly attracted attention (Van den Berg et al., 2003). This capacity refers to achieving consensus between major regional actors on the direction of knowledge-based development and to gaining commitment for daily policies supporting this direction. More specifically, it refers to connecting university, public policy actors and the business sector in producing benefits from collaborative activities in each other's realms – triple helix development (e.g. Etzkowitz, 2008) – and to connecting even more actors, such as societal interest groups and customer groups, in living labs (Leydesdorff, 2012; Marcovitch and Shinn, 2011; OECD, 2007).

3.3 Living Labs

'Living labs' are a physical setting or facility where needs (problems), ideas, and solutions come together through a structured innovation process working with programs and projects, particularly with the input of customer groups (e.g., Guldemond, 2011). Living labs are exemplified by care homes for the elderly, hospitals' surgery rooms, buildings aimed at sustainable energy use, sporting facilities (such as a sailing port, hockey/soccer field) and playing grounds in living quarters. Living labs are also a network of relevant parties, often based upon a public–private partnership.

Living labs have two key attributes: first, customer involvement in an early stage of product development and, secondly, performance in real-life situations and monitoring of it, such as in living, working, health care, travelling, recreation and sports (e.g. Almirall and Wareham, 2008).[2] Customers or users are individual persons, households or workers in their physical environment. They may also be firms, non-profit organizations (like hospitals) and city/regional authorities. It seems that living labs, if well-designed and managed, can provide some solutions to increase efficiency in knowledge valorization with higher levels of market introduction and smaller delay.

4. RESULTS OF VALORIZATION

4.1 Methodology

The analysis dealt with technology projects and involved two steps. A scan of results of almost 370 technology projects was followed by an in-depth

Table 7.2   Scan of project outcomes (take-off in 1995–97)

Outcome	Number (%)
Failure after 5/10 years	54 (26)
Stagnation or development unknown	42 (20)
Continuation after 10 years	66 (32)
Market introduction/use in society	47 (22)
Total projects	209 (100)

Source: Author's calculation based on information from STW and website information.

study of a sample of 51 of these projects. Technology Foundation STW (various years) in the Netherlands provides for each technology project that it subsidizes a short description and evaluation of results at five or (if relevant) ten years after take-off of the project. This information, in some cases together with web-based information, enabled the identification of different outcomes of the projects.

We assigned the outcome label 'market introduction/use in society' (Tables 7.2 and 7.3) to projects that have led to a product, process or method that was brought to market or to use in society. The label was also assigned if software (as the main part of a project) was brought to market in open source ways. Failure was assigned in a situation of 'not having reached the stage of market introduction/use in society' due to ceasing the project (line). This outcome happened early after take-off in only a few cases, i.e. with ceasing the project (subsidization) before the official end date or directly after (four years); in most cases, however, it took a longer time before the line of the project was stopped.

Aside from the two categories of end results, we distinguished between 'stagnation or development unknown' for older projects and 'continuation' for all projects. Using the first category served to identify the projects facing *non-linear* developments in which the original project line was abandoned but the project knowledge was adopted by projects at the collaborating firm, mainly through PhD students accepting a job there after completing thesis research. In addition, two different periods of project take-off were selected in the analysis, i.e. the years 1995 to 1997 and 2000 to 2002. A reason for taking two different periods was the change in economic climate in the early 2000s. Each period covered a sufficient amount of projects in terms of differentiation in the Netherlands, i.e. general and technical universities, and different regions.[3]

The second step of the study, an analysis of factors that hinder valorization, made use of in-depth interviews with research project leaders at university (mostly full professors). These interviews yielded data about

Table 7.3   Scan of project outcomes (take-off in 2000–02)

Outcome	Number (%)
Failure after 5 years	41 (26)
Continuation	94 (59)
Market introduction/use in society	23 (15)
Total	158 (100)

Source: Author's calculation based on information from STW and website information.

51 projects that satisfied three criteria: representing old and younger projects, representing market introduction and failure (delay), and covering a limited number of technology segments, i.e. medical and industrial biotechnology, medical technology (instruments/software), new materials and nanotechnology, systems for sustainable energy, and automotive. The interviews were semi-structured. They systematically addressed potential barriers to valorization, and took 60 to 90 minutes each.

4.2   Results: Failure and Market Introduction

Failure was faced by a minority of the projects – 26 per cent in both cohorts (Tables 7.2 and 7.3). Conversely, market introduction was also faced by a minority of the projects: 22 per cent among older projects and 15 per cent among younger ones. Aside from the downturn in the economy, the latter results also followed from the relatively short time-period in consideration. The category 'stagnation or development unknown' is substantial among older projects at 20 per cent.

Valorization in technology seems to be a long-lasting process. In almost a third of the older projects (32 per cent) R&D was still continued after 10 years (Table 7.2). For example, in medical life sciences, e.g. drugs development and tissue-engineering, 15 to 20 years is not exceptional. Shorter times tend to be involved if R&D is user-driven and taking place in close collaboration with a firm/customer group from the beginning, but also if the invention is a new application of already proven knowledge.

5.   BARRIERS TO KNOWLEDGE VALORIZATION

Table 7.4 reports various factors that hinder knowledge valorization, as forwarded in interviews with research managers at the university. Note that the small number of projects investigated for the second period calls for a cautious interpretation. Broadly speaking, almost 60 per cent of

Table 7.4   Barriers to valorization of projects as forwarded by research managers

Barriers	1995–97 projects No. (%)	2000–02 projects No. (%)	Details
Cognitive distance			
Profile of invention	11(17.4)	3 (8.1)	Too much risk-taking for firms (SMEs); radicalness of invention; no mass-market involved; high price for additional new attributes
Value system, needs and routines at university	18 (28.6)	8 (21.6)	Small affinity with and small attention to valorization (general universities); too small budgets for technology transfer; reorganization of research groups; unfavourable reward structure and career for employees in valorization
Turbulence in university-business interaction caused by firms	6 (9.5)	4 (10.8)	Sudden change in collaboration due to firm reorganization or merger/acquisition (reduction of R&D); sudden loss of attention for invention due to new, superior, technology
Opportunistic behaviour of firms	2 (3.2)	1 (2.7)	Gaining intellectual ownership; investment driven by immediate profit-seeking
Total	37 (58.7)	16 (43.2)	
Regional system			
Business ecosystem	2 (3.2)	3 (8.1)	Small ecosystems (critical mass) (southeast regions) and difficulty in attracting research departments of MNCs
Financial factors	7 (11.1)	4 (10.8)	Limited supply of large amounts of venture capital; lack of investment subsidy (in core) enhancing relocation to other regions
Business accommodation	4 (6.3)	3 (8.1)	Shortage of low rent incubators and incubators close to academic hospital; shortage of follow-up accommodation after incubation

Table 7.4   (continued)

Barriers	1995–97 projects No. (%)	2000–02 projects No. (%)	Details
Regional system			
Remaining factors	5 (7.9)	4 (10.8)	
Totals	18 (28.5)	14 (37.8)	
National system			
Legislation and regulation	4 (6.3)	1 (2.7)	Sudden bans on specific animal experiments
Value system and culture	3 (4.8)	4 (10.8)	Lack of entrepreneurial culture and risk-taking
Remaining	1 (1.6)	2 (5.4)	
Totals	8 (12.7)	7 (18.9)	
All inhibiting factors	63 (100)	37 (100)	

Source: Author's interviews with managers at university (51 projects).

all factors mentioned for the first period resided in the university and university-business interaction, connected to problems of cognitive distance. Regional factors amounted to almost 30 per cent. Cognitive distance factors tended to lose importance in the second period (fallen back from 59 to 43 per cent). This change indicated a somewhat better match of the university value system, needs and routines with requirements needed in collaborative valorization with firms, and an increased application of 'open innovation' models, mainly in the southeast of the country in the micro-electronics and mechatronics cluster.

An unfavourable profile of the invention is one of the factors preventing a strong interest from businesses, but it tends to lose importance, falling from 17 to 8 per cent of all hindering factors mentioned. Details on what unfavourable profiles might be are given in Table 7.4, as are details on other factors. Shortage in the value system at university is the largest category and tends to decrease in importance only slightly, from 29 to 22 per cent of all factors addressed. In addition, turbulence in interaction with firms causing 'sudden' changes in existing firm collaboration, and opportunistic firm behaviour tend to be of minor importance. Turbulence in firms tends to be, however, quite stable in importance, around 10 per cent in both periods.

Among *regional* factors, we may identify differences between the regions involved, i.e. the metropolitan core area, and the southeast of the country. Financial factors tend to be the most important ones in both periods (11 per cent). A limited supply of large venture capital investment (shortage of organizational power) is seen as a barrier in both regions, whereas lack of investment subsidies holds only in the core area, causing the risk of losing grown-up spin-off firms to other regions, attracted by investment subsidies there. With regard to the second period, barriers in the regional business ecosystem take 8 per cent of all factors, as does the category 'business accommodation'. The influence of the *national* system tends to slightly increase, i.e. from 13 to 19 per cent, mainly due to a value system and culture in which entrepreneurship and risk-taking are not highly ranked.

We may conclude this preliminary analysis with the remark that factors connected with cognitive distance between university and businesses are predominant in hindering valorization, but the situation is improving. At the same time, shortages in the region and on the national level tend to increase in importance.

6.   CAN LIVING LABS PROVIDE SOLUTIONS?

As previously indicated, key in living labs is the involvement of customers, with the aim to develop better new products, processes, etc. and to achieve higher efficiency in valorization processes. Ideally, living labs accommodate and coordinate user-driven, open innovation, involving all relevant players in the value network, while benefiting from support of information and communication technology (EC, 2010). Living labs may be located within the university organization, but they may also be completely outside the university organization, yet with university involvement in valorization. We first discuss in this section the different aims of the players involved and major differences between living labs, and then we move attention to expectations about providing solutions to the problem of barriers to valorization. The section closes with questions that still need to be answered.

The aims of living labs as these have unfolded in practice in recent years are still somewhat fluid and different for diverse players (e.g. Følstad et al., 2009; Dutilleul et al., 2010). The various categories of players may be involved for different reasons as indicated below:

- *Customers (user groups)* Through co-creation and feedback in testing they influence the quality of new products and services they will use, such that their needs are better served (e.g., Bogers et al., 2010).

- *Firms* Through co-creation they get the opportunity to produce goods and services that better match with customer needs, while shortening the time between invention and market introduction; by using customer feedback they may increase efficiency. Firms range from MNCs to SMEs.
- *Knowledge institutes* Bring more knowledge, more quickly, to market; impacts of inventions and new findings can be tested in reality leading to more valid results and improved understanding.
- *Intermediary and coordinating organizations* Support the establishment and performance of 'living labs' with particular services.
- *Financial players* Support 'living labs' by providing financial arrangements and investment necessary to allow for R&D and customer interaction.
- *Local/regional authorities* May provide legitimation as a neutral actor to a 'living lab'; they may also act as a co-creator of innovative public services, for example in primary services (e-governance), healthcare and childcare.

The above list illustrates the multi-actor character of living labs. Accordingly, involvement of too many (different) actors and a strong dependence on one large actor may cause imbalances in the living labs networks and hence complexity in management of these networks (van Geenhuizen, 2011). However, living labs may be different in this respect. The same seems true for the technologies and applications involved. Living labs differ in complexity of technology and applications, dependence on fast changes in the technology itself and on constraints in technology applications from regulation and legislation, and issues of intellectual ownership.

Given the limited understanding of complexity in living labs and concomitant differences between living labs to date, we can only propose a list of preliminary benefits of living labs in supporting knowledge valorization (Table 7.5).

First, living labs provide good potentials, principally because customers are involved and user-driven models are followed. Accordingly, time-consuming ways of searching for a business partner and bringing knowledge to market can be avoided by universities and firms, and early customer involvement will increase university understanding of the market and marketing. In particular, living labs seem to enable the smoothening of university-industry relationships through an increased mutual understanding of differences in values and needs and through emerging changes in attitudes and routines. In addition, the concomitant

Table 7.5   Potential contribution of living labs in overcoming barriers to valorization

Challenge	Potential contribution
Reduce cognitive distance in university-industry interaction	Early customer involvement causing a quicker and more efficient valorization (reducing market risk); increase of knowledge at university on markets and marketing Synergy and serendipity in learning, due to collaboration of different players
Improve financial factors and reduce financial risks	Creation of new models of investment and venture funds stimulated by collaboration of a variety of players In particular, the rise of new models of 'frontloading' spreading financial risks over the main players from the start (low financial risk is important for participation of SMEs)
Increase of 'critical mass' in (regional) business ecosystem	A larger and more diversified base for learning in co-design, validation and testing, by connecting local living labs with national and international ones (southeast regions)

collaboration of diverse partners may produce synergy and serendipity in learning, contributing to more efficient innovation.

Second, we may also expect the creation of new models of investment and financing, and the spread of financial risks over all partners from the start of projects; this instead of financial risks only for universities and spin-off firms for a long time. This change may increase involvement particularly of SMEs. Third, living labs may be connected to similar initiatives in other regions and countries, thereby increasing the 'small critical mass' from which particular regions seem to suffer. A concomitant increase in diversity of information and knowledge may contribute to more efficient innovation.

How successfully living labs perform in reality, however, remains to be seen. Documented experience is still scarce, particularly on critical issues like power distribution in the networks and cost and revenue distribution. Therefore, the rest of this section reports various missing insights into living labs. We identify three points.

First, the best composition of players to be involved as partners in living labs, and ways to align and maintain these players in a stable multi-actor situation, are virtually unknown. It is sometimes difficult to commit the university to enable knowledge flows from outside to enter and internal knowledge flows to go outside into relevant networks; the traditional role of the university seems still difficult to change. Faculties, in particular, need to be partly transformed from relatively closed organizations to organizations acting as interfaces with outside networks of collaborating partners. In addition, to include large multinational firms may introduce other difficulties or challenges. They may, for example, require particular privileges compared to small firms. Related with these situations is lack of insight into the best rules for access and exit of partners, such as open/ closed and fixed/fluid.

Secondly, the best way of governing living labs and the best model of distributing costs and revenues over the partners are almost unknown. The best governance model could be a bottom-up model because the first initiatives are mostly bottom-up. However, it is plausible that in the early stage of living labs a mix of bottom-up and top-down is the best, while in later stages pure bottom-up models may be most adequate. Also, best governance models may be different for 'labs' that are within the university organization compared to external labs. Similarly, there is no experience with how to distribute costs (risks) and revenues over the partners in the best fashion, particularly in a public–private partnership construction. The possibility of 'frontloading' seems realistic, in which investment risks (costs) are distributed over the main partners from the early stages; in such a situation, spin-off firms and other SMEs can be freed from unbearable high risks in their early years. However, whether it really works like this and under what conditions 'frontloading' can be accepted by living lab partners need further investigation.

As a third point, intellectual property (IP) issues in living labs are as important as in the traditional situation, but seem to be more complicated because of a larger number of partners involved. There is not much insight into this new complexity. In addition, dealing with legal liability issues seems more important in living labs because customer groups are often involved from the start. For example, experiments with patients may lead – aside from beneficial results – to unexpected harmful health effects. Similar to IP issues, there is not much insight into dealing with complexity in legal liability issues.

7.   CONCLUDING REMARKS

Like various small economies in Europe, the Netherlands is facing a high level of scientific performance but a low level of bringing inventions to market, particularly through SMEs. In this context, the chapter responded to two knowledge gaps: first, a lack of knowledge on the practice of valorization at universities including barriers to valorization, and secondly, a lack of knowledge on living labs as a proposed solution to better connect key players and to involve customers from the beginning.

A sample of about 370 technology projects in the Netherlands served the analysis of market introduction, failure, and other outcomes of knowledge valorization. Both failure and market introduction were experienced by a minority of projects. The largest category of outcomes was continuation, pointing to long time-lines of valorization. Managers in valorization at university indicated that most barriers were connected with differences in value systems between university and business, such as evidenced by a negative reward structure for employees engaged in valorization research and too small budgets for valorization at university, but over time this situation tended to improve. At the same time, regional factors tended to become more important as barriers to valorization, such as shortcomings in financial arrangements and in the business eco-system. Living labs appeared to have large potential to fight barriers to valorization, thanks to their user-driven open innovation model, through which cognitive distance between universities and firms may be reduced, and market and financial risks may be more equally distributed – the last change is particularly important for SMEs to become involved. In addition, connecting living labs in different cities may cause critical mass to grow and information diversity may increase in collaborative learning.

However, major evaluation studies need to be undertaken before living labs can be adopted as a policy tool on a broad scale. Evaluation studies are necessary, first, to identify the best composition of partners and ways to align and maintain them as partners in the network, including rules for access and exit, and secondly, to identify the best models of governance, including the distribution of costs and revenues, and of 'frontloading' as a way of dealing with financial investment risks. Third, evaluation studies are also necessary to identify the best ways of dealing with intellectual property issues and issues of legal liability among the network partners.

The empirical work in this chapter contains some limitations. The first one follows from the use of data from one particular source of financing technology projects, with its specific criteria in granting project financing. Other financing programmes may produce a somewhat different picture. However, the in-depth interviews were structured in such a way that a broader picture of financing programmes could be reached. Accordingly, the results of the analysis of barriers to valorization have larger implications. Secondly, the study on barriers had to be narrow with regard to technologies and applications. Fields such as micro-electronics and information and communication technology have remained outside the study, causing a limitation of its implications. Given the previous results and implications, the following research avenues can be envisaged regarding knowledge valorization. First, in the empirical study the emphasis was on science-based research. The next step in the research could have a stronger focus on user-driven projects. Secondly, the current study was descriptive in nature. The next step could focus on testing causal models of knowledge valorization using a larger database, which allows assessment of the influence of barriers among other factors on outcomes of valorization.

ACKNOWLEDGEMENT

The study has benefited from a subsidy by NICIS (Netherlands Institute of City Innovation), including four cities in the Netherlands (Amsterdam, Delft, Eindhoven, and Maastricht), Delft University of Technology, and the Ministry of Education, Culture and Science.

NOTES

1. Different from knowledge commercialization, the term knowledge valorization is more comprehensive as it also includes non-commercial (societal) applications.
2. 'Field labs', compared with 'living labs', can be seen as a broader category of initiatives, not necessarily dealing with co-creation and monitoring in real-life situations, but mainly dealing with testing of innovations in practice. 'Living labs' are basically concerned with up to 24-hour monitoring of performance of particular user-groups in daily living, working or recreation situations concerning products and services that are highly personalized. Despite this distinction, in part of the literature both terms are used interchangeably.
3. The analysis of outcomes of technology projects covers technical universities and general universities, the last only through beta-faculties and medical schools/hospitals; altogether the study includes six universities in the core area (100% coverage) and three universities at a substantial distance from this area in the eastern and southern part of the country (75% coverage).

REFERENCES

Almirall, E., and Wareham, J. (2008), 'Living labs and open innovation: roles and applicability', *The Electronic Journal for Virtual Organizations and Networks*, **10**, 21–46.

Ambos, T.C., Mäkelä, K., Birkinshaw, J., and D'Este, P. (2008), 'When does university research get commercialized? Creating ambidexterity in research institutions', *Journal of Management Studies*, **45** (8), 1424–47.

Asheim, B., Coenen, L., and Vang, J. (2007), 'Face-to-face, buzz and knowledge bases: sociospatial implications for learning, innovation and innovation policy', *Environment and Planning C: Government and Policy*, **25**, 655–70.

Asheim, B.T., Lawton Smith, H., and Oughton, C. (2011), 'Regional innovation systems: theory, empirics and policy', *Regional Studies*, **45** (7), 875–91.
Bathelt, H., Malmberg, A., and Maskell, P. (2004), 'Clusters and knowledge: local buzz, global pipelines and the process of knowledge creation', *Progress in Human Geography*, **28**, 31–56.
Bekkers, R., and Bodas Freitas (2008), 'Analysing knowledge transfer channels between universities and industry: to what degree do sectors also matter?', *Research Policy*, **37**, 1837–53.
Bercovitz, J., and Feldman, M. (2008), 'Academic entrepreneurs: organizational change at the individual level', *Organization Science*, **19** (1), 69–89.
Berg, L. van den, van der Meer, J., and Pol, P. (2003), 'Organising capacity and social policies in European cities', *Urban Studies*, **40**, 1959–78.
Bergman, E.M. (2011), 'Knowledge links between European universities and firms: a review', *Papers in Regional Science*, **89** (2), 311–33.
Bjerregaard, T. (2010), 'Industry and academia in convergence: micro-institutional dimensions of R&D collaboration', *Technovation*, **30** (2), 100–108.
BogeBoudreau, K.J., and Lakhani, K.R. (2009), 'How to manage outside innovation', *MIT Sloan Management Review*, **50**, 69–76.
Bogers, M., Afuah, A., and Bastian, B. (2010), 'Users as innovators: a review, critique, and future research directions', *Journal of Management*, **36** (4), 857–75.
Bruneel, J., d'Este, P., and Salter, A. (2010), 'Investigating the factors that diminish the barriers to university – industry collaboration', *Research Policy*, **39**, 858–68.
Charles, D., and Howells, J. (1992), *Technology Transfer in Europe. Public and Private Networks*, London: Belhaven Press.
Chesbrough, H. (2003), *Open Innovation: The New Imperative for Creation and Profiting from Technology*, Boston (MA): Harvard Business School Press.
Chesbrough, H., Vanhaverbeke, W., and West, J. (eds) (2006), *Open Innovation: Researching a New Paradigm*, Oxford: Oxford University Press.
Cooke, P., Heidenreich, M., and Braczyk, H.J. (2004), *Regional Innovation Systems: The Role of Governance in a Globalised World* (2nd edition), London: Routledge.
D'Este, P., and Patel, P. (2007), 'University-industry linkages in the UK: what are the factors underlying the variety of interactions with industry?', *Research Policy*, **36**, 1295–313.
Dahlander, L., and Gann. D.M. (2010), 'How open is innovation?', *Research Policy*, **39** (6), 699–709.
DiGregorio, D., and Shane, S. (2003), 'Why do some universities generate more start-ups than others?', *Research Policy*, **32** (2), 478–96.
Dutilleul, B., Birrer, F.A.J., and Mensink, W. (2010), 'Unpacking European living labs: analysing innovation's social dimension', *Central European Journal of Public Policy*, **4**, 60–85.
EC (2010), *Advancing and Applying Living Lab Methodologies. An Update on Living Labs for User-Driven Open Innovation in the ICT Domain*, Brussels: EC Directorate General for the Information Society and Media.
Etzkowitz, H. (2003), 'Research groups as "quasi firms": the invention of the entrepreneurial university', *Research Policy*, **32**, 109–21.
Etzkowitz, H. (2008), *The Triple Helix: University-Industry-Government Innovation in Action*, London: Routledge.
Feldman, M. (1999), 'The new economics of innovation, spillovers and agglomeration', *Economics of Innovation and New Technology*, **8**, 5–25

Florida, R. (2002), 'The economic geography of talent', *Annals of the Association of American Geographers*, **92**, 743–55.

Følstad, A., Brandtzaeg, P.B., Börjeson, M., Gulliksen, J., and Näkki, P. (2009), 'Towards a manifesto for living labs co-creation', *Human Computer Interaction – Lecture Notes, Interact*, **5727**, 979–80.

Geels, F.W. (2004), 'From sectoral systems of innovation to socio-technical systems insights about dynamics and change from sociology and institutional theory', *Research Policy*, **33**, 897–920.

Geenhuizen, M. van (2003), 'How can we reap the fruits of academic research in biotechnology? In search of critical success factors in policies for new-firm formation', *Environment and Planning C*, **21**, 139–55.

Geenhuizen, M. van (2011), 'Knowledge valorization requires a stronger embedding. On the way to larger benefits from universities in city and regions', Delft-Den Haag: TU Delft-NICIS.

Geenhuizen, M. van, and Nijkamp, P. (2007), 'Technological innovation, socio-economic change and quality of life in an age of globalization', *Studies in Regional Science*, **37** (2), 307–13.

Guldemond, N.A. (2011), Position paper, TU Delft on Co-creation and e-Heath for 'Active and Healthy Ageing', TU Delft, accessed 5 June 2011 at www.tudelft.nl.

Huggins, R., and Johnston, A. (2009), 'The economic and innovation contribution of universities: a regional perspective', *Environment and Planning C: Government and Policy*, **27**, 1088–106.

Hussler, C., Picard, F., and Tang, M.F. (2010), 'Taking the ivory from the tower to coat the economic world: regional strategies to make science useful', *Technovation*, **30**, 508–18.

Innovation Platform (2009), *From Aims to a Position Ahead. Enhancing Knowledge Circulation* (in Dutch), The Hague: Innovation Platform.

Kim, Y. (2011), 'The ivory tower approach to entrepreneurial linkage: productivity changes in university technology transfer', *The Journal of Technology Transfer* (2011, online first).

Leydesdorff, L. (2012), 'The triple helix, quadruple helix, . . ., and an N-tuple of helices: explanatory models for analyzing the knowledge-based economy?', *Journal of Knowledge Economics*, **3** (1), 25–35.

Looy, B. van, Landoni, P., Callaert, J., Pottelsberghe, B. van, Sapsalis, E., and Debackere K. (2011), 'Entrepreneurial effectiveness of European universities. An empirical assessment of antecedents and trade-offs', *Research Policy*, **40** (4), 553–64.

Marcovitch, A., and Shinn, T. (2011), 'From the triple helix to a quadruple helix? The case of dip-pen nanolithography', *Minerva* (online first).

Markman, G., Gianiodis, P., Phan, P., and Balkin, D. (2004), 'Entrepreneurship from the ivory tower: do incentive systems matter?', *The Journal of Technology Transfer*, **29** (3), 353–64.

Markman, G., Siegel, D.S., and Wright, M. (2008), 'Research and technology commercialization', *Journal of Management Studies*, **45** (8), 1401–23.

McDowell, K. (2010), 'Commercialization of university research. University of Austin, Texas', accessed 5 June 2011 at www.eda.gov.

Mora-Valentin, E., Montoro-Sanchez, A., and Guerras-Martin, L. (2004), 'Determining factors in the success of R&D cooperative agreements between firms and research organizations', *Research Policy*, **33** (1), 17–40.

Nooteboom, B. (2009), *A Cognitive Theory of the Firm: Learning, Governance and*

Dynamic Capabilities, Cheltenham, UK and Northampton, MA, USA: Edward Elgar.

NOWT (Netherlands Observatory of Science and Technology) (2011), *Science and Technology Indicators*, Leiden-Maastricht: CWTS and UNU-MERIT.

O'Shea, R., Allen T.J., Chevalier, A., and Roche, F. (2005), 'Entrepreneurial orientation, technology transfer and spin-off performance of US universities', *Research Policy*, **34**, 994–1009.

OECD (2007), *Higher Education and Regions: Globally Competitive and Locally Engaged*, Paris; OECD.

Porter, M. (2003), 'The economic performance of regions', *Regional Studies*, **37**, 549–78.

Pro Inno Europe (2011), *Innovation Union Scoreboard*, Maastricht.

Rasmussen, E., Moen, Ø and Gulbrandsen, M. (2006), 'Initiatives to promote commercialization of university knowledge', *Technovation*, **26** (4), 518–33.

Shane, S. (2004), *Academic Entrepreneurship. University Spin-offs and Wealth Creation*, Cheltenham, UK and Northampton, MA, USA: Edward Elgar.

Soetanto, D., and Geenhuizen, M. van (2007), 'Technology incubators and knowledge networks: a rough set approach in comparative project analysis', *Environment and Planning B* (Planning and Design), **34**, 1011–29.

Statistics Netherlands (2010), *The Regional Economy 2009* (in Dutch), Voorburg/Heerlen: Statistics Netherlands.

Technology Foundation STW, various years, *Reports on Utilisation, 2006–2007–2008* (in Dutch), Utrecht: STW.

Thomke, S., and Von Hippel, E. (2002), 'Customers as innovators: a new way to create value', *Harvard Business Review*, **80** (1), 91–7.

Tidd, J., and Bessant, J. (2009), *Managing Innovations. Integrating Technological, Market and Organizational Change*, 4th edition, John Wiley.

Tijssen, R.J.W, Leeuwen, T.N. van, and Wijk, E. van (2009), 'Benchmarking university-industry research cooperation worldwide', *Research Evaluation*, **18**, 13–29.

Tödtling, F., and Trippl, M. (2005) 'One size fits all? Towards a differentiated regional innovation approach', *Research Policy*, **34**, 1203–19.

Utterback, J. (1996), *Mastering the Dynamics of Innovation*, HBS Press.

Von Hippel, E. (2005), *Democratizing Innovation*, Cambridge, MA: MIT Press.

West, J., and Gallagher, S. (2006), 'Patterns of open innovation in open source software', in H. Chesbrough, W. Vanhaverbeke and West, J. (eds), *Open Innovation: Researching a New Paradigm*, Oxford: Oxford University Press, pp. 82–108.

8. The influence of cross-border knowledge interaction on the relation between key subsystems of the RIS and innovation performance of Dutch SMEs

Patricia van Hemert, Peter Nijkamp and Enno Masurel

1. INTRODUCTION

It is now widely recognized, in turbulent market economies, that innovation is the source of existence for firms, regardless of their size or other attributes. The prerequisite of every innovation is either the generation of new knowledge or, alternatively, and more typically, the combination of existing pieces of knowledge in novel, entrepreneurial ways (Schumpeter, 1934; Drucker, 1985). Innovations are to an increasing extent also seen as the result of an interactive process of knowledge generation, diffusion and application. This specifically applies to small and medium-sized enterprises (SMEs) that, due to their lack of financial and human capital resources, often do not have direct access to R&D. What is often neglected in the literature is to what extent different kinds of innovation rely on specific knowledge sources and links. This possibility has been recognized only fairly recently (Tödtling et al., 2009; Freel and de Jong, 2009). In particular for SMEs, tacit knowledge and trust based relationships are considered essential for successfully carrying out innovation activities (Howells, 2002; Gertler, 2003). The exchange of tacit knowledge presupposes trust and personal contacts which are, according to the literature on regional innovation systems (RIS), essentially facilitated by spatial proximity (Storper, 1997; Morgan, 2004). In the past decade, the systems of innovation approach has substantially enhanced our knowledge about the nature of the innovation process. The strong focus of the RIS on tacit knowledge and trust based relationships, and localized knowledge spillovers, suggest that the RIS architecture is ideal for the study of the innovation process of SMEs. This chapter uses the basic structuring of the RIS as suggested by Autio (1998) and Trippl (2010) to study the effect of knowledge interaction on innovation performance in Dutch SMEs. Although the RIS focuses on local interactions generally, this study is especially interested in the cross-border knowledge interactions of SMEs because, increasingly, the idea is gaining ground that more often than not a RIS is inserted into a complex web of relations to national and international organizations and innovation systems (Trippl, 2010; Trippl and Tödtling, 2007).

The sample used in this research is drawn from a survey among Dutch SMEs that participated in a government subsidy programme which was aimed to improve knowledge relations between universities and other knowledge institutions and SMEs. In the period 2006–09, the SMEs that were questioned successfully applied for the subsidy, which consisted of a sum of money of €2,500 or €7,500 that went by the name of 'small' or 'large' innovation voucher respectively. Because of communication problems or time limitations, however, not all SMEs actually used the subsidy. For this study, we only regarded the survey results of SMEs that used their voucher. The sample is thus unique because it is comprised of those companies that see value in innovation and in government programmes of this kind. A moderated hierarchical regression approach is used to analyse the moderating effect of cross-border knowledge interactions. Furthermore, the mediating effect of cross-border is tested through the use of structural equation modelling (SEM) to study if the influence of cross-border interactions on the relation between RIS innovation sources and innovation performance of SMEs is essential. The study is structured as follows: Section 2 reviews the literature and provides theoretical expectations. Section 3 introduces the research methods, including the models, variable definitions and measurements, and the sample used in this study. Section 4 presents and analyses the results. Section 5 summarizes the results, and discusses the implications for theory and managerial practice. Section 6 suggests possible directions for future research.

2.   LITERATURE REVIEW AND RESEARCH HYPOTHESES

2.1   Literature on Innovation Systems and Knowledge Networks

For a proper understanding of our analysis, it is important to understand some of the key assumptions of the innovation system and the basic structuring of regional innovation systems (RIS). The innovation systems approach highlights that innovation is an evolutionary, non-linear and interactive undertaking that requires intensive communication and cooperation between firms and other organizations such as universities and other public research facilities, technology centres, educational establishments, financing institutions, standard setting bodies, industry associations and government agencies (Edquist, 1997, 2005). Regional innovation systems (RIS) traditionally highlight the disparities in innovation across regions (Autio, 1998; de la Mothe and Paquet, 1998; Howells, 1999; Acs, 2000; Cooke et al., 2000, 2004; Doloreux, 2002; Fornahl and Brenner, 2003; Asheim and Gertler, 2005; Doloreux and Parto, 2005; Tödtling and Trippl, 2005; Asheim and Coenen, 2006), whereas national innovation systems (NIS) show that countries differ enormously with respect to their economic structures, R&D bases, institutional set-ups and innovation performances (Edquist, 2001). Due to its regional unit of analysis, the RIS literature has focused more specifically on knowledge spillover and interaction processes.

Key assumptions of the RIS are (Trippl and Tödtling, 2007): innovation activities exhibit a very distinctive geography (see amongst others, Howells, 1999; Breschi, 2000; Paci and Usai, 2000); knowledge spillovers are often spatially bounded (i.e. localized) (Jaffe, 1989; Jaffe et al., 1993; Audretsch and Feldman, 1996; Anselin et al., 1997; Bottazzi and Peri, 2003); tacit knowledge remains important for successfully carrying out innovation (Howells, 2002; Gertler, 2003), and the exchange of tacit knowledge presupposes trust and personal contacts which are essentially facilitated by spatial proximity (Storper, 1997; Morgan, 2004); and subnational territories tend to differ strongly in their institutional setting and political decision-making abilities (Cooke et al., 2000). We argue in this chapter that the assumptions of the RIS seem particularly relevant for the study of innovation in SMEs, since SMEs are considered to operate primarily on a local level due to a lack of human capital and financial resources. As a result, SMEs rely heavily on localized knowledge spillovers, tacit knowledge and trust-based relationships for their innovation activities. Figure 8.1 gives an overview of the structuring of a RIS. On the basis of Figure 8.1, we can argue that three subsystems are essential for a RIS and thus for SMEs: the knowledge generation and diffusion subsystem; the knowledge application and exploitation subsystem; and the regional policy subsystem. The focus of the RIS on knowledge, business and policy subsystems is similar to the ideas of the 'triple-helix' literature, which also highlights the importance of knowledge, business and policy interactions for innovation (e.g. Etzkowitz and Leydesdorff, 1997). We have added in our own modification of Trippl and Tödtling (2007) the regional financial subsystem, which is generally considered to be at the basis of any business environment and thus innovation system.

In the ideal case, there are different types of relations within and between

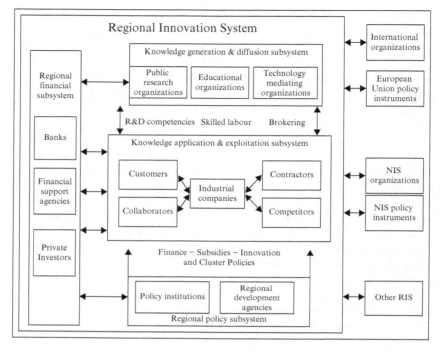

Source: Author's modification of Trippl and Tödtling (2007).

Figure 8.1 Key elements of regional innovation systems

the RIS subsystems enumerated above, which facilitate a continuous flow of knowledge, resources and human capital. The relation dimension of a RIS is of key importance (Trippl and Tödtling, 2007; Trippl, 2010). We argue that this is also true for innovation performance of SMEs. Intensive local knowledge interactions and transfer processes are at the heart of dynamic regions, giving rise to systemic innovation activities. SMEs rely for a large part on those (tacit) local knowledge interactions and transfer processes for their innovation performance, because due to their small size and limited financial resources they rely more on their external environment for knowledge input and support than large firms, who are better able to internalize their innovation activities. This study underlines that the regional level plays a key role for the generation of new knowledge and its economic exploitation, but ongoing globalization tendencies and technological change make it hard to believe that knowledge interactions are local only. The literature about inflow of international knowledge and expertise, brought about by the extra-local contacts of regional firms and knowledge providers (Bunnel and Coe, 2001; Oinas and Malecki, 2002; Maskell et al., 2006), underlines the complex web of relations to national and international organizations and innovation systems of the RIS. However, only few efforts have been made so far to explore the question of whether and under which conditions a RIS can transcend national borders (Trippl, 2010). This study aims to add to this literature by exploring which types of knowledge interactions are of relevance for cross-border RIS. We will particularly analyse the relationship between the four subsystems of the RIS as depicted in Figure 8.1 on the innovation performance of Dutch SMEs, and the influence of cross-border interactions on this relation. In the following section, the hypotheses will be discussed.

2.2 Hypotheses: Knowledge Transfer Through Sources of Information

Knowledge generation and diffusion subsystem (KGDS)

Trippl (2010) suggests that the KGDS, or the knowledge infrastructure dimensions of a RIS, is made up of all those organizations that are engaged in the production and diffusion of knowledge, expertise and skills. Key actors are public research institutions, technology mediating organizations (technology licensing offices, innovation centres, etc.) as well as educational bodies (universities, polytechnics, vocational training institutions, etc.) and workforce mediating organizations. Within the systems-of-innovation approach, the creation, selection and transformation of knowledge takes place within a complex matrix of interactions between different actors (firms, universities and other research organizations, educational organizations, financial organizations, public support organizations, etc.), and within a diverse economic, institutional, social, political, cultural, and geographical context. Tödtling et al. (2009) particularly highlight local knowledge externalities or spillovers from universities and research organizations to firms, whereby they argue that, different from market links, in these cases there is often no contract or formal compensation for the acquired knowledge. Local knowledge spillovers are further regarded by the literature to particularly result from various kinds of mechanism such as patents, and knowledge exchange through mobile labour, or through informal contacts (Feldman, 2000). On the basis of the ideas about the knowledge infrastructure dimensions of a RIS, we have formulated the following hypothesis:

H1   The knowledge generation and diffusion subsystem (KGDS) is positively associated with SMEs' innovation performance

Knowledge application and exploitation subsystem (KAES)

The KAES reflects the firm or business dimensions of a RIS. It comprises the companies, their clients, suppliers, competitors as well as their industrial cooperation partners, i.e. the industrial clusters located in the region. Tödtling et al. (2009) refer in the case of market relations to the buying of technology and knowledge in various forms such as the buying of machinery, ICT equipment or software, or the buying of licences. The relation or knowledge transfer is static because the technology or knowledge is traded more or less in ready form. In this study, however, SMEs are central and their financial resources are often limited. As the firms' ability to attract and maintain a highly qualified labour force is important (Bougrain and Haudeville, 2002), with regard to SMEs, more important than attracting pure R&D may therefore be the existence of a skilled and technically qualified workforce. Further, as already indicated, firms, especially smaller ones, generally cannot rely solely on their internal knowledge and competences in their innovation process but are forced to seek complementary information from their environment. With regards to market relations, previous research has particularly emphasized the importance of vertical relationships with suppliers and customers as an important source of innovation-related inputs (von Hippel, 1988; Lundvall, 1992), but sometimes horizontal relationships with competitors are also of importance (Hamel et al., 1989). Our second hypothesis is therefore formulated as follows:

H2   The knowledge application and exploitation subsystem (KAES) is positively associated with SMEs' innovation performance

Regional policy subsystem (RPS)

The regional policy subsystem can promote regional competitiveness by fostering innovation, networks and clusters (Asheim et al., 2003; Nauwelaers and Wintjes, 2008). The RPS includes public authorities, regional development agencies and other policy agents engaged in formulating and implementing innovation policies and cluster strategies. The innovation systems literature draws heavily on the institutionalist school of thought and its line of reasoning (Hodgson, 1988, 1999; Johnson, 1992; Edquist and Johnson, 1997), emphasizing the impact of formal and informal institutions on innovation activities. However, policy interventions and actions undertaken at the national and European levels can also constitute important external impulses, influencing the development and dynamics of a RIS (Cooke et al., 2000; Asheim et al., 2003). We thus assume that regional and national policies also influence innovation performance of SMEs, and have formulated the third hypothesis as follows:

H3   The regional policy subsystem (RPS) is positively associated with SMEs' innovation performance

Regional financial subsystem (RFS)
The various subsystems are also dependent on the existence of a sufficient level of financial resources and legal competencies at the regional level. Many firms that are innovative, growing and seeking to internationalize, encounter problems in obtaining sufficient finance. This is not in itself an indication of a market failure. If markets are working efficiently, firms that do not have viable products or markets or are inefficient with no competitive advantage will face difficulties in obtaining finance. However, a market failure may indeed occur if viable businesses are unable to obtain the amounts of finance they need. This may be because of problems arising from unwillingness by the suppliers of finance to take the risk that would be involved, or it may be the result of the challenges financiers face in obtaining the information about a firm, which they need in order to be able to make an informed investment decision. If such market failures occur, there are often calls for policy intervention to resolve the problem. This is why in representations of RIS architecture the regional financial subsystem is often not regarded, yet we argue that for a RIS to function successfully the regional financial subsystem is essential. Our fourth hypothesis is thus formulated as follows:

H4   The regional financial subsystem (RFS) is positively associated with SMEs' innovation performance

2.3   Hypotheses: Cross-Border Interactions

Different types of relations within and between the RIS subsystems are considered to facilitate a continuous flow of knowledge, resources and human capital. In general, this relational dimension is local, but increasingly various forms of partnerships between research organizations, educational bodies and transfer agencies from adjoining areas seem necessary to mobilize synergies and to amplify the combination of capabilities in knowledge generation and diffusion. On a regional level, the emergence of a cross-border RIS could thus constitute an increase in the exchange of goods and knowledge, labour mobility and direct investments, offering opportunities for mobilization of synergies and shared growth effects. In the literature, cross-border areas are defined as spaces that consist of neighbour territories belonging to different nation states. Trippl (2010), in this respect, especially highlights the high levels of economic integration and innovation-related intersections that characterize cross-border RIS areas. In this study, cross-border interactions are a particular focus of attention, which can take the form of bundling of scientific and economic strengths, complementary expertise and innovation capabilities. There is a widespread consensus amongst researchers in innovation studies that intense knowledge flows between various actors constitute a crucial 'building block' of regional innovation systems. According to Trippl (2010) there is no doubt that economic relations and processes of collective learning should also be regarded as an indispensable condition for the rise and dynamic evolution of cross-border RIS. Trippl (2010) thus argues that the extent and the precise nature of transborder linkages matter in a fundamental way when it comes to evaluate the development potential and future prospects of cross-border RIS. We therefore argue that cross-border interactions can greatly strengthen the relationship between the subsystems of a RIS and the innovation performance of SMEs. Our final set of hypotheses is therefore formulated as follows:

H5   The greater the cross-border interactions, the stronger the relationship between key subsystems of the RIS and SMEs' innovation performance

H6   SMEs' innovation performance is likely to be positively influenced by their cross-border interactions

H7   SMEs that make active use of key subsystems of the RIS are likely to have increased innovation performance only through their cross-border interactions

3.   RESEARCH METHOD

3.1   Conceptual Framework

Figure 8.2 shows the conceptual framework of cross-border knowledge interaction in the innovation process of SMEs that will be investigated in this study. We base this on the RIS architecture proposed by Trippl and Tödtling (2007), and aim to look particularly at SMEs. Further, on the basis of the classifications of Tödtling et al. (2009) we discern a more static knowledge transfer phase, as well as a more dynamic phase of collective learning (i.e. the dimensional stage). Both phases have an effect on the SMEs' innovation performance, but in the second dynamic phase we predict that the learning effect is moderating rather than direct. Next, the possibility of a mediating effect of cross-border interactions

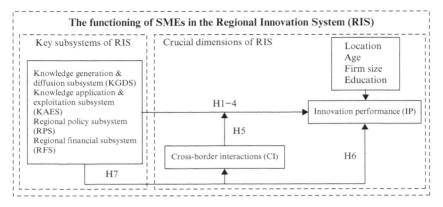

Figure 8.2   Conceptual model based on the systems of innovation and innovation networks approaches

between sources of innovation and innovation performance will be tested through Hypotheses 6 and 7. Further, we assume that location of the firm, age of the owner/manager, firm size, and education of the owner/manager may influence the relationship between RIS subsystems and innovation performance of SMEs, and they are therefore included as control variables in the model to eliminate or reduce the bias arising from these effects.

3.2   Variable Definitions

Dependent and independent variables

The dependent variable in this study is innovation performance, which is a sum-variable consisting of variables that measure radical innovation, i.e. the development of new products, services or processes, and incremental innovation, i.e. the improvement of existing products, services or processes, as well as the SMEs' percentage increase in sales in 2009 from new or improved products, services or processes (see Table 8.1 for further details). A technologically new product is a product whose technological characteristics or intended uses differ significantly from those of existing products (OECD, 1997). A technologically improved product refers to an existing product whose performance has been significantly improved or upgraded (OECD, 1997). Further, the OSLO Manual (OECD, 1997) proposes that innovation performance can best be measured by the proportion of sales as a result of technologically new or improved products. This indicator has been widely adopted in innovation studies (Evangelista et al., 2001). The independent variables in this study are the three subsystems

Table 8.1   Description of the variables used in this study

Variable	Description	Scale of measurement
Dependent variables		
Innovation performance	Sum-variable measuring the innovation and sales performance of SMEs:	
	Radical innovation	
	Mean-variable consisting of:	
	Development of new products or services	1 = no
		2 = don't know/no answer
		3 = yes
	Development of new production or service processes	1 = no
		2 = don't know/no answer
		3 = yes
	Incremental innovation	
	Mean-variable consisting of:	
	Improvement of existing products or services	1 = no
		2 = don't know/no answer
		3 = yes
	Improvement of existing production or service processes	1 = no
		2 = don't know/no answer
		3 = yes
	Sales performance	
	Percentage increase in sales in 2009 from new or improved products/services/processes from the period 1 January 2006 until 1 January 2010	1 = decrease
		2 = none
		3 = don't know/no answer
		4 = very low percentage
		5 = low percentage
		6 = average
		7 = high percentage
		8 = very high percentage
Independent variables		
Knowledge generation & diffusion subsystem (KGDS)	Mean-variable measuring use of knowledge infrastructure that SMEs normally use for innovation:	
	University	1 = no
		2 = yes
	University of professional education	1 = no
		2 = yes

Table 8.1 (continued)

Variable	Description	Scale of measurement
Independent variables		
	Research institutions (TNO, EIM, etc.)	1 = no
		2 = yes
	Commercial research organizations	. 1 = no
		2 = yes
Knowledge application & exploitation subsystem (KAES)	Mean-variable measuring use of firm or business dimensions of SMEs:	
	Customers	1 = no
		2 = yes
	Suppliers	1 = no
		2 = yes
	Employees	1 = no
		2 = yes
	Concern or umbrella company	1 = no
		2 = yes
	Other firms/competitors	1 = no
		2 = yes
Regional policy subsystem (RPS)	Sum-variable measuring the policy dimensions of a RIS for SMEs:	
	Government (for example Agentschap.nl or Syntens)	1 = no
		2 = yes
	Trade organizations	1 = no
		2 = yes
	Chamber of Commerce	1 = no
		2 = yes
Regional financial subsystem (RFS)	Sum-variable measuring the financial dimensions of a RIS for SMEs:	
	Financial institutions (banks, etc.)	1 = no
		2 = yes
	Audit firms	1 = no
		2 = yes
	Private investors	1 = no
		2 = yes
Cross-border interactions (CI)	Interaction-variable measuring the extent of local interactions of firms:	
	Extent to which employees (including owner/manager of SME) have contact with professional networks	1 = not
		2 = don't know/no answer
		3 = irregular
		4 = yearly
		5 = monthly
		6 = weekly
		7 = daily
	Contact with international networks	1 = no
		2 = yes

Table 8.1   (continued)

Variable	Description	Scale of measurement
Control variables		
	Location	1 = outside university city
		2 = inside university city
	Age	1 = 20–29
		2 = 30–39
		3 = 40–49
		4 = 50–59
		5 = 60–69
		6 = 70–79
		7 = >79
	Firm size	1 = 1–9 (micro)
		2 = 10–49 (small)
		3 = 50–250 (medium)
	Education	1 = primary school
		2 = lower vocational training
		3 = MAVO/MULO/VMBO
		4 = vocational training
		5 = HAVO/VWO/HBS
		6 = university of professional education
		7 = university
		8 = PhD

of a RIS discussed in the literature review, i.e. the knowledge generation and diffusion subsystem, the subsystem of knowledge application and exploitation, and regional policy subsystem. This study further adds a fourth subsystem, namely the regional financial subsystem. All subsystem variables are mean-variables consisting of two or more variables that are representative for a specific subsystem and that SMEs may normally use for innovation. Individually, they are all dummy variables that take the value of 2 if the SME uses the source for knowledge for innovation, or otherwise 1.

Moderator/mediator and controls
The moderating variable is cross-border interactions. The RIS literature emphasizes the critical role of local interaction and knowledge circulation facilitated by mutual trust, common conventions and norms (Saxenian, 1994; Storper and Venables, 2004). This study argues that this line of argumentation particularly holds for SMEs, which are largely dependent on local resources and knowledge input. In the recent past, however, the relevance of non-local knowledge relations has been accentuated (Amin and Cohendet, 2004; Maskell et al., 2004), complementing local ones (Bathelt et al., 2004; Gertler and Levitte, 2005). This chapter therefore argues that with ongoing globalization and digitalization, innovative SMEs cannot draw on local knowledge only but rely heavily upon a substantial inflow of external knowledge and expertise to complement the locally available competencies. A RIS is thus considered to have various connections to international actors and innovation systems (Trippl and Tödtling, 2007; Trippl, 2010). In this study, the cross-border interaction variable is measured by dividing the SME's network intensity, i.e. the extent to which employees (including the owner/manager of the SME) have contact with professional networks, and the SME's contact with international networks, which is a dummy variable that take the value of 2 if the SME uses international networks for innovation activities, or otherwise 1.

Also, several control variables are used in the model. The first control is the use of the dummy location to test for proximity effects, whereby location in a university city takes the value of 2, or otherwise 1. A number of studies have demonstrated through econometric methods that there are considerable local knowledge externalities or spillovers, in particular from universities and research organizations to firms (for example, the studies applying the knowledge production function approach, e.g. Audretsch and Feldman, 1996; Anselin et al., 1997; Bottazzi and Peri, 2003). Age and firm size are used as controls to test for the effects of firm behaviour. Given a wide choice of alternative ideas, SMEs with increasing invention experience are more likely to select the ideas of others from a comparison group that is at the frontier of knowledge and solution development (Lewin and Massini, 2004). The age of the owner/manager and years of firm existence may therefore be considered to affect the model. Further, larger firms may be argued to have a larger innovation network. Finally, the education level of the owner/manager of the SME serves as a proxy for the quality of the firm's human resources, which is an important determinant of innovation output in the literature (Rothwell and Dodgson, 1991; Jones, 2001). More highly educated entrepreneurs may be more likely to stimulate learning in their organization.

3.3 Data Description

Our sample consists of 416 Dutch SMEs that have participated in a subsidy scheme of the Ministry of Economic Affairs that goes by the name of the 'innovation vouchers programme'. In 2006, the government of the Netherlands officially launched this subsidy programme, which aimed to promote knowledge transfer to SMEs by means of 'innovation vouchers' in order to encourage the flow of information from knowledge institutes (KIs) to SMEs. Our database consists of SMEs that applied for a small or large innovation voucher in the period 2006–08, hence after the programme was officially launched. An innovation voucher is a (relatively small) sum of money made available by the Dutch government, with the particular aim to improve access for SMEs to the knowledge available within (public) KIs. Per year about 3000 small vouchers and 3000 large vouchers were made available by the Dutch government. The database is considered particularly valuable because it consists of SMEs that have the intention to be innovative, and aim to improve contacts with one or more KIs. In this study, the focus is on innovative SMEs that demonstrate 'active strategic commitment to research and technological change' (Motwani et al., 1999), and exploit external opportunities for inward investment and information gathering (Heunks, 1998). In this survey, a majority of firms are micro-sized, with 1–9 employees (60 per cent). More importantly, of the 416 respondents that replied to our questionnaire, a majority (68.9 per cent) indicated that they had previous contacts with the KI of their choice, because the vouchers were easily accessible. There was no assessment upfront for SMEs. The sample is thus not representative for SMEs in the Netherlands generally, because it is comprised of those companies that, often, already have innovation contacts with KIs and see value in government programmes of this kind.

Quantitative data was collected by means of a survey which was both made available online and sent as a paper version to 2253 SMEs in July 2010. The general aim of the survey was to research the innovation sources and networks of Dutch SMEs and study their influence on the performance of these firms. The questionnaire design was partly based on the Dialogic (2008) evaluation in order to allow for comparison. Test questionnaires were sent to colleagues and SMEs in June, and on the basis of their comments the questionnaire was further improved. Address details were made available by Agentschap.NL, which is a division of the Dutch Ministry of Economic Affairs that is in charge of the innovation voucher programme. The majority of respondents returned the questionnaire by mail. A stamped-addressed return envelope was sent with it to increase the response rate. Also, per valid questionnaire, €1 was donated to a

Table 8.2   Mean, standard deviations, and correlations (N=320)

Variable	1	2	3	4	5	6	7	8	9	10
1. IP	1.000									
2. KGDS	0.093[c]	1.000								
3. KAES	0.257[a]	0.076	1.000							
4. RPS	0.068	0.096[c]	0.184[a]	1.000						
5. RFS	0.120[b]	0.088	0.104[c]	0.218[a]	1.000					
6. CI	0.254[a]	0.195[a]	0.131[b]	−0.010	0.081	1.000				
7. Location	0.082	−0.029	0.078	−0.062	−0.115[b]	0.017	1.000			
8. Age	0.026	0.052	0.006	0.033	0.034	0.135[b]	0.004	1.000		
9. Firm size	0.015	0.015	0.009	0.038	−0.001	0.044	−0.031	−0.084	1.000	
10. Education	0.080	0.024	0.069	0.050	0.021	0.054	0.180[a]	0.016	0.033	1.000
Mean	12.934	1.179	1.361	1.220	1.027	6.388	0.284	3.313	1.541	5.978
S.D.	2.780	0.364	0.241	0.263	0.109	3.551	0.452	1.084	0.725	1.154

Note: [a] $p<0.01$; [b] $p<0.05$; [c] $p<0.10$.

good cause (Cordaid Micro Credit). It turned out that the paper version was preferred because it gave the respondents more freedom to add a comment, remark, or clarification. In total 416 valid questionnaires were returned by January 2011. The response rate of 18.5 per cent is comparable with the general response rate from questionnaires, which is between 5 and 15 per cent (Miles and Huberman, 1999). All questionnaires were manually entered into an SPSS-database. Further, as this study focuses on innovative SMEs, SMEs that applied for a small or large voucher, but did not use the voucher, because of, for example, time limitations (a voucher is valid for one year only), were deleted from the sample.

Table 8.2 reports the basic statistics for the variables used in the analysis. Based on the correlation coefficients for the SI variables that achieve a statistical significance at the 5 per cent significance level, the knowledge application and exploitation subsystem (KAES) in particular is used as a source of innovation ($r = 0.257$, $p < 0.01$). Further, SMEs that use the KAES tend to also use regional policy subsystems (RPS) ($r = 0.184$, $p < 0.01$), and, to a lesser extent, regional financial subsystems ($r = 0.104$, $p < 0.10$), which indicates the existence of strong market relationships between SMEs. At the same time, SMEs collaborating via the knowledge generation and diffusion subsystem (KGDS) tend to have particularly strong correlations with cross-border interactions ($r = 0.195$, $p < 0.01$), suggesting that cross-border interactions take place largely within the knowledge infrastructure dimension of a RIS in our sample. There is no significant correlation of the control variables with SMEs' innovation performance, which suggests that the control variables do not affect our model.

4.   ANALYSIS

4.1   Results: CI as Moderator Between RIS and IP

The model in this study is estimated by OLS-based hierarchical regression. In Table 8.3 the results of the hierarchical regression analysis are shown for IP. Model 1 contains the control variables location, age, firm size, and education. In Model 2, cross-border interaction (CI) and the RIS subsystem variables (KGDS, KAES, RPS, and RFS) are entered into the model. The terms of interaction between the RIS subsystem variables and the CI variable are added in Model 3. Because the interaction terms are usually highly correlated with CI or the knowledge exchange variables, this study follows the procedure suggested by Friedrich (1982) to reduce or eliminate any contamination of the results due to multi-collinearity. This approach first standardizes the variables, and then forms the cross-product terms. Table 8.3 indicates that adding the subsystem and CI variables (Model 2) to the model with only the controls (Model 1) increases the R^2 by about 12 per cent. The F-value (8.38) for the incremental R^2

Table 8.3   Moderated hierarchical regression analysis of innovation performance (N=320)

Variable	Model 1	Model 2	Model 3	VIF
Location	0.071	0.067	0.060	1.072
Age	0.026	−0.010	−0.028	1.044
Firm size	0.017	0.002	−0.021	1.031
Education	0.066	0.039	0.043	1.061
KGDS		0.029	0.227***	2.479
KAES		0.208***	0.196***	1.081
RPS		0.014	0.003	1.136
RFS		0.083	0.103*	1.180
CI		0.213***	0.198***	1.093
CI*KGDS			−0.258***	2.411
CI*KAES			−0.005	1.075
CI*RPS			−0.093	1.268
CI*RFS			−0.004	1.418
R^2	0.012	0.130	0.168	
Adj-R^2	−0.001	0.104	0.133	
F-value	0.960	5.133***	4.770***	
ΔR^2		0.118	0.039	
F-value for ΔR^2		8.382***	3.570***	

Note: *** $p < 0.01$; ** $p < 0.05$; * $p < 0.10$.

achieves a statistical significance at the 1 per cent level. An inspection of the coefficient estimates of the RIS subsystem variables shows that these variables explain the change in innovation performance for KAES. This result implies that only the market subsystem increases the innovation performance of innovative SMEs when the analysis does not account for the effect of CI. Adding the interaction terms (Model 3) to Model 2 further increases the R^2 by about 4 per cent. The F-value (3.57) for the incremental R^2 value achieves statistical significance at the 1 per cent level, which indicates that the interaction terms of both the RIS subsystem variables and the CI variable have explanatory powers with regard to the change in the SMEs' innovation performance. Model 3 can thus be used to discuss the interaction effect between CI and RIS subsystems on SMEs' innovation performance. The variance inflation factors (VIF) for all coefficient estimates in Model 3 are below 10, indicating that multi-collinearity does not contaminate the results as suggested by Mason and Perreault (1991). A significant negative interaction effect appears between knowledge generation and diffusion subsystem (KGDS) and cross-border interaction (CI) (Beta = -0.258, p < 0.01), providing support for the fifth hypothesis. At a high level of CI, the relationship between KGDS and IP is negative and significant. From the results, it appears that knowledge interactions with international networks are particularly relevant for the knowledge dimension of the RIS, but that these interactions do not (yet) lead to high innovation performance in our sample.

4.2 Results: CI as Mediator Between RIS Subsystem and IP

Measurement and model validation

This study employs path analysis with latent variables (PALV) in SEM (undertaken with AMOS 18.0 with the Maximum Likelihood (ML) method). When using AMOS, Anderson and Gerbing (1988) recommend a two-step approach. This approach requires that, before SEM analysis is conducted, in Step 1 the latent constructs are tested to find out if they are statistically adequate for SEM analysis. This is done by means of Confirmatory Factor Analysis (CFA), whereby the latent variables are integrated into a measurement model and tested with AMOS. The results of the CFA are shown in Table 8.4.

Overall, the results of the CFA show that all the theoretical constructs defined by this chapter are confirmed by, and fit, the sample well. Step 2 concerns the PALV, which is a type of causal modelling technique integrating path analysis and CFA, rooted in a latent model, for not only the examination of causal relationships among latent constructs but also the estimation of observed variables (Raykov and Marcoulides, 2001).

Table 8.4   Results of confirmatory factor analysis (N = 320)

Construct and items	Standardized loading
RIS subsystem	
KGDS	0.22
KAES	0.50**
RPS	0.37**
RFS	0.31**
Innovation Performance (IP)	
Radical innovation	0.42
Incremental innovation	0.64***
Sales performance	0.61***
Controls	
Location	$0.31^{n.s.}$
Age	$0.02^{n.s.}$
Firm size	$0.04^{n.s.}$
Education	0.57
CFA diagnostics	
$R^2 = 38.755$, df $= 41$, p $= .571$, GFI $= .972$, AGFI $= .958$, RMSEA $= .000$	

Note: *** $p<0.01$; ** $p<0.05$; * $p<0.10$.

It can be inferred that, if a PALV theoretical model is statistically speci-fied and fitted to the associated samples, and its estimates are present at a significant level, the defined causal correlations can be said to exist in both theoretical and statistical terms. Within SEM, Jöreskog and Sörbom (1986) and Hu and Bentler (1999) suggest some cut-off criteria: The R^2 test statistic is at an insignificant level or CMIN/df < 2 if considering the complexity of the model; the Goodness of Fit Index (GFI) and adjusted GFI (AGFI) are over 0.9; the Normed Fit Index (NFI) is over 0.90; or in the case of a smaller sample size, the threshold of Comparative Fit Index (CFI) is at the 0.95 level; and, for root mean square error of approxima-tion (RSMEA), lower is better: a benchmark of 0.05 is often used. All are met or exceeded by the model.

Hypothesis tests
The hypothesis tests for mediation compare the strength of hypothesis H6 (i.e. SMEs' innovation performance (IP) is likely to be positively influenced by cross-border interaction (CI)) with those of H7 (i.e. SMEs that actively use RIS subsystems are likely to have increased innovation performance only through their CI). According to the causal relationship defined in the research framework, this study examines the mediated

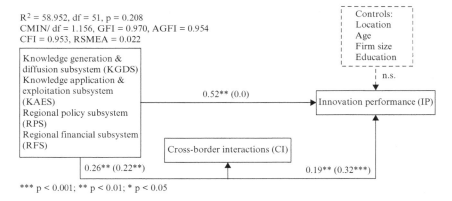

Figure 8.3   The (standardized) proposed model for causal relationship analyses

effects of absorptive capacity on innovation performance (see Figure 8.3).

We first impose the constraint criterion that the path RIS → IP is set to 0 (zero) (thus assuming that the possible direct effect of RIS subsystems on IP should be disregarded). The model fit diagnostics of Model 1 show that the hypothetical model's statistical specification is not satisfied and thus fails to fit the sample (df = 52, R^2 = 75.841 with p = 0.0.017). Other indices, including GFI = .963, AGFI = .944, CFI = 0.858 and RSMEA at the 0.038 level, reach or exceed the normal benchmarks of model goodness of fit. With a sample size of n = 320, such residual covariances appear to conform to a normal distribution that is reflective of the model's statistical correctness (Jöreskog and Sörbom, 1986). Model 2 investigates the possible direct effects on innovation performance from sources of innovation (RIS → IP) in order to justify the mediated role played by the absorptive capacity (ACAP) variable. Table 8.5 provides the chi-square difference test results for Model 1 and Model 2, where Model 2 (referred to as the competing model) includes a direct path RIS → IP, while Model 1 (the hypothetical model) excludes it. Only Model 2 is statistically appropriate, and comparing the model schemes of Model 1 and Model 2 is thus not necessary. The existence of path RIS → IP cannot be ignored.

For Hypothesis 6, we examined the possible direct effects on innovation performance (IP) from cross-border interactions (CI). The defined path CI → IP appears to be statistically significant. The standardized path coefficient of CI → IP in Model 2 is 0.26 (p < 0.05), which indicates that IP is positively influenced by the variance in CI. Hypothesis 6 is thus supported by the sample. However, Hypothesis 7 is rejected, as the model

Table 8.5   Results of model comparison (path coefficients in standardized mode)

Diagnosis and measurements	Model 1	Model 2	ΔR^2
Model fit			
R^2	75.841	58.952	16.889
Df	52	51	1
p-value	n.s. (0.017)	0.208	n.a.
Path coefficients			
RIS → CI	0.22**	0.26**	
CI → IP	0.32***	0.19**	
RIS → IP	n.a.	0.52**	

Notes:
R^2 difference test: ΔR^2 = 2.61**. Model 1: excluding the path 'SI → IP'; Model 2: including the path 'SI → IP'.
*** $p < 0.001$; ** $p < 0.01$; * $p < 0.05$.

proves insignificant. To conduct hypothesis tests for this study, we also introduced control variables as confounders into the proposed model. This arrangement was employed to examine the possibility of an authentic relationship between innovation and firm performance according to the theoretical model. The non-significance of this latent variable shows that the introduction of those confounders does not contribute any significant obscuring or accentuating effects to the direct relationship between RIS subsystems and innovation performance that we have shown to be non-existent (see Table 8.6). This lends further weight to the non-existence of a direct mediating role of CI in SMEs according to our sample's statistical behaviour

5.   DISCUSSION

The results of our analyses generally support the existence of considerable knowledge spillovers from sources of innovation to firms (Audretsch and Feldman, 1996; Anselin et al., 1997; Bottazzi and Peri, 2003). Market sub-systems generally have the strongest relationship with SMEs' innovation performance. Apparently our sample SMEs are mainly part of a dense network of organizations that focus on commercialization. Interaction in market subsystems is regional and/or national, rather than international by nature. This is also true for the regional policy subsystem and the financial subsystem. It could be argued that for these subsystems mutual

Table 8.6 SEM results of the structural paths including the control variables (standardized mode)

Variables	Model 1		Model 2	
	Beta	p-value	Beta	p-value
RIS → CI	0.221	0.039	0.255	0.026
KGDS	0.271		0.254	
KAES	0.363	0.028	0.478	0.019
RPS	0.438	0.049	0.350	0.023
RFS	0.397	0.034	0.332	0.019
CI → IP	0.323	0.000	0.187	0.045
RIS → IP	n.a.	n.a.	0.517	0.022
Radical innovation	0.444		0.444	
Incremental innovation	0.574	0.000	0.609	0.000
Sales performance	0.654	0.000	0.622	0.000
Controls → IP	0.224	0.261	0.192	0.472
Location	0.731		0.571	
Age	0.014	0.903	0.009	0.920
Firm size	0.238	0.970	−0.019	0.852
Education	0.247	0.362	0.316	0.489

trust and common conventions and norms are more important, which emphasizes the critical role of local interactions and knowledge circulation here. Cross-border interactions in our sample only have an effect on the relationship between the knowledge infrastructure dimension of a RIS and SMEs' innovation performance. This effect is negative, which suggests that cross-border interactions take place in knowledge generation and diffusion subsystems (KGDS) for exploratory purposes and (thus) fail to connect to the local market, policy and financial subsystems for commercialization of their innovations. Or, as suggested by Enright (2003), regions covered by our sample have little experience in commercializing scientific discoveries, have a weak culture of risk taking, or lack crucial factors such as venture capital or a support structure specialized in promoting academic spin-offs. Trippl and Tödtling (2007) in this respect suggest a far-reaching transformation of the RIS by means of the creation of a variety of new organizations, processes of institutional (un)learning and socio-cultural shifts.

Our study supports that knowledge industries cannot draw on local knowledge only but also rely upon the inflow of external knowledge and expertise to complement the locally available competencies. This finding is supported by previous study that hypothesized that high-tech companies and knowledge intensive service firms are more engaged in cross-border innovation networking than low-tech firms (van Geenhuizen, 2008). A reason why cross-border interactions only take place in the knowledge infrastructure dimension may be that these cross-border interactions are not essential for SMEs' innovation performance as our SEM analysis showed, but nevertheless greatly enhance the strength of the RIS. Our study shows that cross-border interactions as suggested by Trippl (2010) are indeed a reality that deserve research attention, because they can lead to a stronger RIS. Trans-frontier economic relations and knowledge linkages can take different forms, including among others cross-border labour mobility, co-patenting and co-publications, formal and informal networking in the field of technology and innovation, trade relations, etc. (see, for instance, van Houtum and van der Velde, 2004; van Houtum and Gielis, 2006; Maggioni and Umberti, 2007; Tödtling and Trippl, 2007). The extent and the precise nature of trans-border linkages matter in a fundamental way when it comes to evaluating the development potential and future prospects of cross-border RIS. In this study, cross-border interactions take the form of professional international networks. More detailed information about the nature of the knowledge that is interacted in the networks is however not available. It could be argued that in our sample the knowledge infrastructure subsystem exchanges in particular codified knowledge, which would facilitate cross-border interaction compared with the other subsystems. In the commercialization phase, knowledge exchange maybe requires higher trust due to a stronger emphasis on secrecy. However, future research is necessary to further investigate this assumption.

6.   CONCLUSIONS

This study has addressed the question of whether relationships exist between different RIS subsystems and the innovation performance of innovative SMEs in the Netherlands, and what the role of cross-border interaction (CI) is on their relationship. For Dutch SMEs, the knowledge application and exploitation, or market, subsystem is most important for high innovation performance. This subsystem is still mainly local and/ or national. Nevertheless, in order to be innovative, SMEs increasingly look for and find inspiration abroad. The RIS literature acknowledges that knowledge interactions with international partners and knowledge sources are highly relevant (Trippl and Tödtling, 2007). Such linkages are very important for a region, because through such links scientific knowledge and managerial know-how as well as qualified labour are acquired.

Our study supports the importance of linkages for a RIS. Dutch SMEs that participate with knowledge institutions often do so through cross-border linkages. So far, however, they generally fail to commercialize their innovations and increase their innovation performance. Our results in this respect highlight the existence of two stages of innovation, the exploration phase and the exploitation stage, which seem to require a different knowledge environment. Exploration in firms is stimulated by the inflow of external knowledge and expertise to complement and enrich the locally available knowledge and competencies. It can lead to entirely new innovations, or the introduction of cross-border innovations to the local market. Exploitation or the commercialization of innovations, however, may require higher levels of trust and tacit knowledge interactions. Exploitation may thus be a stage that requires proximity of economic actors, while for the exploration stage, proximity may hamper innovation, and innovation should be stimulated through cross-border interactions, which lead to higher creativity and local economic advantage. Future research is necessary to investigate if exploration indeed requires more trust and tacit knowledge, or if such trust relationships also exist on a cross-border level. Our results could also point towards weak commercialization capabilities of firms that work actively with actors from the knowledge generation and diffusion subsystem, for example spin offs. This may be a weak point of the firms, but it may also point towards a region's weak commercialization capabilities. A range of policy actions and government programmes might be necessary in this context to better support the commercialization of (scientific) discoveries, amongst others through venture capital.

ACKNOWLEDGEMENTS

We are very grateful to Agentschap.NL for access to their database. The study would not have been possible without their support.

REFERENCES

Acs, Z. (ed.) (2000), 'Regional innovation', *Knowledge and Global Change*, London: Pinter.

Amin, A. and P. Cohendet (2004), *Architectures of Knowledge*, Oxford: Oxford University Press.

Anderson, J.C. and D.W. Gerbing (1988), 'Structural equation modelling in practice: a review and recommended two-step approach', *Psychological Bulletin*, **103** (3), 411–23.

Anselin, L., A. Varga and Z. Acs (1997), 'Local geographic spillovers between university research and high technology innovations', *Journal of Urban Economics*, **42** (3), 422–48.

Asheim, B. and L. Coenen (2006), 'Contextualising regional innovation systems in a globalising learning economy: on knowledge bases and institutional frameworks', *Journal of Technology Transfer*, **31**, 163–73.

Asheim, B. and M. Gertler (2005), 'The geography of innovation: regional innovation systems', in J. Fagerberg, D.C. Mowery and R.R. Nelson (eds), *The Oxford Handbook of Innovation*, Oxford: Oxford University Press.

Asheim, B., A. Isaksen, C. Nauwelaers and F. Tödtling (eds) (2003), *Regional Innovation Policy for Small-Medium Enterprises*, Cheltenham, UK and Northampton, MA, USA: Edward Elgar.

Audretsch, D. and M. Feldman (1996), 'Innovative clusters and the industry life cycle', *Review of Industrial Organisation*, **11** (2), 253–73.

Autio, E. (1998), 'Evaluation of RTD in regional systems of innovation', *European Planning Studies*, **6** (2), 131–40.

Bathelt, H., A. Malmberg and P. Maskell (2004), 'Clusters and knowledge: local buzz, global pipelines and the process of knowledge creation', *Progress in Human Geography*, **28** (1), 31–56.

Bottazzi, L. and G. Peri (2003), 'Innovation and spillovers in regions: evidence from European patent data', *European Economic Review*, **47** (4), 678–710.

Bougrain, F. and B. Haudeville (2002), 'Innovation, collaboration and SMEs internal research capabilities', *Research Policy*, **31**, 735–47.

Breschi, S. (2000), 'The geography of innovation: a cross-industry analysis', *Regional Studies*, **34**, 213–29.

Bunnel, T. and N. Coe (2001), 'Spaces and scales of innovation', *Progress in Human Geography*, **25** (4), 569–89.

Cooke, P., P. Boekholt and F. Tödtling (2000), *The Governance of Innovation in Europe: Regional Perspectives on Global Competitiveness*, London: Pinter.

Cooke, P., M. Heidenreich and H. Braczyk (2004), *Regional Innovation Systems: the Role of Governance in a Globalized World*, London: Routledge.

De la Mothe, J., and G. Paquet (eds) (1998), *Local and Regional Systems of Innovation*, Boston: Kluwer Academic Publishers.

Dialogic (2008), *Evaluatie innovatievoucherregeling 2005/2006*, Utrecht: Dialogic.

Doloreux, D. (2002), 'What we should know about regional innovation systems of innovation', *Technology and Society*, **24**, 243–63.

Doloreux, D. and S. Parto (2005), 'Regional innovation systems: current discourse and unresolved issues', *Technology in Society*, **27**, 133–53.

Drucker, P.F. (1985), 'The discipline of innovation', *Harvard Business Review*, **63** (3), 67–72.

Edquist, C. (1997), *Systems of Innovation: Technologies, Institutions and Organizations*, London: Pinter.

Edquist, C. (2001), 'The systems of innovation approach and innovation policy: an account of the state of the art', *DRUID conference working paper*, 12–15 June, Aalborg.

Edquist, C. (2005), 'Systems of innovation – perspectives and challenges', in J. Fagerberg, D. Mowery and R. Nelson (eds), *The Oxford Handbook of Innovation*, Oxford: Oxford University Press, pp. 181–208.

Edquist, C. and B. Johnson (1997), 'Institutions and organizations in systems of innovation', in C. Edquist (ed.), *Systems of Innovation*, London: Pinter.

Enright, M. (2003), 'Regional clusters: what we know and what we should know', in J. Bröcker, D. Dohse and R. Soltwedel (eds), *Innovation Clusters and Interregional Competition*, Berlin: Springer.

Etzkowitz, H., and L. Leydesdorff (1997), *Universities in the Global Economy: A Triple Helix of University–Industry–Government Relations*, London: Cassell Academic.

Evangelista, R., S. Iammarino, V. Mastrostefano and A. Silvani (2001), 'Measuring the regional dimension of innovation: lessons from the Italian innovation survey', *Technovation*, **21** (11), 733–45.

Feldman, M. (2000), 'Location and innovation: the new economic geography of innovation spillovers, and agglomerations', in G. Clark, M. Feldman and M. Gertler (eds), *The Oxford Handbook of Innovation*, Oxford: Oxford University Press, pp. 373–94.

Fornahl, D. and T. Brenner (eds) (2003), *Cooperation, Networks and Institutions in Regional Innovation Systems*, Cheltenham, UK and Northampton, MA, USA: Edward Elgar.

Freel, M. and J.P. de Jong (2009), 'Market novelty, competence-seeking and innovation networking', *Technovation*, **29** (12), 873–84.

Friedrich, R.J. (1982), 'In defense of multiplicative terms in multiple regression equations', *American Journal of Political Science*, **26** (4), 797–833.

Gertler, M. (2003), 'Tacit knowledge and the economic geography of context or the undefinable tacitness of being (there)', *Journal of Economic Geography*, **3**, 75–99.

Gertler, M. and Y. Levitte (2005), 'Local nodes in global networks: the geography of knowledge flows in biotechnology innovation', *Industry and Innovation*, **12** (4), 487–507.

Hamel, G., Y.L. Doz and C.K. Prahalad (1989), 'Collaborate with your competitors – and win', *Harvard Business Review*, 190–96.

Heunks, F.J. (1998), 'Innovation, creativity and success', *Small Business Economics*, **10**, 263–72.

Hodgson, G. (1988), *Economics and Institutions: A Manifesto for a Modern Institutional Economics*, Cambridge: Polity Press.

Hodgson, G. (1999), *Economics and Utopia*, London: Routledge.

Howells, J.R. (2002), 'Tacit knowledge, innovation and economic geography', *Urban Studies*, **39** (5/6), 871–84.

Howells, J. (1999), 'Regional systems of innovation', in D. Archibugi, J. Howells, and J. Michie (eds), *Innovation Policy in a Global Economy*, Cambridge: Cambridge University Press, pp. 67–93.

Hu, L.-T. and P.M. Bentler (1999), 'Cutoff criteria for fit indexes in covariance structure analysis: conventional criteria versus new alternatives', *Structural Equation Modeling*, **6** (1), 1–55.

Jaffe, A. (1989), 'The real effects of academic research', *American Economic Review*, **79** (5), 957–70.

Jaffe, A., M. Trajtenberg and R. Henderson (1993), 'Geographic localization of knowledge spillovers as evidenced by patent citations', *Quarterly Journal of Economics*, **79**, 577–98.

Johnson, B. (1992), 'Institutional learning', in B.-Å. Lundvall (ed.), *National Systems of Innovation. Towards a Theory of Innovation and Interactive Learning*, London: Pinter.

Jones, P. (2001), 'Are educated workers really more productive?', *Journal of Development Economics*, **64** (1), 57–79.

Jöreskog, K.G. and D. Sörbom (1986), *LISREL VI: analysis of linear structural relationships by maximum likelihood, instrumental variables, and least squares methods*, Scientific Software.

Lewin, A.Y. and S. Massini (2004), 'Knowledge creation and organizational capabilities of innovating and imitating firms', in H. Tsoukas and N. Mylonopoulos (eds), *Organizations as Knowledge Systems: Knowledge, Learning and Dynamic Capabilities*, New York: Palgrave MacMillan, pp. 209–37.

Lundvall, B.-Å. (1992), *National Systems of Innovation*, London: Pinter.

Maggioni, M. and E. Uberti (2007), 'Inter-regional knowledge flows in Europe: an econometric analysis', in K. Frenken (ed.), *Applied Evolutionary Economics and Economic Geography*, Cheltenham, UK and Northampton, MA, USA: Edward Elgar.

Maskell, P., H. Bathelt and A. Malmberg (2004), 'Temporary clusters and knowledge creation: the effects of international trade fairs, conventions and other professional gatherings', *SPACES 2004-4*, Philipps University Marburg.

Maskell, P., H. Bathelt and A. Malmberg (2006), 'Building global knowledge pipelines: the role of temporary clusters', *European Planning Studies*, **14** (8), 997–1013.

Mason, C.H. and W. Perreault (1991), 'Collinearity, power and the interpretation of multiple regression analysis', *Journal of Marketing Research*, **28**, 268–80.

Miles, N. and F. Huberman (1999), *Qualitative Data Analysis: An Expanded Sourcebook*, Thousand Oaks: Sage Publications.

Morgan, K. (2004), 'The exaggerated death of geography: learning, proximity and territorial innovation systems', *Journal of Economic Geography*, **4**, 3–21.

Motwani, J., T. Dandridge, J. Jiang and K. Soderquist (1999), 'Managing innovation in French small- and medium-sized enterprises', *Journal of Small Business Management*, **37** (2), 106–14.

Nauwelaers, C. and R. Wintjes (eds) (2008), *Innovation Policy in Europe*, Cheltenham, UK and Northampton, MA, USA: Edward Elgar.

OECD (1997), *The Oslo Manual: The Measurement of Scientific and Technological Activities*, Paris: OECD.

Oinas, P. and E. Malecki (2002), 'The evolution of technologies in time and space: from national and regional to spatial innovation systems', *International Regional Science Review*, **25** (1), 102–31.

Paci, R. and S. Usai (2000), 'Technological enclaves and industrial districts: an analysis of the regional distribution of innovative activity in Europe', *Regional Studies*, **34**, 97–114.

Raykov, T. and G.A. Marcoulides (2001), 'Can there be infinitely many models equivalent to a given covariance structure model?', *Structural Equation Modelling*, **8**, 142–9.

Rothwell, R. and M. Dodgson (1991), 'External linkages and innovation in small and medium-sized enterprises', *R&D Management*, **21** (2), 125–37.

Saxenian, A. (1994), *Regional Advantage: Culture and Competition in Silicon Valley and Route 128*, Cambridge, MA: Harvard University Press.

Schumpeter, J.A. (1934), *The Theory of Economic Development*, Cambridge MA: Harvard University Press.

Storper, M. (1997), *The Regional World*, New York: Guilford Press.

Storper, M. and A. Venables (2004), 'Buzz: face-to-face contact and the urban economy', *Journal of Economic Geography*, **4** (4), 351–70.

Tödtling, F. and M. Trippl (2005), 'One size fits all? Towards a differentiated regional policy approach', *Research Policy*, **34** (8), 1203–19.

Tödtling, F., P. Lehner and A. Kaufmann (2009), 'Do different types of innovation rely on specific kinds of knowledge interactions?', *Technovation*, **29**, 59–71.

Trippl, M. (2010), 'Developing cross-border regional innovation systems: key factors and challenges', *Tijdschrift voor Economische en Sociale Geografie*, **101** (2), 150–60.

Trippl, M. and F. Tödtling (2007), 'Developing biotechnology clusters in non-high technology regions – the case of Austria', *Industry and Innovation*, **14** (1), 47–67.

van Geenhuizen, M. (2008), 'Knowledge networks of young innovators in the urban economy: biotechnology as a case study', *Entrepreneurship & Regional Development*, **20**, 161–83.

van Houtum, H. and R. Gielis (2006), 'Elastic migration: the case of Dutch short-distance transmigrants in Belgian and German Borderlands', *Tijdschrift voor Economische en Sociale Geografie*, **97**, 195–202.

von Hippel, E. (1988), *Sources of Innovation*, Oxford: Oxford University Press.

9. Region-specific productivity competitiveness and the university-industry interface

Vadim Grinevich

1. INTRODUCTION

There has been considerable interest in the United Kingdom concerning industry-university links as a mechanism of enhancing innovation and improving productivity competitiveness of local industries. In the last two decades the UK regions have been increasingly encouraged to promote university-industry knowledge transfer partnerships and networks, centres of excellence and high-technology clusters (Sainsbury, 2007; Wilson, 2012). The policy focus on the link between the university and productivity performance is because the university is often seen as one of the contributors to industrial innovation (Cooke et al., 1997; Lundvall, 1992; Nelson, 1993), with the latter being widely acknowledged as a key source of economic growth (Romer, 1990; Aghion and Howitt, 1992; Grossman and Helpman, 1991).

As far as spatial dimension of the university-industry interface is concerned, the respective literature indicates that knowledge flows from the university are often geographically localised (Jaffe, 1989; Anselin et al., 1997, Jaffe et al., 1993; Singh et al., 2010). In a parallel stream of research, a number of studies report little or no localisation effects at all when these are measured in terms of economic performance of firms and industries, such as business start-up rates, employment, sales and profitability (Bania et al., 1993; Siegel et al., 2003; Löfsten and Lindelöf, 2005). Also, the literature on sectoral patterns of industry-university links indicates its region-invariant technology-specific nature (Faulkner and Senker, 1994; Cohen et al., 2002; Nomaler and Verspagen, 2008), which can make it very difficult to use university-industry links as an instrument of regional policy.

Given this diverse evidence on the extent of regional economic impact of university-industry links, and the highly important role which is attached to the university in the UK regional economic agenda, our main objective in this chapter is to investigate whether the region-specific extent of industry-university interactions can, indeed, be linked to the size of sectoral productivity gains achieved at a regional level. We assume that the underlying pattern of university-industry links is mainly defined by sector-specific needs for knowledge. However, region-specific competitiveness characteristics of the innovation system, including those related to the history of relationship between the science base and local industries, the policy context and the structure and capabilities of regional university systems, may well result in some deviations from this pattern and lead to region-specific productivity gains enjoyed by industry.

The rest of the chapter is organised as follows. In the following section we discuss our key assumptions and hypotheses with reference to the relevant literature on the university-industry relationships. We then describe the data and methodology used at each stage of analysis, followed by a discussion of the empirical results and conclusion.

2. UNIVERSITY ENGAGEMENT WITH INDUSTRY: ANALYTICAL ASSUMPTIONS AND HYPOTHESES

2.1 Making a Distinction Between Regional and Sectoral Effects

The university is one of the main organisational elements of the innovation system. As such, it is involved through market and non-market linkages in dynamic relationships with other innovation agents such as firms and non-firm organisations (Freeman, 1987; Lundvall, 1992; Nelson, 1993). These linkages can be realised through a number of channels such as educating people, increasing the stock of codified knowledge, technological problem solving, spin-out activities, various public space functions and informal arrangements such as clubs, forums and networks (Cooke et al., 1997; Lester, 2003). This view is strongly supported by the extensive literature on the extent and variety of industry-university interactions, which can be approached from the point of view of industry or academia (Agrawal and Henderson, 2002; Arundel and Geuna, 2004; Cohen et al., 2002; D'Este and Patel, 2007; Faulkner and Senker, 1994; Schartinger et al., 2001; Abreu et al., 2009; Abreu and Grinevich, 2010).

Innovation processes differ greatly both across regions and across sectors, which is reflected by two broad streams of the innovation system literature representing location-focused models such as those stressing the role of innovation characteristics found together only within the boundaries of a nation state (Lundvall, 1992; Nelson, 1993; Edquist, 1997) or rooted inside certain regions (Cooke et al., 1997; Braczyk et al., 1998; Cooke, 2001; Asheim and Isaksen, 2002) and models where the focus is on either the role of sectors (Breschi and Malerba, 1997; Malerba, 2005) or technologies involved (Carlsson, 1995; Jacobsson, 2002). In this regard, it is important to distinguish between regional and sectoral effects of the university engagement with industry.

A large body of empirical research indicates that knowledge flows from the university tend to be geographically localised. For instance, Jaffe (1989) in his highly influential paper based on the knowledge production function framework finds that geographic coincidence between universities and industrial laboratories contributes to corporate patenting activity in addition to the main spillover effect of university research. The geographical coincidence effect is, however, shown to significantly vary across technological areas, implying that spillovers are limited to specific technical areas and are not just the diffuse effect of a large research university. Jaffe's conclusions are reinforced by Acs et al. (1992) and Anselin et al. (1997) who use a similar methodology but introduce other measures of innovative output, such as innovation counts and R&D employment.

A number of other spatial studies have also concluded that the degree of localisation of knowledge spillovers varies significantly across technological areas and industrial sectors. Acosta and Coronado (2003), who use non-patent scientific citations to get a picture of science-industry links in Spanish regions, find that differences in industry specialisation of the regions may condition university-industry knowledge flows. In a series of studies on the proportion of firm's products and processes which could not have been developed without academic research, Mansfield (1991, 1995, 1998) concludes that geographic proximity plays a lesser role for basic research than it does for applied research. Also, Abramovsky et al. (2007) find a strong technology specific dimension of university knowledge spillovers.

In parallel, the literature on sectoral effects of university knowledge flows reports clear differences between sectors in terms of the extent and nature of their engagement with the university and their capability to transfer knowledge from the scientific to economic domain (Faulkner and Senker, 1994; Arundel et al., 1995; Arundel and Geuna, 2004; Marsili, 2001; Cohen et al., 2002; Nomaler and Verspagen, 2008). The relevance of academic knowledge for industry and its nature are argued to be mainly driven by the technological requirements of industrial sectors rather than localisation effects. It implies that the pattern and effects of industry-university links are primarily shaped by the relationship between industry demand for and supply of academic knowledge, with the location of the two sides of this relationship being of secondary importance.

Based on the innovation system approach and discussion above, we conceptualise that regional systems of innovation develop from the different composition of sectors, with some of the latter being critically important in driving regional innovation and economic performance. The university may be only one of many institutions and actors contributing to the creation and development of innovation activities within those sectors; among other possible sources of innovation may be suppliers, customers, consultancies and competitors. In general, the underlying pattern of industry-university interactions can be assumed to be linked to region-invariant sectoral needs for university knowledge. However, the way these needs are realised may reflect regional characteristics of innovation systems, including those related to the history of relationship between the science base and local industries, the policy context, as well as the structure and capabilities of regional university systems (Malerba, 2005; Leslie and Kargon, 1996; Mowery and Sampat, 2005; Saxenian, 1994). These may contribute to region-specific competitiveness effects in relation to the organisation of innovative and production activities of region-based sectors, which eventually may influence sectoral economic indicators on a regional level.

2.2 Analytical Approach

As we argue that the underlying patterns of university interactions with industry are mainly shaped by sector specific technical requirements for knowledge inputs, we imply that these region-invariant technology driven links represent the main route by which the university can contribute to the innovation and productivity performance of a given region. Given that the sector related route of the university-industry interface is very well documented by both spatial and sectoral studies, we leave it outside the scope of this chapter and concentrate on a much more debated issue of region-specific effects of the university-industry interface.

As discussed above, the literature on the localised knowledge spillovers implies that a region that aims to improve its economic performance should simply focus on upgrading its science base. However, the very same literature suggests a cross-boundary nature of industry-university effects. Furthermore, a number of studies report small or statistically insignificant evidence of knowledge spillovers when these are measured in terms of the economic performance of sectors or firms. For instance, Bania et al. (1993) identify "serious leaks" in the pipeline between the university research and local commercialisation measured in terms of manufacturing start-up rate in US metropolitan statistical areas; Beeson and Montgomery (1993) find only mixed evidence that the university R&D funding had a measurable impact on US local labour market characteristics; Florax and Folmer (1992), who use private sector investments as an indicator of knowledge impact in the Dutch regions, argue that knowledge-intensive industries do not need to locate in the proximity of the university as they can still get indirect access to the university knowledge by locating in central places of the spatial system. Also, Löfsten and Lindelöf (2005) investigate the differences in economic performance between new technology based firms located on and off science parks in Sweden. They find no significant differences between these two groups of firms in terms of sales growth and profitability. Similarly, Siegel et al. (2003), in their review of the UK evidence on the performance of new technology firms on and off science parks, conclude that the returns to being located on the science park are negligible.

In this context, we aim to further add to this debate on region-specific effects of university-industry links. We assume that the extent to which sector-specific needs for knowledge and technology are met by the university may vary across regions, depending on the local history of university-industry links, the local policy context and the structure and quality of the local university system. Our objective is to investigate whether these deviations from region-invariant patterns of university-industry links are significant enough to contribute to region-specific competitiveness effects. The latter normally encapsulate all factors which are not directly related to the regional industrial structure. These may include resource endowment, geographical, historical and institutional factors including those related to the regional science base and region-specific patterns of industry-university links.

In its most schematic form, our analytical approach is presented by Figure 9.1. We first assume that the observed patterns of economic performance of a given sector in a given region are shaped by both sector specific factors and region-specific competitiveness effects. We then disentangle these effects from each other. As discussed above, we focus on region specific effects only (corresponding to the shaded left-hand side area of Figure 9.1) and whether these effects can be explained by regional variations in the extent of the industry-university interface. We now proceed to outline a number of relevant hypotheses.

Hypotheses
The university is fundamentally engaged in research and education and, therefore, provides critical resources for innovation such as talent and knowledge. At the same time, the university is only one of many sources of knowledge that can be deployed by businesses in their pursuit of competitive advantage. The previous research indicates that the university alone

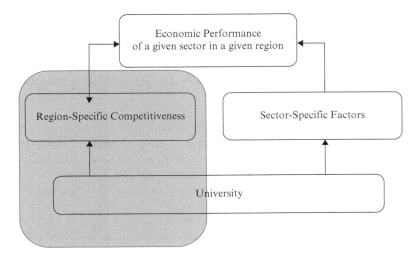

Note: The shaded area indicates the analytical focus of this chapter.

Figure 9.1   Analytical framework

is typically a less important source of knowledge for firms than suppliers, customers, competitors and other firms (Arundel and Geuna, 2004). This is mainly because most innovation and business challenges require a combination of alternative sources of knowledge, including the university. It is often argued that the ability of industries to build networks with a wide range of innovation players, at different geographical levels, could be an important factor of innovation and competitiveness (Fogarty and Sinha, 1999; Christopherson et al., 2008; Abreu et al., 2007, 2011). Thus,

Hypothesis 1   The extent of interconnectedness of local industry with multiple innovation players, including the university, both locally and externally, is likely to have a positive effect on region-specific economic competitiveness

As reviewed above, the literature on the localised economic effects of the university-industry links indicates very little or no economic benefits at all from co-locating industry activities in proximity to the university. This suggests the presence of multiple diversions of knowledge traffic (when measured in economic terms) between the local university and local businesses. It is also argued that the economic effects of the industry-university co-location may be negligible compared to those for the co-location between producers and suppliers or producers and customers (Breschi and Lissoni, 2001). Furthermore, a few studies show that locating outside any cluster may bring more economic advantages than being inside a cluster (Oakey and Cooper, 1989; Suarez-Villa and Walrod, 1997). Therefore,

Hypothesis 2   The extent of co-location of local industry and the university is likely to be an insignificant factor in explaining region-specific economic competitiveness

Research quality of the local university system is conceptualised as one of the factors of region-specific economic competitiveness, falling within the resource endowment category. Also, there is some empirical evidence from firm-level studies that the economic impact of the university is not observed in the case of weak research output of the university (Audretsch and Lehman, 2006). Thus, we test:

Hypothesis 3   The extent of high quality research in the local university system is likely to have a positive effect on region-specific economic competitiveness

Developing closer links between the university and industry is one of the pillars of the UK's innovation strategy (Lambert, 2003; Sainsbury, 2007; Wilson, 2012). The government has introduced "third stream" or "third leg funding" (in addition to teaching and research), which is specifically designed to help the university increase its capability to address the needs of businesses. In each UK region, the university has been increasingly encouraged to be more entrepreneurial and embark on commercialisation of academic research. We analyse the relevance of such policies, by introducing:

Hypothesis 4   The extent of commercialisation in the local university system is likely to have a positive effect on region-specific economic competitiveness

3.   METHOD

3.1   Measuring Region-Specific Competitiveness of Industry

Given that the UK regional policy agenda pays particular attention to productivity performance indicators (DCLG, 2006), we use labour productivity as our measure of economic performance of a given sector in a given region (corresponding to the top block in Figure 9.1). Labour productivity is, in turn, defined as the ratio of gross value added to employment. Correspondingly, our analysis seeks to understand the relationship between the extent of university-industry links at a regional level and region-specific productivity competitiveness of industry. It is the latter which represents the dependent variable in our analysis of economic effects of the university-industry interface.

In order to estimate the region-specific competitiveness component of the aggregate economic performance of a given industry, we run a shift-share regression model. The model was originally specified by Marimon and Zilibotti (1998) It is sometimes described as "an elegant new way" of isolating regional effects from the rest (Meunier and Mignolet, 2003) and has been widely applied in many recent regional studies (Toulemonde, 2001; Blien and Wolf, 2002; Fritz and Streicher, 2005). Thus,

$$\dot{p}\,(i, j, t) = h\,(i) + m\,(i, j) + l\,(t) + a\,(i, t) + b\,(j, t) + v\,(i, j, t)$$
(9.1)

where the dependent variable $\dot{p}\,(i, j, t)$ represents the growth rate of labour productivity in industry i in region j in year t, and defined as the log difference of the respective labour productivity levels in two points in time (t and $t - 1$). The independent variables are sectoral, temporal and regional dummies, such as:

$h\,(i)$ denoting a time invariant sector-specific effect that is common to all regions,

$m\,(i, j)$ denoting a time invariant effect specific to a given sector i and given region j,

$l\,(t)$ denoting a time effect, which is not specific to a sector or region,

$a\,(i, t)$ denoting interaction of a fixed sector and a time effect, common to all regions,

$b\,(j, t)$ denoting interaction of a fixed region and a time effect, common to all sectors within a given region, and

$v\,(i, j, t)$ representing an idiosyncratic disturbance.

The model is estimated using restricted least squares, taking the sample average as reference points (Marimon and Zilibotti, 1998). Based on this model, we construct a virtual labour productivity series, which indicates industry productivity levels that would have been observed in each region in the absence of any region-specific effects and, therefore, would have been determined by a combination of national sectoral trends and regional industry mix only. In technical terms, we set $b(j, t) = m(i, j) = v(i, j, t) = 0$ for all i, t. The respective virtual growth rate of productivity ($\dot{p}^{virt}$) for industry i, region j and year t looks as follows:

$$\dot{p}^{virt} = h(i) + l(t) + a\,(i,t) \tag{9.2}$$

We then generate the respective virtual labour productivity series. The virtual value for labour productivity in year one is obtained by applying the virtual productivity growth rate over the period between year zero and year one to the actual value of labour productivity in year zero. Correspondingly, the virtual value for labour productivity in year two is calculated on the basis of the respective virtual productivity value for year one, and so on.

Comparing actual and virtual productivity levels gives us the measure of region-specific productivity competitiveness effects. By definition, this measure is clear of national business cycle and sectoral trends and represents a pure gain (or loss) in productivity made by a given industry on a regional level due to region-specific competitiveness effects. To obtain a region-specific competitiveness indicator (C_{ij}) for the period longer than one year, we take the log difference between the respective average values of actual and virtual productivity levels, such as

$$C_{ij} = \log(\overline{P}_{ij}) - \log(\overline{P}_{ij}^{virt}) \tag{9.3}$$

where $\overline{P}_{ij}$ denotes average productivity level over a given period.

In our analysis of labour productivity we use UK Annual Business Inquiry in relation to regional employment data[1] and UK Regional Accounts in relation to Gross Value Added (GVA) estimates.[2] This makes it possible to easily trace our measure of labour productivity to official UK statistics. We also use the 60-industry database by the Groningen Growth and Development Centre to obtain UK sector-level deflators.[3] The employment and GVA data are analysed at a region-sector level. The regions are identified at the level of UK Government Office Regions (the Eastern, the East Midlands, London, the North East, the North West, the South East, the South West, the West Midlands and Yorkshire and the Humber) and devolved administrations (Northern Ireland, Scotland and Wales). As far as industries are concerned, these are aggregated to the two digit standard industrial classification (SIC) level.

3.2 Main Empirical Model and Measurement of Independent Variables

Having identified the region-specific competitiveness indicator (C_{ij}) as our dependent variable, we now present our main empirical model. It is estimated using ordinary least squares (OLS) and in its generalised form specified as follows:

$$C_{ij} = \beta_0 + \sum_{k=1}^{k} \beta_k (\log X_{ij} - \log X_{in}) + \sum_{m=1}^{m} \varphi_m (\log U_j - \log U_n) + \varepsilon_{ij} \quad (9.4)$$

where X represents sector-level variables related to the extent of industry engagement with the university and other innovation system players, U relates to relevant characteristics of regions and their university system, β and φ are estimated parameters, ε is an error term, subscripts i and j refer to sector and region respectively, and subscripts k and m indicate the number of the respective variables.

We conduct our analysis in the context of UK regional productivity performance in the late 1990s and early 2000s. To arrive at the variables on the extent of university-industry links during that period we use data from several sources such as the 1998–2000 Community Innovation Survey (CIS3),[4] the 2001 Higher Education – Business and Community Interaction Survey (HE-BCI)[5] and the 2001 Research Assessment Exercise (RAE).[6] In addition, we use data from the UK 2001 Census and UKBORDERS[7] to introduce spatially informed variables.

The independent variables in Equation 9.4 are intended to capture the relative extent of the university-industry interface on a regional level. We measure all explanatory variables as regional deviations from the respective national average levels. As we design proxies to test Hypothesis 1, we rely on our analysis of the CIS3 data on the importance of alternative sources of knowledge for industry innovation. From the CIS3 we confirm that the university knowledge is almost never used by industry in isolation from other sources of knowledge, such as company channels and intermediaries.

This complementary role of the university is illustrated by Table 9.1. It reports the extent of industry engagement with several mutually exclusive combinations of knowledge sources for innovation. To be consistent with the labour productivity measure, it is reported in terms of employment weight of the firms engaged. This provides a good estimate of total business employment within a given sector which is potentially affected by knowledge transfer spillovers. The reported descriptive statistics cover five broad sectors such as high technology and conventional manufacturing, high-technology knowledge intensive services (KIS), other (non high-technology) KIS and conventional services.[8] The sources of knowledge include the science base (such as higher education institutions, government and private research organisations and R&D labs), the company related intelligence (such as suppliers, clients, competitors and from within the company sources) and intermediaries (such as consultants, public sector offices, professional conferences and trade associations).

It is very clear that the use of the science base sources in combination

Table 9.1   Use of knowledge for industry innovation (employment weight
of relevant firms by broad sector, %)

	High Tech Mfg	Conventional Mfg	High Tech KIS	Other KIS
At least one science base source and no other sources	0.0	0.0	0.2	0.0
At least one company source and no other sources	2.6	2.9	2.0	2.1
At least one intermediary source and no other sources	1.0	1.0	1.1	0.8
At least one company source and one intermediary source and no other sources	16.8	26.8	24.6	26.8
At least one company source and one science base source and no other sources	0.7	0.3	0.1	0.2
At least one intermediary source and one science base source and no other sources	0.0	0.1	0.0	0.1
At least one source in each category – companies, intermediaries and science base	61.6	39.3	57.7	24.8

Source: Author's calculations using CIS3.

with intermediaries and company sources dominates the pattern of industry engagement with alternative sources of knowledge. In high-technology
manufacturing and high-technology services, the firms resorting to this
tri-source combination account for over 57 per cent of the total employment; the results for conventional manufacturing are also very impressive
(around 40 per cent). We can also see that "at least one company source
and one intermediary source" is the second most widespread combination of knowledge sources used by industries, in terms of its employment
coverage. The use of other combinations of knowledge sources is almost
negligible.

Therefore, to test Hypothesis 1 on the region-specific economic effects of industry interconnectedness with different innovation players, we select two explanatory variables. The first one characterises each of the sectors in terms of the employment weight of the firms using in their innovation activities at least one company source, one intermediary source and one science base source, and the second variable is the employment weight of the firms using at least one company source and one intermediary source.

In relation to Hypothesis 2 on the region-specific economic effects of industry clustering around the university, we use a variable which measures the density of industry employment in university locations in each of the regions. It is measured as number of employees of a given sector per square kilometre of the university local authority area. In the context of our empirical model, for each of the sectors we look at region-specific deviations in employment density in university locations from the respective national average indicator, and estimate whether these deviations are significant enough to have an effect on region-specific competitiveness.

To test Hypothesis 3 on the region-specific economic effects of research quality of the local university system, we introduce two region level variables. The first variable controls for the concentration of research quality in university locations and is measured as the total "research quality mass" per square kilometre of the total university local authority area. For a given region, the measure of the research quality mass is obtained by grossing up the results of the UK Research Assessment Exercise to the whole population of academics. The second variable measures the average RAE score per academic in each of the regions. This is to control for so called "star scientist" effects (Zucker and Darby, 2006). Keeping the concentration of research and other variables constant, an increase in the average research quality per academic will indicate a decrease in total number of academic staff. Therefore, this variable helps to pick up the effect of university systems with relatively small numbers of academics, which are, however, extremely strong in terms of research output.

Finally, for Hypothesis 4 on the region-specific economic effects of university commercialisation activities, we also use two variables to measure the extent of pro-business orientation of the university. The design and interpretation of these variables is similar to that for the research quality proxies above. For each region, the first variable measures the level of income generated by the university from its commercialisation activities (such as business contracts, consultancy, equipment-related services, and spin-outs) per square kilometre of a given region. The second variable is the average third stream income per academic. Again, this is to control for the effects of relatively small but very productive academic teams in terms of their commercialisation output.

In addition, we introduce a regional dummy to control for some unobserved influences in labour productivity patterns between the Greater South East (GSE) and the rest of the country. The GSE consistently demonstrates highest productivity levels, with the rest of UK regions trailing behind with a substantive margin of more than 20–50 per cent (BIS and ONS, 2010).

Table 9.2 presents further details on the way in which the variables above are computed. For the "use of knowledge" variables, the respective coefficients will read as a per cent change in region-specific productivity of a given industry as the respective "use of knowledge" ratio increases by one percentage point (for example, from 1.16 to 1.17). As far as the remaining variables are concerned, the respective coefficients report the per cent change of region-specific productivity of a given industry as a result of a 1 per cent increase in the respective region-specific explanatory variable.

4.   THE RESULTS

4.1   Region-Specific Competitiveness Effects

Our results indicate that there is a considerable heterogeneity in the labour productivity performance of industry across the UK, with many of its changes at a regional level being of an idiosyncratic nature, that is caused by $v\ (i, j, t)$ as specified by Equation 9.1. For a panel of 41 industries in twelve UK regions in the period 1998–2002, we find that the full shift-share regression model explains, as either sectoral, or regional, or temporal effects, around 24 per cent of the labour productivity growth variance. To put it in the contet, our value of R^2 is higher than that reported by Toulemonde (2001) for the employment growth model for Belgian regions, but significantly lower than the estimates by some other relevant international studies of employment trends (Meunier and Mignolet, 2003; Marimon and Zilibotti, 1998). This indicates that compared to employment growth labour productivity changes are more sensitive to region-specific competitiveness factors.

The extent of region-specific competitiveness effects is illustrated by Figure 9.2. It positions the sectors analysed according to their virtual (axis X) and actual (axis Y) productivity performance as described in Section 3.1. The diagonal line on this figure indicates the points where the actual and virtual values would coincide, implying zero region-specific effects. Sectors located above this line enjoy region-specific productivity gains; those below suffer from losses. The further the perpendicular

Table 9.2   Description of the variables included in the analysis

Variable	Mean	Description	Source
Regional sectors' variables			
Use of knowledge sources			
At least one company source and one intermediary source	1.16	Specified as a per cent deviation from the UK average such as (Xij/Xin), for a given sector *i* in region *j* this is employment share of firms using this source of knowledge.	CIS3
At least one company source, one intermediary source and one science base source	0.91	Specified as a per cent deviation from the UK average such as (Xij/Xin), for a given sector *i* in region *j* this is employment share of firms using this source of knowledge.	CIS3
Co-location effects			
Employment density in university locations	0.44	Specified as log difference such as ln(Xij/Xin), for a given sector *i* in region *j* this is employment per square km of the local authority area of all region's universities, as indicated by their full postcode.	UK 2001 Census, UKBORDERS
Regional variables			
University system characteristics			
Concentration of research mass	0.62	Specified as log difference such as ln(Ur/Un), for a given region *j*, this is $\Sigma\, m*r*t$ per square km of the local authority area of all region's universities, as indicated by their full postcode, where *m* is a research assessment exercise score, *r* is the proportion of the assessed research staff who received that score and *t* is total number of research active staff.	RAE 2001, UKBORDERS

Table 9.2   (continued)

Variable	Mean	Description	Source
University system characteristics			
Research output per academic	−0.01	Specified as log difference such as ln(Ur/Un), for a given region *j*, this is $(\Sigma\ m^*r^*t)/t$, where *m* is a research assessment exercise score, *r* is the proportion of the assessed research staff who received that score and *t* is total number of research active staff.	RAE 2001, UKBORDERS
Commerciali-sation income generated per area	0.14	Specified as log difference such as ln(Ur/Un), for a given region *j* this is total monetary value of third stream activities in all region's universities per square kilometre of the respective region; the third stream activities included are contracts with businesses, equipment related services for businesses, consulting and spin-outs.	HE-CBI 2001–02, UKBORDERS
Commerciali-sation income per academic	−0.06	Specified as log difference such as ln(Ur/Un), for a given region *j* this is total monetary value of third stream activities in all region's universities per academic employee; the third stream activities included are contracts with businesses, equipment related services for businesses, consulting and spin-outs.	HE-CBI 2001–02
Other variables			
Greater South East		Whether a given observation comes from the Greater South East of England (including London, the South East and the Eastern Region).	

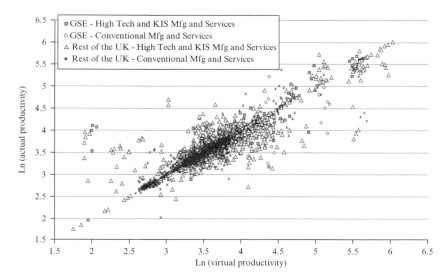

Notes: Both virtual and actual productivity are measured as a four-year average of the respective productivity levels (£'000/employee) over the period 1998–2002.

Source: Author's calculations using ABI/Regional Accounts.

Figure 9.2   Region-specific competitiveness effects

distance between the diagonal and the sectoral point on the figure, the more noticeable the respective region-specific effects are. The pattern of region-specific productivity gains and losses is quite heterogeneous across regions and sectors. We can see a noticeable presence of region-specific effects across both high-technology and conventional sectors in both the Greater South East and the rest of the country.

4.2   The Role of the University-Industry Interface

The results of our main empirical model (Equation 9.4) are reported in Table 9.3. It covers a set of three regression runs with different temporal dimensions of the dependent variable. The first regression is concerned with the average region-specific productivity gain over 1998–2002, the second one relates to the period 1998–2000, which is closest to the CIS data coverage, and the last one is for the period immediately after the CIS3 coverage. In each of the regressions we use the robust estimator of variance to take account of heteroscedasticity arising from the heterogeneity of data we deal with.

Table 9.3 *Region-specific productivity effects and the university: the regression results*

	(1) Productivity gain 1998–2002	(2) Productivity gain 1998–2000	(3) Productivity gain 2001–02
Use of knowledge sources			
At least one company source and	0.0161**	0.0161***	0.0152**
one intermediary source	(0.00524)	(0.00500)	(0.00601)
At least one company source,	0.0425*	0.0443*	0.0384
one intermediary source and	(0.0218)	(0.0227)	(0.0222)
one science base source			
Co-location effects			
Employment density in university	−0.0311	−0.0318	−0.0308
locations	(0.0330)	(0.0340)	(0.0328)
University system characteristics			
Concentration of research mass	0.0599*	0.0595*	0.0609*
	(0.0291)	(0.0288)	(0.0305)
Research output per academic	0.421*	0.414*	0.463*
	(0.196)	(0.215)	(0.231)
Commercialisation income per	−0.0395**	−0.0387**	−0.0414**
area	(0.0175)	(0.0171)	(0.0187)
Commercialisation income per	0.0681*	0.0590*	0.0790**
academic	(0.0322)	(0.0318)	(0.0352)
Greater South East	0.00511	0.00276	0.00487
	(0.0320)	(0.0325)	(0.0299)
Constant	−0.0498	−0.0492	−0.0469
	(0.0353)	(0.0355)	(0.0384)
Observations	412	412	412
R-squared	0.042	0.051	0.036

Notes:
Robust standard errors in parentheses.
*** $p < 0.01$, ** $p < 0.05$, * $p < 0.1$.
Productivity gain = ln(actual 4-year average productivity level/virtual 4-year average productivity level).

The results are supportive of Hypothesis 1, indicating that the effects of industry engagement with the university via tri-source links (covering company, intermediary and science base sources) are positive. However, these effects are found to be less significant compared to those resulting from industry engagement with company and intermediary sources only. Both effects are especially strong in relation to the CIS3 period 1998–2000.

We do not find a significant relationship between the university-centred industry clustering and region-specific productivity gains, which confirms Hypothesis 2. In keeping with our previous research, this supports the argument that mapping where industries are should not be confused with what industries do (Abreu et al., 2007). The results may also suggest the presence of intra-industry mechanisms which could make it possible for economic benefits arising from industry-university clustering in a given region to materialise somewhere else.

Consistent with Hypothesis 3, our results indicate that both the concentration of research quality mass and research productivity of academic staff are positively and significantly related to region-specific productivity gains made across all sectors. The size of the coefficients is particularly high for the research output per academic, suggesting the presence of the "star scientist" effects of the university system.

We find only a partial confirmation of Hypothesis 4. On the one hand, higher commercialisation income per academic is positively associated with region-specific productivity competitiveness across all sectors. On the other hand, regions with relatively high levels of the university generated income per square kilometre reveal relatively lower region-specific gains in industry productivity. Effectively, these results suggest that region-specific competitiveness of industry is likely to be higher in places where the university has the relatively small commercialisation rate measured in terms of the number of employees involved and where the generated commercialisation income per head is higher. Also, these results may be one more indication of the leaks in the pipeline between the local university and the performance of the local industry. Finally, the effects of the GSE dummy are found positive but not significant enough.[9]

5. CONCLUSION

In this chapter we analyse region-specific productivity competitiveness of industry in combination with the patterns of university-industry links. The work has been motivated by the ongoing policy and academic debate on the role of the university in regional economic development. As we analyse regional productivity effects of university-industry links, we first identify the extent to which regional productivity performance of industry can be attributed to region-specific competitiveness effects. We then estimate the relationship between the latter and the extent of industry engagement with the university at a regional level.

We find that most of productivity growth fluctuations on a regional level are of an idiosyncratic nature and, therefore, can only be attributed to a unique combination of regional, sectoral and temporal effects. Our results, therefore, imply that a carefully designed regional policy which takes into consideration every peculiar aspect of regional geographic, historical, institutional and resource conditions may enhance regional competitiveness and productivity growth performance. Most recently, the Regional Development Agencies which have been responsible for producing regional development strategies in the UK have been abolished and replaced with so called Local Enterprise Partnerships (HMT, 2010). Interestingly, the latter are supposed to deliver more localised and specific development plans, which could potentially be an important factor in enhancing regional competitiveness.

The evidence on the extent of industry engagement with the university demonstrates that the university is an important player in regional innovation systems. The value of the university to businesses is especially high when its knowledge inputs are closely interconnected with those from other sources, such as other businesses and intermediary organisations. Networking and the critical role of intermediaries or knowledge gatekeepers are indeed often referred to by businesses when they are asked about their links with the university (Abreu et al., 2008). We find that increased interconnectedness of industry with all three main groups of innovation system players, such as other businesses, intermediary organisations and the university is positively associated with region-specific productivity gains enjoyed by industry.

We also show that the concentration of high quality research mass and the quality of individual research output are positively related with region-specific productivity competitiveness across all sectors. The impact will arguably vary by type of research undertaken by the university (basic versus applied), but this is beyond the scope of this chapter. As far as pro-business orientation of the university system is concerned, it can be associated with region-specific losses in productivity unless third stream income is generated by a relatively small number of academics and the value of the knowledge commercialisation income per head is relatively high.

Overall, the results present a strong argument in favour of policy mechanisms which promote networks and increase interconnectivity among multiple innovation system players, both locally and externally. In this regard, the focus should be on equipping businesses with better skills and expertise to help them form sustainable multi-level networks, rather than pushing the university further along the path of commercialisation. The presence of star quality academic entrepreneurs, who are capable of generating high value income, can be a noticeable feature of region-specific competitiveness profile. However, it is even more important for the university to keep concentrating on the quality of its academic research. This argument is also supported by the evidence from economically advanced regions in some other countries, such as the Netherlands, Finland and Sweden (Abreu et al., 2011).

The results of our analysis have important implications for the conceptualisation of the university and its role in regional economic growth. We clearly find a spatial dimension to the economic role of the university. However, the patterns discovered are very complex, calling for more research on the mechanisms by which the university, through engagement with business innovation, can affect regional economic performance.

ACKNOWLEDGEMENTS

Our special thanks to Oliver Fritz, Olivier Meunier and Themis Apostolidis for their practical advice on the modelling and geo-conversion aspects of this research. We also acknowledge the UK Office for National Statistics as follows: "This work contains statistical data from ONS which is Crown copyright and reproduced with the permission of the controller of HMSO and Queen's Printer for Scotland. The use of the ONS statistical data in this work does not imply the endorsement of the ONS in relation to the interpretation or analysis of the statistical data. This work uses research datasets which may not exactly reproduce National Statistics aggregates."

NOTES

1. The Annual Business Inquiry (ABI) is an integrated survey of employment and accounting information from businesses and other establishments in most sectors of the UK economy. For further details see http://data.gov.uk/dataset/annual_business_inquiry.
2. UK Regional Accounts represent regional specification of the national GVA and Gross Disposable Household Income accounts, which are available from http://www.ons.gov.uk/ons/taxonomy/index.html?nscl=Regional+Accounts.
3. The Groningen Growth and Development Centre database is a comprehensive internationally comparable dataset on industrial performance at a detailed industry level for 27 member states of the Organisation for Economic Co-operation and Development (OECD). For further details see http://www.ggdc.net/dseries/60-industry.html.
4. The Community Innovation Survey by the UK Office for National Statistics is a business survey of innovation inputs, outputs and constraints. It also collects information on the industry engagement with the university for the purposes of innovation. The survey was originally carried out every four years, but since 2005 it has taken place every two years. The CIS3 covers the period from 1 January 1998 to 31 December 2000, which roughly corresponds to the 1998–2001 period from our ABI dataset. For further details see http://www.bis.gov.uk/policies/science/science-innovation-analysis/cis.
5. The Higher Education-Business and Community Interaction Survey (HE-BCI) is conducted by the Higher Education Council for England and covers 164 higher education

institutions in the UK. It asks university managers about strategic aims and levels of infrastructure development of universities as well as financial outputs of different knowledge transfer activities. The regional HE-BCI data are available from the 2001–02 academic year. For further details see http://www.hefce.ac.uk.

6. The Research Assessment Exercise (RAE) is conducted by UK Higher Education Funding bodies to produce quality profiles of research activity of UK universities. Further details are at http://www.rae.ac.uk.

7. UKBORDERS provides access to digitised boundary datasets. Further details are at http://edina.ac.uk.

8. Used for illustration purposes, these broad sectors are derived from the Eurostat/OECD classification of the high-technology and knowledge-intensive sectors (Appendix A). The latter was specially designed for the two-digit SIC level and widely applied in international comparisons (Felix, 2007). In relation to manufacturing, this classification is based on the ratio of R&D expenditure to value added and the ratio of R&D expenditure to production, or R&D intensities. In relation to services, the knowledge intensity is interpreted as a combination of knowledge embedded in new equipment, personnel, and R&D intensity.

9. As our explanatory variables are mainly related to the university and knowledge transfer indicators there is a risk that the estimated model may suffer from omitted variable bias. In addition, the explanatory power of the model is not particularly high, varying in the range from 0.036 to 0.051. As a robustness check, we perform the Ramsey (1969) regression specification test for omitted variables to diagnose the likelihood of the respective bias. The test results fail to reject the null hypothesis that the model has no omitted variables. This implies that the relatively large unexplained variation in the regional competitiveness effect is due to the systematic impact of omitted variables, which, as a group, remain uncorrelated with any of our explanatory variables, and, of course, some random noise (Jargowsky, 2005).

REFERENCES

Abramovsky, L., R. Harrison and H. Simpson (2007), 'University research and the location of business R&D', *The Economic Journal*, **117** (March), C114–C141.

Abreu, M. and V. Grinevich (2010), 'Personal, institutional and spatial determinants of academic entrepreneurship in the UK', paper presented at the 50th Anniversary European Congress of the Regional Science Association International, Jönköping, Sweden, 19–23 August.

Abreu, M., V. Grinevich, M. Kitson and M. Savona (2007), 'Absorptive capacity and regional patterns of innovation', DIUS Research Report 0811, Department for Universities, Innovation and Skills.

Abreu, M., V. Grinevich, A. Hughes, M. Kitson, and P. Ternouth (2008), 'Universities business knowledge exchange', Report by the Council for Industry and Higher Education and Centre for Business Research, London/Cambridge, UK.

Abreu, M., V. Grinevich, A. Hughes and M. Kitson (2009), *Knowledge Exchange Between Academics and the Business, Public and Third Sectors*, UK Innovation Research Centre, University of Cambridge and Imperial College London.

Abreu, M., V. Grinevich, M. Kitson and M. Savona (2011), 'The changing face of innovation policy: the implications for the Northern Ireland Economy', Report by the Programme on Regional Innovation, University of Cambridge, for the Department of Enterprise, Trade and Investment, Northern Ireland.

Acosta, M. and D. Coronado (2003), 'Science-technology flows in Spanish regions. An analysis of scientific citations in patents', *Research Policy*, **32**, 1783–803.

Acs, Z., D. Audretsch and M. Feldman (1992), 'Real effects of academic research: comment', *American Economic Review*, **82** (1), 363–7.

Aghion, P. and P. Howitt (1992), 'A model of growth through creative destruction', *Econometrica*, **60** (2), 323–51.

Agrawal, A. and R. Henderson (2002), 'Putting patents in context: exploring knowledge transfer from MIT', *Management Science*, **48**, 44–60.

Anselin, L., A. Varga and Z. Acs (1997), 'Local geographic spillovers between university research and high technology innovations', *Journal of Urban Economics*, **42**, 422–48.

Arundel, A. and A. Geuna (2004), 'Proximity and the use of public science by innovative European firms', *Economics of Innovation and New Technology*, **13** (6), 559–80.

Arundel, A., G. van de Paal and L. Soete (1995), 'Innovation strategies of Europe's largest firms: results of the PACE Survey for information sources, public research, protection of innovation, and government programmes', PACE Final report, MERIT.

Asheim, B. and A. Isaksen (2002), 'Regional innovation systems: the integration of local "sticky" and global "ubiquitous" knowledge', *Journal of Technology Transfer*, **27**, 77–86.

Audretsch, D. and E. Lehman (2006), 'What determines the variation in entrepreneurial success', Proceedings – Community Affairs Department Conferences, Federal Reserve Bank of Kansas City, July.

Bania, N., R. Eberts and M. Fogarty (1993), 'Universities and the start ups of new companies: can we generalise from Route 128 and Silicon Valley?', *The Review of Economics and Statistics*, **75** (4), 761–6.

Beeson, P. and E. Montgomery (1993), 'The effects of colleges and universities on local labour markets', *Review of Economics and Statistics*, **75** (4), 753–61.

BIS and ONS (2010), 'Regional economic performance indicators: regional competitiveness and state of the regions', Department for Business, Innovation and Skills and Office for National Statistics, 10/259, May.

Blien, U. and K. Wolf (2002), 'Regional development of employment in Eastern Germany: an analysis with an econometric analogue to shift-share techniques', *Papers in Regional Science*, **81**, 391–414.

Braczyk, H.J., P. Cooke, and M. Heidenreich (1998), *Regional Innovation Systems: The Role of Governance in a Globalised World*, London and Pennsylvania: UCL.

Breschi, S. and F. Lissoni (2001), 'Knowledge spillovers and local innovation systems: a critical survey', *Industrial and Corporate Change*, **10** (4), 975–1005.

Breschi, S. and Malerba, F. (1997), 'Sectoral innovation systems: technological regimes, Schumpeterian dynamics, and spatial boundaries,' in Edquist, 1997.

Carlsson, B. (1995), *Technological Systems and Economic Performance: The Case of Factory Automation*, Dordrecht: Kluwer.

Christopherson, S., M. Kitson and J. Michie (2008), 'Innovation, networks and knowledge exchange', *Cambridge Journal of Regions, Economy and Society*, **1** (2), 165–73.

Cohen, W., R. Nelson and J. Walsh (2002), 'Links and impacts: the influence of public research on industrial R&D', *Management Science*, **48** (1), 1–23.

Cooke, P. (2001), 'Regional innovation systems, clusters, and the knowledge economy', *Industrial and Corporate Change*, **10** (4), 945–74.

Cooke, P., M. Uranga and G. Etxebarria (1997), 'Regional innovation systems: institutional and organisational dimensions', *Research Policy*, **26**, 475–91.
D'Este, P. and P. Patel (2007), 'University-industry linkages in the UK: what are the factors underlying the variety of interactions with industry?', *Research Policy*, **36**, 1295–313.
DCLG (2006), 'PSA Target 2 – Regional Economic Performance', Department for Communities and Local Government, UK.
Edquist, C. (1997), *Systems of Innovation: Technologies, Institutions and Organisations*, London: Pinter.
Faulkner, W. and J. Senker (1994), 'Making sense of diversity: public–private sector research linkages in three technologies', *Research Policy*, **23**, 673–95.
Felix, B. (2007), 'Employment and earning in high-tech sectors', *Statistics in Focus: Science and Technology*, **32**, 1–7.
Florax, R. and H. Folmer (1992), 'Knowledge impacts of universities and industries: an aggregate simultaneous investment model', *Journal of Regional Science*, **32** (4), 437–66.
Fogarty, M. and A. Sinha (1999), 'Why older regions can't generalize from Route 128 and Silicon Valley: university-industry relationships and regional innovation systems', in L. Branscomb, F. Kodama and R. Florida (eds), *Industrializing Knowledge. University-Industry Linkages in Japan and the United States*, Cambridge, MA: The MIT Press.
Freeman, C. (1987), *Technology Policy and Economic Performance: Lessons from Japan*, London: Pinter.
Fritz, O. and G. Streicher (2005), 'Measuring changes in regional competitiveness over time. A shift-share regression exercise', InTeReg Working Paper No. 20–2005, Institute of Technology and Regional Policy, Vienna.
Grossman, G. and E. Helpman (1991), *Innovation and Growth in the Global Economy*, Cambridge, MA: MIT Press.
HMT (2010), *Budget 2010*, HM Treasury.
Jacobsson, S. (2002), 'Universities and industrial transformation: an interpretative and selective literature study with special emphasis on Sweden', *Science and Public Policy*, **29** (5), 345–65.
Jaffe, A. (1989), 'Real effects of academic research', *American Economic Review*, **79** (5), 957–70.
Jaffe, A., M. Trajtenberg and R. Henderson (1993), 'Geographic localization of knowledge spillovers as evidenced by patents citations', *The Quarterly Journal of Economics*, **108** (3), 577–98.
Jargowsky, P.A. (2005), 'Ecological fallacy' in K. Kempf-Leonard, *Encyclopaedia of Social Measurement – 1*, Amsterdam and London: Elsevier/Academic Press.
Lambert, R. (2003), *Lambert Review of Business-University Collaboration*, Final Report, HM Treasury, London, UK.
Leslie, S.W. and R.H. Kargon (1996), 'Selling Silicon Valley: Frederick Terman's model for regional advantage', *The Business History Review*, **70** (4), 435–72
Lester, R. (2003), 'Universities and local systems of innovation: a strategy approach', *Workshop on High-Tech Business: Clusters, Constraints, and Economic Development*, Robinson College, University of Cambridge.
Löfsten, H. and P. Lindelöf (2005), 'R&D networks and product innovation patterns – academic and non-academic new technology-based firms on science parks', *Technovation*, **25** (9), 1025–37.

Lundvall, B.-Å. (ed.) (1992), *National Systems of Innovation: Towards a Theory of Innovation and Interactive Learning*, London: Frances Pinter.

Malerba, F. (2005), 'Sectoral systems: how and why innovation differs across sectors', in J. Fagerberg, D. Mowery and R. Nelson (eds), *The Oxford Handbook of Innovation*, Oxford: Oxford University Press.

Mansfield, E. (1991), 'Academic research and industrial innovation', *Research Policy*, **20**, 1–12.

Mansfield, E. (1995), 'Academic research underlying industrial innovations: sources, characteristics and financing', *Review of Economics and Statistics*, **77**, 55–65.

Mansfield, E. (1998), 'Academic research and industrial innovation: an update of empirical findings', *Research Policy*, **26**, 773–6.

Marimon, R. and F. Zilibotti (1998), '"Actual" versus "virtual" employment in Europe. Is Spain different?', *European Economic Review*, **42**, 123–53.

Marsili, O. (2001), *The Anatomy and Evolution of Industries: Technical Change and Industrial Dynamics*, Cheltenham, UK and Northampton, MA, USA: Edward Elgar.

Meunier, O. and M. Mignolet (2003), 'Regional employment disparities in Belgium: some empirical results', paper by Centre de Recherche sur l'Economie Wallone (CREW), University of Namur, Belgium.

Mowery, D. and B. Sampat (2005), 'Universities in national innovation systems', in J. Fagerberg, D. Mowery and R. Nelson (eds), *The Oxford Handbook of Innovation*, Oxford: Oxford University Press.

Nelson, R. (ed.) (1993), *National Innovation Systems: A Comparative Analysis*, Oxford: Oxford University Press.

Nomaler, O. and B. Verspagen (2008), 'Knowledge flows, patent citations and the impact of science on technology', *Economic Systems Research*, **20** (4), 339–66.

Oakey, R. and S. Cooper (1989), 'High technology industry, agglomeration and the potential for peripherally sited small firms', *Regional Studies*, **23**, 347–60.

Ramsey, J. (1969), 'Tests for specification errors in classical linear least-squares regression analysis', *Journal of the Royal Statistical Society. Series B (Methodological)*, **31**, 350–71.

Romer, P.M. (1990), 'Endogenous technological change', *The Journal of Political Economy*, **98** (5), part 2, S71–S102.

Sainsbury, D. (2007), 'The race to the top: a review of Government's science and innovation policies', Lord Sainsbury of Turville, HM Treasury.

Saxenian, A. (1994), *Regional Advantage: Culture and Competition in Silicon Valley and Route 128*, Cambridge, MA: Harvard University Press.

Schartinger, D., A. Schibany and H. Gassler (2001), 'Interactive relations between universities and firms: empirical evidence for Austria', *Journal of Technology Transfer*, **26**, 255–69.

Siegel, D., P. Westhead and M. Wright (2003), 'Science parks and the performance of new technology-based firms: a review of recent U.K. evidence and an agenda for future research', *Small Business Economics*, **20**, 177–84.

Singh, J., M. Marx and L. Fleming (2010), 'Patent citations and the geography of knowledge spillovers: disentangling the role of state borders, metropolitan boundaries and distance', INSEAD Faculty and Research Paper, 03/ST.

Suarez-Villa, L. and W. Walrod (1997), 'Operational strategy, R&D and intra-metropolitan clustering in a polycentric structure: the advanced electronics industries of the Los Angeles Basin', *Urban Studies*, **34** (9), 1343–80.

Toulemonde, E. (2001),'"Actual" versus "virtual" employment in Belgium', *Regional Studies*, **25** (6), 513–18.

Wilson, T. (2012), 'A review of business-university collaboration', Department for Business, Innovation and Skills.

Zucker, L. and M. Darby (2006), 'Movement of star scientists and engineers and high-tech firm entry', NBER Working Papers 12172, National Bureau of Economic Research, Inc.

10. Exploring knowledge-transfer dynamics in a South European region: breadth, intensity and informality of university-industry interactions in Andalusia

Hugo Pinto and Manuel Fernández-Esquinas

INTRODUCTION

Innovation studies and policies are increasingly interested in knowledge valorization of the capabilities available in universities. Although the knowledge reservoir accumulated by the academic sector may have considerable value for firm innovation, in many regional environments firms experience significant gaps in turning research results into business, especially in peripheral regions where most firms are small and medium sized and do not work on knowledge-intensive processes.

In these regional contexts it is important to take into account the fact that valorization is diverse and occurs through several channels. Knowledge-transfer processes between universities and firms largely exceed the restricted vision of science commercialization that is based on IPR licensing and spin-off creation. Firms draw from universities in multiple ways, including human-resources training, use of university facilities, contract research, consultancy, public–private partnerships, collaborative projects and exchange of personnel, among others. In addition, informal interpersonal contacts are believed to play an important role in university-industry links. Therefore it is especially relevant to investigate the conditions that favour the diversity of contacts and collaborative activities between sectors.

This chapter focuses on the dynamics of knowledge valorization in regional development by exploring a diversified set of interactions between firms and the academic sector. Knowledge transfer is understood here as a diversified process that includes the most science-intensive mechanisms, such as patenting, collaborative projects and research contracts, but also stresses the importance of services and personal interactions.

The study provides evidence of knowledge-transfer flows from the perspectives of both actors involved in the process: firms and research teams. In addition to a detailed description of channels, the analysis pays special attention to several key aspects of the dynamics of knowledge transfer: the breadth of university-industry interactions, the intensity of the interactions and the importance of informal relations. The statistical exploration identifies the main features of firms and research teams that influence these dynamics.

Two surveys representing innovative firms and university research groups in Andalusia have been used as data sources. Andalusia is a large region of Southern Spain with a population and territorial scale similar to some smaller European countries. The regional innovation system is characterized by having a large university system and a diversified productive structure, but also an industrial base with a majority of small firms in low- and medium-tech sectors and services. This region is considered a relevant case for understanding knowledge valorization since it provides a comprehensive vision of the role of universities in a catch-up innovation system.

The chapter is organized as follows. Firstly, some findings in the literature about knowledge transfer are briefly reviewed. Secondly, the methodology is explained, underlining the regional context, the data collection and the definition of variables. Thirdly, results from the econometric analysis are presented. The chapter concludes with some policy implications.

BACKGROUND

Heterogeneity of University-Industry Interactions and Implications for Regional Development

The relevance of knowledge transfer has been underlined in the last two decades by a stream of innovation-related literature that stresses the crucial role of scientific knowledge to economic development. The notions of Triple Helix (Etzkowitz and Leydesdorff, 1997), Mode 2 of knowledge production (Gibbons et al., 1994) and innovation systems (Lundvall, 1992) share a common vision of contemporary science and innovation where interactions between several actors are required. A relevant linkage is between universities and public research organizations (PROs)[1] on the one side, and firms on the other. Policies are concerned with enhancing the effectiveness of the channels by which universities interact with companies based on the assumption that companies increase innovation by acquiring knowledge from external sources. Nevertheless, the connection between these two worlds is not obvious in many regional environments, especially in peripheral regions where most firms are small and medium sized and do not work on knowledge-intensive processes. In these regions knowledge transfer seldom occurs through commercialization by means of patent licensing and creation of spin-offs. Instead universities are important actors for knowledge valorization in regional economic development. Local firms use the variety of skills, human resources and facilities available in academic organizations to enhance the economic value of their productive processes.

Studies of university-firm interactions show important limitations in addressing the diversity of mechanisms for knowledge transfer in certain regional environments. Theoretical discussions and empirical research in this field are based on approaches that commonly depart from one of the two sides, the firm or the university, and consequently pay attention to different influencing factors. Firstly, universities and firms are very different actors in terms of capacities and motivations. They also act within different institutional spheres and are subject to divergent norms and expectations. The main stream of literature concentrating on the company perspective has been based on the relevance of absorptive capacity. It is assumed that the existence of a critical level in size, cognitive abilities and organizational arrangements specialized in R&D (Cohen and Levinthal, 1990) facilitates the interconnections between the worlds of science and industry. Therefore the interactions between firms and universities are more evident in regions with a significant number of firms working in medium- and high-technology sectors or large companies with their own R&D departments (Saxenian, 1994). The main stream of studies on university-industry links from the university perspective has focused on commercialization. Many of these studies are rooted in the specific configuration of the social system of science, where publication of research results and acknowledgement by academic peers form the basis for career progression (Merton, 1973). An important part of the discussions has been centred on the challenges created by the rise of knowledge commercialization in traditional academic settings. This approach to technology transfer has privileged the observation of certain kinds of knowledge-transfer mechanisms and has diminished the visibility and policy support for other forms (Molas-Gallart et al., 2002).

Secondly, empirical research on university-industry interactions is also problematic. Many studies do not capture the valorization that arises from knowledge-transfer processes. It has been difficult to obtain data sets reflecting links with SMEs and firms that work in sectors that are not R&D intensive, such as the service sector. Instead many studies are based on firms with R&D departments, large firms or firms in high-tech sectors (Escribano et al., 2009). Empirical studies for observing the variety of channels used by academic researchers also lack adequate data sources. Activities other than commercialization are not easily registered by technology transfer offices (TTOs) or by university administrators. In addition, many of them are carried out informally and are not reported by individual academics.

The limitations of empirical research on university-industry interactions have important implications for regional development, especially for peripheral regions[2] that try to catch up with the productive processes of more developed countries. In these regions the characteristics of both the productive sector and the university system mean that the diversity of channels for knowledge transfer acquires a special significance.

Being a peripheral region means a lack of industrial agglomeration. Peripheral regions are dominated by SMEs operating in traditional sectors. There is a high presence of service-sector companies oriented to the local market whose productive processes do not have a high technological content. There are few firms that are important players in the global technology market. Firms with a significant number of research staff or specialized R&D departments are also scarce. Most of the SMEs in peripheral regions have difficulties absorbing the knowledge available in universities and have limitations in using academic patents and benefiting from research results. Instead many companies find other resources within universities, such us expert knowledge or specialized training that helps them to improve their productive processes. In many regions it is difficult to find consulting companies specializing in high-tech or private laboratories to carry out analysis and testing services. Local firms often find the technical assistance they need in regional universities.

On the other hand peripheral regions also tend to concentrate scientific capabilities in universities. The majority of scientists, PhD holders, qualified R&D staff and technological infrastructures are located in the academic sector. Regional innovation policies seek to capitalize on public investment by making available to companies the knowledge reservoir of the academic sector. In these contexts universities must adapt their potential supply to the demand arising from regional companies. Academic researchers who wish to make practical use of their capabilities or need funding from the private sector must be willing to diversify their services. It is also relevant to underline that academic patents available in peripheral regions are usually scarce since the universities have been traditionally oriented to education and publishing.

Therefore in these regional contexts it is crucial to pay attention to the value that the different forms of knowledge transfer may have for enhancing the innovation capacity of firms.

The Shaping of Knowledge-Transfer Dynamics

Discussions on knowledge valorization have highlighted both the importance of the heterogeneity of channels and the diversity of factors that influence the many forms of knowledge transfer. However, empirical studies that link both aspects have not been carried out until very recently. The so-called 'first generation' of studies on university- industry interactions (Gulbrandsen et al., 2011) has succeeded in mapping the variety of channels. These studies also found a positive relationship between links with universities and firm innovation. A 'second generation' of university-industry studies has emerged alongside continued attempts to analyse the complex array of relations using data sources specially gathered for observing multi-channel interactions. These studies reflect the heterogeneity, the multiplicity of possible outcomes and the high presence of nonlinear associations that are present in the process (for a review see Larsen, 2011). Analyses are evolving to a more advanced stage aimed at understanding the various channels through which knowledge transfer takes place and the causal influences that derive from multiple sources.

Recent research has underlined issues of particular importance in increasing the benefits of knowledge transfer. In this study several aspects have been selected because of their special relevance for regional development: the conditions required for bridging the gap by developing an initial contact, the breadth and intensity of interactions between universities and firms, and the relevance that informality has in these interactions.

Firstly, a key issue in making academic resources available to firms is the breakdown of structural separation between the two sectors. The university and business worlds are subject to very different institutional frameworks and incentive structures. While academic work is based on open communication of research results, companies are oriented to the appropriation of knowledge aimed at gaining competitive advantages. Cognitive abilities in both sectors also differ. There is evidence that one of the key determinants for facilitating transfer is previous experience of collaboration (D'Este and Patel, 2007). Facilitating the start of such relationships is therefore very important. Given that certain features of firms and university researchers contribute to maintaining the structural separation, an important issue is the investigation of the characteristics of both sectors that might actually allow the start of collaboration. These can be interpreted as constituting a threshold: once the first contact is established it can open doors to additional forms of knowledge transfer.

A second important issue is the diversity and breadth of interactions between universities and companies. Literature in this field underlines that the use of different kinds of partnership is an important factor in promoting knowledge transfer. From the company's point of view, participating in different types of relations can help to manage conflict about the orientation of the activities (Bruneel et al., 2010) and creates opportunities for organizational learning due to exposure to both face-to-face interactions and contractual interactions. The breadth of relationships can also generate synergies between different forms of collaboration. Performing a wider range of activities can reinforce the company's ability to detect opportunities with the resources accumulated in academia (Laursen and Salter, 2006). Seen from the viewpoint of the university, diversity can also lead to higher profits. Liaison with companies in a flexible manner and encompassing a variety of tasks can generate additional financial resources and job opportunities for university graduates. On the other hand the diversity of contacts makes it easier for researchers to exercise a monitoring task that tailors research to the demands of the environment and increases its potential impact (Lissoni, 2010).

The third important issue is the strength or intensity of interactions. A greater number of contacts, involving either formal agreements or informal support, can contribute to reinforcing the mutual capabilities of companies and universities and increase the chances of profit. An increased number of interactions can create routines for collaboration, increases mutual understanding of benefits and facilitates the identification of common goals. A larger intensity of interactions can be interpreted as evidence that companies and universities have internalized knowledge transfer as a strategic instrument for their work processes (Giuliani and Arza, 2009; Giuliani et al., 2010).

The fourth issue for facilitating the transfer of knowledge through university-industry interactions is the possibility of maintaining close relationships (Debackere and Veugelers, 2005). Informal personal linkages can be crucial to improving the effectiveness of formal contracts. Informal relationships have a function that is associated with increased trust between universities and companies (Østergaard, 2009). Trust is very important in processes with uncertain outcomes. Therefore maintaining informal ties can facilitate an understanding of expectations and also the connection of interests between stakeholders. It also facilitates the exchange of information that is necessary to carry out complex tasks. Finally, the fluidity of informal interactions also helps to build confidence for long-term relationships.

The above knowledge-transfer dynamics can be influenced by many factors that determine the relationship between universities and companies. In the business sector there is evidence of the special importance of the so-called absorptive capacities and business strategy with respect to openings in the search for external knowledge (Lee, 2010). In academic organizations, crucial factors are associated with a series of individual and institutional characteristics. There is evidence that age, scientific discipline, work organization and the role of TTOs determines the behaviour of university researchers in maintaining links with firms (Audretsch and Aldridge, 2009). Additionally, there is growing evidence of the importance that geographical location plays for both collectives (Arundel and Geuna, 2004; D'Este and Iammarino, 2010).

However, research in this field remains confronted with significant challenges. On the one hand there is a lack of specific studies tailored to business and academic groups located in regions in different stages of development, especially in regions that are less knowledge intensive. In the university sector it is also difficult to obtain information from many areas, such as the humanities and social sciences, and to appreciate the organizational features of the work process. On the other hand there are few integrated observations that take into account the specificities and constraints that simultaneously affect the two collectives. The lack of empirical evidence with regard to the chain of influences and different logics of firms and university researchers thus makes it difficult to define clear guidelines for regional innovation policies.

This chapter aims to provide evidence of various forms of knowledge valorization in a peripheral regional context. The strategy of the study is to use a cross-fertilization of perspectives regarding the theoretical basis for selecting dependent and independent variables. To do this, first the variety of channels is described and the most important are detected. An indicator set designed specifically to study the diversity of university-industry interactions is used. Second, the study examines the dynamics of interactions, looking specifically at those factors that reflect the existence of a minimum contact (or the threshold to maintaining a relationship), the breadth, intensity and informality of interactions. Analyses have been designed to detect influential factors that are specific to the university and those that are specific to the company.

METHODOLOGY

Research Site and Data Sources

The empirical site is the Spanish region of Andalusia. Andalusia is a large region in terms of territory and population with more than nine million people, 18 per cent of the population of Spain, and almost 90 000 square kilometres in size. In the last two decades economic growth has been intense. Currently the 75 per cent European Union (EU) average of GDPpc has been surpassed, which places the region above the 'convergence' category for structural funds. From being one of the poorest European regions, Andalusia was able to structure an active network of innovation actors (Pinto et al., 2012). Nevertheless it remains a disadvantaged region of Spain and Europe in terms of innovation (Pinto, 2009). Andalusia is an example of a catch-up region in the context of the European Union: historically it has lacked industrial agglomeration, although recently there has been industrial dynamism together with innovation policies that try to facilitate convergence towards more developed economies. Agriculture and tourism are very relevant to the regional economy but other sectors such as food processing, chemicals, automotive auxiliary industries and energy are also important. The industrial base is diversified but dominated by traditional activities and SMEs. The regional university system is made up of nine public universities that employ close to 17 000 professors and researchers (Fernández-Esquinas et al., 2008), together with 1200 who are part of public research organizations (CICE, 2006). Most of the research capabilities are concentrated in the public research sector.[3] Using Andalusia as a research site has the potential to contribute to the understanding of knowledge valorization processes in other catch-up innovation systems.

The data sources derive from two surveys of 737 firms and 765 research groups conducted in 2008 and 2009. For the firms survey, a registry of firms produced by regional government agencies was used (Network of Technological Areas of Andalusia – RETA). It comprises 1844 firms that have received some type of public aid for innovation in the period from 1999 to 2005 or that have indicated interest in receiving innovation advice. This source does not represent all firms from the region, only those with a potentially innovative profile. It is therefore assumed that a certain bias arises when compared to the whole industrial sector.[4] Nevertheless this data source is suitable for observing the different patterns of interaction and the possible factors that operate within them because of the diversity of firms included. Firstly, it includes companies with differing innovative capabilities. Manufacturing and service firms are present in low-tech sectors, as well as firms conducting highly scientific activities (for example R&D projects for firms in the aerospace industry). This means that only a relatively small proportion of them have an R&D department. Secondly, it incorporates a broad diversity of sizes, from small family businesses to large firms. Thirdly, companies are not concentrated in industrial centres or technology parks near universities but are dispersed among the diverse urban and rural areas of the region. We therefore consider this source as an 'operative population' which fits the goals of this study since it contains the segment of the productive sector with a higher tendency towards collaboration.

From the above population a sample of 800 firms was selected. The selection was done randomly with a proportional distribution between strata made up of the activity sector and the province where the firm is located. The fieldwork was done through face-to-face interviews at the firms' offices using a professional group of survey takers. When firms declined to participate a substitution sample, chosen randomly using the same criteria, was used. The acceptance rate in the first wave was 76 per cent. The acceptance rate in the second wave was 72 per cent. The total sample included 737 firms.

For the survey of research groups an official registry of the public R&D system was used, including both universities and PROs. Since almost the entire scientific community employed by the public sector is made up of research groups, which are registered in order to receive funding, it is believed that using them as the unit of analysis makes it easier to observe their interactions with the firms.[5] In addition research groups include people from all professional categories, from research assistants to professors, and provide better coverage than a survey targeting individuals. The reference population is made up of 1769 research groups registered in 2006. The regional government provided the names of the group leaders and other basic information.

The sampling used was stratified using proportional allocation based on scientific areas. A simple random selection in each stratum resulted in a proportional distribution of the sample by types of centre. The survey was conducted using a personal interview at the workplace of the group director or, in case of absence, another member assigned by the group director. After two waves of fieldwork 765 groups had responded to the survey. The majority were from universities (89 per cent). With regard to the scientific areas, the sample reflects the distribution of the academic community: there are groups in 'Humanities and Artistic Creation' (28 per cent), followed by 'Health and Life Sciences', 'Technologies' and 'Social Science, Economics and Legal' (all at 13 per cent) and 'Experimental Sciences' (11 per cent). The majority of the groups are mid-sized: between 6 and 10 members (43 per cent) and between 11 and 15 members (24 per cent).

Indicator Set and Descriptive Results for University-Firm Interactions

Departing from a review of the literature on diversity of knowledge-transfer activities, the indicator set considers four groups of variables: (a) R&D activities and formal consulting work, (b) training and transfer of personnel, (c) commercialization activities and (d) other contacts (Table 10.1). After doing several pre-tests for adapting the multiple possibilities to a questionnaire format, twelve possible types of interaction were

Table 10.1   *Types of university-firm interaction (existence of interactions reported by research groups and firms)*

Domains	Variables	Research groups*	Companies*
R&D activities and formal consulting work	Consultancy work and advice from a university or public research centre	38.0	21.8
	Contracted or commissioned R&D projects (financed exclusively by the firm)	34.8	14.0
	Joint R&D projects (shared financing or with public support)	30.6	22.1
Training and transfer of personnel	Training of university personnel and internships at the firm	20.4	27.5
	Temporary exchange of personnel	12.4	7.1
	Specific training for the firm provided by the university	24.2	15.2
Commercialization related to IPR	Use or rental of facilities or equipment by a firm	8.4	8.1
	Exploitation of a patent or utility model, joint patents	10.1	4.6
	Creation of, or collaboration in the creation of, a new firm (spin-offs and start-ups)	6.1	3.9
Other contacts	Participation in a joint venture involving hybrid research centre	2.4	3.7
	Informal relations	45.0	32.2
	Other types of co-operation activities	2.7	1.9
	Non-academic knowledge diffusion activities (**)	30.6	–

Notes: * % of research groups and firms that declared they had at least one interaction.
** Participation in workshops, fairs and encounters in co-operation with firms (only for research teams).

Source: Personal elaboration from surveys carried out by IESA (IESA, 2009a, 2009b).

selected. Additionally, in the case of research teams, another category was added to include non-academic knowledge-diffusion activities since these are more frequent among these groups. For each type of interaction both firms and research groups were asked if they had had this relationship in the previous five years and how many times. This formulation is aimed at contrasting the same activity for each of the two types of actors and allows providing a detailed descriptive measurement of the 'diversity' of channels for knowledge transfer.[6]

Descriptive results from the survey of firms show that the highest scores are for the informal relations type (32 per cent of the firms indicate that they have these kinds of relations) followed by training of university postgraduates and internships at the firm (27 per cent). This last case is especially relevant since the regional government provides easy access to this kind of training for university postgraduates. Furthermore, it is a common way of discovering future employees and eliminates the pit-falls of personnel selection processes. The rest of the interactions can be divided into three groups (percentage of firms in each relationship and mean for the number of times during the period of reference show the same pattern):

- Consulting activities, joint research projects and training of firm workers by the university are carried out by between 15 per cent and 25 per cent of all firms.
- Between 5 per cent and 15 per cent of firms have participated in contract R&D projects, use of university facilities and personnel exchange.
- Less than 5 per cent of the firms have participated in spin-offs or start-ups, licensing or sale of patents and joint ventures.

Other types of collaborative activities – encompassing participation in meetings, seminars, diffusion, publications and so on – are carried out by not more than 2 per cent of firms.

The importance of training contracts and consulting is worth noting. Exploitation of intellectual property is clearly a minor activity even in those firms that could be considered as the most innovative in the region. Overall 421 (57 per cent) firms state that they have no type of collaboration. 305 (41 per cent) firms say they have some type of collaboration beyond informal relations. Only 11 firms declare having only informal relations, meaning that this indicator shows that the relations are linked to the other activities.

Descriptive results from the research side show a similar structure of links between research groups and firms. Again informal links (45 per cent) stand above the rest. The remaining indicators can be grouped into three categories:

- A high number have carried out technology consulting for firms (38 per cent) and research projects contracted by firms (34.8 per cent). Groups that undertake joint research projects with firms (30.6 per cent) also stand out, and are in the same proportion as those that organize non-academic knowledge diffusion activities with firms (meetings, conferences, fairs, and so on).
- There is a notable presence of activities related to human resources that flow both ways: specific training by the group for a firm (24.2 per cent), internships for group members in firms (20.4 per cent) and exchange of scientific and technical personnel (12.4 per cent).
- Participation of firms in the exploitation of group patents occurs in 10.1 per cent of the cases, being more common than renting facilities or equipment (8.4 per cent) and the creation of spin-offs or technology companies in collaboration with a firm (6.1 per cent).

425 cases, or 55.5 per cent of the sample, had participated in at least one of the activities, not including informal relations. Only 13 cases declared that they had exclusively informal contacts, while the number of groups that had not participated in any type of relationship was 327 (42.7 per cent).

Dependent and Independent Variables

The four main aspects related to knowledge-transfer dynamics as specified above have been reflected in the transformation of the original sets of variables. The calculations made it possible to prepare appropriate variables for causal analysis. The econometric analysis is intended to understand the process of knowledge transfer in this regional context, starting from the possibility offered by the two data sets to compare the influences of the relevance of several dimensions from companies' and research groups' perspectives.[7] Four dependent variables were constructed for both collectives, with the following interpretations:

- Existence of interactions for knowledge transfer (KT). This is a binary variable that assumes value 1 if the research group or the firm has engaged in any knowledge-transfer activity and 0 if not. This variable can be interpreted as a minimum level of engagement. The goals of the analysis are to understand the factors that increase the probability of engaging or not in knowledge transfer. Influences from the independent variables reflect the conditions that function as a 'threshold' from which a relationship departs.

- Breadth of interactions (DIVKT). This is a variable that reflects the variety of transfer channels used in relation to the total available channels. The variable has been calculated based on the existence of the referred types of relations in binary form. It has been assumed that value is 0 if a specific channel was not used and 1 if it was used. The variable is constructed by simply summing the binary results for all channels so that each company or research group receives a value ranging from 0, if they have not used any channel, to 11 (12 in the case of research groups) if they have used all available channels. The variable can be interpreted as showing that companies or groups that have used more channels behave more openly in relation to knowledge-transfer activities.
- Intensity of interactions (NUMKT). This is a count variable of the total number of interactions reported. This variable reflects the number of times that the company or research group has participated in knowledge-transfer activities, taking into account all possible types. The variable is the total sum of the number of relations expressed in each channel in the specified period. It can be considered as a measure of the level of engagement. The objective of the analysis is to see whether the presence of certain characteristics in groups and companies increases or decreases the intensity of collaboration in both sectors.
- Informality of interactions (INF). This variable is aimed at appreciating the importance of personal informal relations with respect to the total number of interactions undertaken with the other sector. The variable is the ratio between the number of informal relations and the sum of all interactions. Through the analysis it is possible to compare the importance of the fluidity of personal links over those that require a contractual basis.

Although these four variables are connected they account for different aspects of the process.[8] An example is the relation between the intensity of interactions (NUMKT) and the breadth of interactions (DIVKT). There is a positive association between both variables although the correlation and the graphical analysis suggest that there is a common positive movement up until a certain degree of specialization (Figure 10.1). After this point the utilization of more diversity of channels is accompanied by a reduction in the number of knowledge-transfer activities, suggesting that companies and research groups may specialize in certain specific channels. The inclusion of these four dependent variables is thus intended to

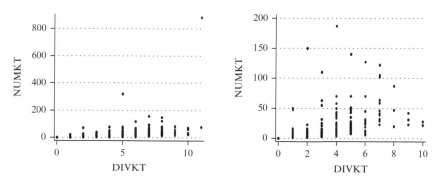

Note: DIVKT: breadth of interactions; NUMKT: intensity of interactions. Research groups (left); Companies (right).

Source: Personal elaboration from surveys carried out by IESA (IESA, 2009a, 2009b).

Figure 10.1   Relation between the intensity and the breadth of knowledge-transfer activities in companies and research groups

give a more complex understanding of influences on knowledge-transfer dynamics.

The set of independent variables was constructed to verify the main determinants in university-firm interactions according to literature in this field. Detailed information on all independent variables is included in the appendix. The variables included in the analysis are the following:

For the companies, the variables pay attention to five dimensions: structural characteristics of the firm (performing manufacturing activities, belonging to business groups, age of the company and number of employees); absorptive capacity (proportion of employees with higher education background, export intensity, existence of internal R&D departments and investment in training); innovation performance (participation in innovative activities and registration of patents); institutional features of knowledge transfer (maturity of relations with universities, strategic importance given to knowledge transfer for competitiveness, relevance of the TTO for establishing relations with universities); and geographical context of the company (location in a science park, geographical proximity to a university, proximity to high-tech multinationals and integration within a cluster).

For the research groups, the independent variables focus on the following dimensions: structural characteristics of the group (specific scientific domains, age of the group); capacity of the group (total number of researchers and staff qualifications); internal dynamics of the R&D work (centralization of decision processes, R&D budget and financing coming from private sources); institutional features of knowledge transfer (importance given to knowledge-transfer activities, maturity in contacts with companies, relevance of TTO for establishing relations with firms); and the group's external interactions (previous relations with firms, existence of contacts outside the region and relations with large firms).

EXPLORING THE DETERMINANTS OF KNOWLEDGE-TRANSFER DYNAMICS

Econometric findings support many of the influences suggested by current research, but in this study a number of specific patterns as well as some contrasts between knowledge-transfer dynamics in companies and research groups can be found.

Table 10.2 summarizes results regarding the four independent variables (KT, DIVKT, NUMKT and INF) by comparing independent variables that are common to both companies and research groups. The values of coefficients resulting from the count models have been grouped in the cells. This comparison creates a mirror image facilitating an evaluation of the aspects that are relevant and suggesting the specific factors on both sides that may be targeted by specific policies.

Regarding the existence of interactions, for both collectives the engagement with external organizations outside the region and the value given to the relationships with other sectors are important inducers for starting contacts. Specifically for firms, employees' qualifications and previous experience are crucial dimensions. For research groups, age is a significant variable for engaging in knowledge-transfer activities. The role of the technology transfer office is substantially more important to research groups than to firms. This result suggests that bridging the gap is associated with openness and the valorization of these activities, adequate qualifications among firms' workers and critical mass in the number of researchers in the research group.

Regarding the breadth of relationships, most of the variables affect both firms and groups: the existence of previous relations, the role of the TTO, relations with other actors outside the region and the value attributed to knowledge-transfer activities. Nevertheless some variables operate in a different way in both collectives: the size of the research group and the number of years since the first contact are important for groups, but not for firms. In contrast, the qualifications of human resources are important for firms, but not for groups. TTOs are important actors for facilitating fluid and diversified contacts, as reflected in the breadth variable. TTOs are also relevant for research groups' first contacts, as reflected in the variable

Table 10.2   Comparing influences on knowledge transfer in companies and research groups (degree of importance of common independent variables on KT dynamics)

Common variables	Existence of KT activities (KT)		Diversity-breadth of KT activities (DIVKT)		Intensity of KT activities (NUMKT)		Importance of informal KT activities (INF)	
	Companies	Research Groups	Companies	Research Groups	Companies	Research Groups	Companies	Research Groups
Age	+	+++	+	−	+	++++	−	−
No of people (EMP/MEMB)	−	+	−	++++	−	++	−−−	−−−−
Qualification of human resources (EMPQ/MEMBQ)	++++	−	++++	−	++++	−	++++	−
No of years since the first contact (KTEXP)	−	−	+	++++	++++	−	−	−−−−
Importance of previous relations for KT activities (PREVREL)	++++	+	++++	++++	++++	++++	+	+++
Importance of TTO for KT activities (KTO)	+	++++	++++	++++	++++	++++	−	−
Relation with the other actors outside the region (KTEXT)	++++	+++	++++	++++	+	++	−−−	+
Strategic value given to KT for competitiveness (KTVAL)	++++	++++	++++	++++	++++	++++	++++	++++

Notes: Symbols: − non-significant negative coefficient; −− significant negative coefficient; −−− significant negative coefficient at 0.05; −−− significant negative coefficient at 0.01; + non-significant positive coefficient; ++ significant positive coefficient at 0.1; +++ significant positive coefficient at 0.05; ++++ significant positive coefficient at 0.01.

Source: Personal elaboration from surveys carried out by IESA (IESA, 2009a, 2009b).

for a minimum contact. Nevertheless they are not relevant for firms' first contacts. Interface organizations are therefore an important inducer for groups to obtain more diversified links, although the institutional aspects are not relevant for the firm sector.

Regarding the intensity of interactions, in general the same pattern can be found as for breadth in most of the independent variables. Nevertheless the number of years since the first contact is important for companies but not for research groups. In addition, relations with other actors outside the region are less important than the pattern shown for the breadth of interactions. Intensity reflects a different pattern regarding the building of trust that is associated with repeated long-term relationships. These long-term relations seem to be a condition for involvement in intense interactions. In addition, intensity is not associated to contacts outside the region. This situation may suggest that companies rely on certain knowledge-transfer processes that are regularly undertaken with regional universities but not with other external actors.

Finally, the influences detected on the variable reflecting informality do not provide a clear pattern. The existence of previous relations is again significant for both companies and research groups to increase informality. The importance of interactions for competitiveness is the main variable associated to informality for both companies and groups. The relevance that knowledge-transfer valorization has for the internal work processes seems to be an inducer for the increased importance of personal and fluid relations.

Table 10.3 summarizes the same four dependent variables but this time only the specific independent variables for both companies and research groups have been selected. For companies specifically, most of the influences are associated to breadth and intensity. The existence of a minimum level of knowledge-transfer activities is associated to localization in a science and technology park. Breadth, or a broader utilization of channels, is positively related with export capacity. Breadth is also associated with innovative activities in firms. Intensity is associated to export behaviour, investment in innovative activities and localization in science and technology parks. Finally, the only specific variable that seems to have a statistically significant coefficient in informality is investment in the training of employees. This has a negative impact in the degree of informality. Interestingly some of the results show the association of firms' innovation performance with some of the knowledge-transfer dynamics. Producing a product innovation for the market in the last five years is associated positively with breadth and intensity but not with the existence of a minimum contact or with the degree of informality. These results therefore reinforce the evidence about the benefits of diversity of channels for enhancing innovative capabilities.

Table 10.3 *Comparing influences on knowledge transfer in companies and research groups (degree of importance of specific independent variables on KT dynamics)*

Specific variables for companies	KT	DIVKT	NUMKT	INF	Specific variables for research groups	KT	DIVKT	NUMKT	INF
Firm in the industrial sector (IND)	–	+	–	+	Natural and life sciences (NATLIFE)	+	++	+	–
Belong to a corporate group (GROUP)	–	+	+	+	Experimental sciences and technologies (EXPTECH)	+	++++	+	+++
% of sales in the international market (EXP)	+	+++	++++	+	Social sciences and humanities (SOCHUM)	–––	–––	+	–––
Existence of R&D department (RDDEP)	+	+	++	–	Centralized leadership (DIR)	+	–	–	+
Investment in training (FORM)	–	+	+	––	Decentralized leadership (LIBER)	++++	++	++++	+
Product innovation in the last five years (INOVACT)	+	++++	++++	–	Total budget for R&D (IDTOTAL)	–	–	+	–

					Budget from private sources (IDPRIV)	Orientation of the group to KT (FOCUSKT)	Co-operation with large companies (KTLARGECOMP)
Patenting activity (PAT)	–	+	– – –	+	–	+	+ + + +	– – –
Location in a S&T park (STP)	+ + +	+	+ + +	+	+	+	+	– –
Proximity to a university campus (PROXUNIV)	+	+	+	+	+	+	–	+
Proximity to high-tech multinational companies (PROXHTMNE)	–	–	–	–		– – –		+
Integration into a territorial cluster (CLUST)	+	+	+	+	+	+	–	+

Note: Symbols: see Table 10.2.

Source: Personal elaboration from surveys carried out by IESA (IESA, 2009a, 2009b).

For research groups specifically, the existence of knowledge-transfer activities seems to be related with the freedom of decision making in research. Breadth is related to decentralized leadership also, and to certain scientific specialties: primarily experimental sciences and technologies and natural and life sciences. Intensity is associated mostly to decentralized leadership and economic resources coming from the R&D sector. The influences on informality are again weaker and less clear. As Heinze et al. (2009) have underlined, complementarities of competencies and leadership in research are determinants that deserve attention. In this case, there is statistical evidence that freedom of individual researchers can be important not only to the engagement in knowledge transfer but also to increasing the number of relations and the degree of informality of these relations.

There is also some evidence that groups from natural and life sciences have more propensity to knowledge transfer than other scientific areas. This is particularly visible in the breadth of channels used but not so much in terms of intensity. Finally, the fact of research groups obtaining an important part of the budget from private sources is clearly associated to intensity, and not so much to the other dynamics. A relevant association is that breath and intensity is not connected positively to co-operation with large companies, but rather the opposite, which reflects the importance of links with SMEs in the regional context.

CONCLUSIONS AND POLICY IMPLICATIONS

The empirical observations have shown that university-firm interactions are a crucial dimension of knowledge valorization. The diversity of mechanisms and activities is relevant to stimulating the acquisition of regional firms' capabilities. Comparing specific observations from research groups and companies on different channels and influences provides evidence about the real dynamics of knowledge transfer.

Firstly, descriptive results show the presence of a broad set of knowledge valorization processes in this peripheral region. Personal contacts are the most frequent interactions for both firms and research groups, although personal contacts are not maintained alone but are linked to other specific activities. Other relevant links are related to human resources and to R&D services. Commercialization does exist although it is limited to a small group of universities and firms. These results suggest that valorization of university resources should be a first step to increasing the knowledge base of firms, and that enhancing both informal activities and absorptive capacities can lead to a more effective way of commercializing knowledge.

Secondly, the estimated models confirm the existence of significant differences between the variables that impact on knowledge-transfer dynamics from the perspective of a company and that of a research group. The analysis shows that absorptive capacities are not the only determinants, but also the strategies and the openness of both actors, together with the existence of fluid personal relations.

These results are not easily generalized to other regional contexts because knowledge transfer is a process that is not only highly dependent on capabilities available in companies and research groups but also on institutional architectures and territorial resources. Nevertheless the case of the Spanish region of Andalusia can provide some insights into the policy implications for enhancing knowledge transfer in regions with similar socio-economic profiles.

Perhaps the most relevant implication from the point of view of the companies is that breadth and intensity of interactions are clearly associated to innovation capabilities and to the orientation of the firm outside the regional market. In addition, some basic features of firms are related to the qualifications of human resources. Location in science and technology parks and the firm's productive processes are also important for bridging the gap, as well as for enhancing intensity and diversity. This suggests that regional governments should diminish the barriers by creating the conditions that act as a threshold and at the same time they should facilitate the existence of multiple and diversified contacts. From the academic perspective the main implications are related to the existence of a minimum critical mass in the organizational units that perform research. This means that individual professors or small groups usually have difficulty engaging in knowledge transfer. The other important implication is related to the institutional environment, in particular the help provided by TTOs for all possible channels, not only some of them, together with the capacity of academic researchers to act in a decentralized way. It is important to underline that the development of specific instruments to stimulate these activities are required from each side. Current policy instruments should address knowledge-transfer dynamics not as a homogeneous process but as a context-dependent process influenced by specific features of companies and academic collectives.

ACKNOWLEDGEMENTS

Hugo Pinto acknowledges the financial support of the Portuguese Foundation for Science and Technology (SFRH/BD/35887/2007). Manuel Fernández-Esquinas acknowledges the support of the Regional R&D Plan of Andalusia. The data for this study are part of the project 'Conditioning factors for the generation and use of scientific knowledge in the regional innovation system on Andalusia' (grant ref. SEJ-2005-801).

NOTES

1. In the interest of clarity the term 'university' is used to mean both higher-education establishments and other public research organizations that have the production of scientific knowledge as one of their main missions.
2. The notion of a peripheral region is associated here with the lack of industrial agglomeration that creates a gap in the economic capacity of more developed regions. The causes of these trajectories may be diverse. In this chapter, we refer to catch-up regions that historically did not have an intense industrialization process and were late in integrating the knowledge economy. In these regions industrial dynamics are different from industrialized settings that have suffered industrial decline and symptoms of structural crisis (Abramovitz, 1986).
3. Investment in the acquisition of scientific capacity during the 1980s and 1990s has led to the concentration of a large part of regional R&D resources in universities (universities account for 45 per cent of R&D expenditure, while 61 per cent of researchers in the region are employed by universities). PROs account for 10 per cent of the expenditure. These consist mainly of CSIC institutes, hospital units and agricultural research institutes. An important change has occurred as a result of the reorganization of R&D and higher education policy in 2003 aimed at orienting universities towards firm innovation. Andalusia is a good example of the rapid transition from traditional policies based on a linear model of innovation to policies aimed at interaction between the public administration, the educational system and industry (CICE, 2006).
4. We must point out that the bias is only in one direction. The majority of small firms in low-technology sectors of the region is not represented. However, almost all of the technology-intensive firms as well as those that carry out significant R&D activities, from the very large to the very small, have received public aid (meaning at least tax breaks) and therefore are included in the data file that we use as our source.
5. The registry of research groups covers more than 90 per cent of the scientific community in the public sector. Researchers who are part of bodies outside of the public sphere or those that do not realize year on year activities in said groups are not included in the registry.
6. Analysis for testing the validity of the indicator set and more extensive descriptive analysis using the same data sources can be found in Ramos-Vielba and Fernández-Esquinas (2010).
7. The estimated models have been analysed in terms of their general capacity to explain the processes, significance of the coefficients, characteristics of the residuals and autocorrelation. The ordinary least squares (OLS) estimator is commonly considered the best linear unbiased estimator. But with the characteristics of the dependent variables the efficiency of the estimates of this estimator is poor compared with alternative methods. PROBIT estimation was used in the case of variable KT. In the case of NUMKT, INF and DIVKT, dependent variables that are count scores of non-negative integers, from zero to many, a count model approach was used. The problem of over-dispersion required the comparison of a Poisson model with a negative binomial (Cameron and Trivedi, 1998). Negative binomial representation was always superior to a Poisson model for the available data. Because of the high number of zeros in the observations the zero-inflated model was also compared with a negative binomial using the Vuong test available in Stata 10.0. Vuong (1989) developed non-nested model tests that were adapted (Greene, 1994; Long, 1997). In general the negative binomial was the estimator that better suited the data. The

negative binomial estimator has been widely used in count models in innovation studies at least since the time of the influential study using patent data by Hausman et al. (1984). In the case of INF, as this variable was not a true count data variable but a transformation, a Tobit specification was performed as a confirmatory method. OLS models were always calculated as indicators to check the overall robustness of the results and to support the analysis of the correct signal of the coefficient.

8. To provide a descriptive overview, for companies the rate of minimal engagement in knowledge-transfer activities is 40 per cent, the mean value for breadth is 1.29 (out of eleven), and the mean value for intensity is 6.94, with the level of informality at 8 per cent. For research groups the level of engagement is 55 per cent, the mean value for breadth of interactions is 2.5 (out of 12), the mean value for intensity is 1.6 and the level of informality is 11.3 per cent.

REFERENCES

Abramovitz, M. (1986), 'Catching up, forging ahead and falling behind', *Journal of Economic History*, **46** (2), 386–406.

Arundel, A. and A. Geuna (2004), 'Proximity and the use of public science by innovative European firms', *Economics of Innovation and New Technology*, **13** (6), 559–80.

Audretsch, D. and T. Aldridge (2009), 'Scientist commercialization as conduit of knowledge spill-overs', *The Annals of Regional Science*, **43** (4), 897–905.

Bruneel, J., P. D'Este and A. Salter (2010), 'Investigating the factors that diminish the barriers to university–industry collaboration', *Research Policy*, **39** (7), 858–68.

Cameron, Colin and Pravin Trivedi (1998), *Regression Analysis of Count Data*, Cambridge: Cambridge University Press.

CICE (2006), *Plan Andaluz de Ciencia, Tecnología e Innovación Tecnológica 2007–2013*, Sevilla: Consejería de Innovación Ciencia y Empresa, Junta de Andalucía.

Cohen W. and D. Levinthal (1990), 'Absorptive capacity: a new perspective on learning and innovation', *Administrative Science Quarterly*, **35** (1), 128–52.

D'Este, P. and S. Iammarino (2010), 'The spatial profile of university-business research partnerships', *Papers in Regional Science*, **89** (2), 335–50.

D'Este, P. and P. Patel (2007), 'University-industry linkages in the UK: what are the factors underlying the variety of interactions with industry?', *Research Policy*, **36** (9), 1295–313.

Debackere, K. and R. Veugelers (2005), 'The role of academic technology transfer organizations in improving industry science links', *Research Policy*, **34** (3), 321–42.

Escribano, A., A. Fosfuri and J. Tribó (2009), 'Managing external knowledge flows: the moderating role of absorptive capacity', *Research Policy*, **38** (1), 96–105.

Etzkowitz, Henry and Loet Leydesdorff (eds) (1997), *Universities in the Global Economy: A Triple Helix of University-Industry-Government Relations*, London: Cassel Academic.

Fernández-Esquinas, M., E. Espinosa de los Monteros, M. Jiménez Buedo y M. Pérez Yruela (2008), *Prospectiva de recursos humanos en el sistema andaluz de universidades*, Córdoba: IESA-CSIC/Consejería de Innovación Ciencia y Empresa, Junta de Andalucía.

Gibbons, Michael, Camille Limoges, Helga Nowotny, Simon Schwartzman, Peter Scott and Martin Trow (1994), *The New Production of Knowledge: The Dynamics of Science and Research in Contemporary Societies*, London: Sage.

Giuliani, E. and V. Arza (2009), 'What drives the formation of "valuable" university–industry linkages? Insights from the wine industry', *Research Policy*, **38** (6), 906–21.

Giuliani, E., A. Morrison, C. Pietrobelli and R. Rabellotti (2010), 'Who are the researchers that are collaborating with industry? An analysis of the wine sectors in Chile, South Africa and Italy', *Research Policy*, **39** (3), 748–76.

Greene, W.H. (1994), 'Accounting for excess zeros and sample selection in poisson and negative binomial regression models', Working paper, Stern School of Business, NYU EC-94-10.

Gulbrandsen, M., D. Mowery and M. Feldman (2011), 'Introduction to the special issue: heterogeneity and university-industry interactions', *Research Policy*, **40** (1), 1–5.

Hausman, J., B.H. Hall and Z. Griliches (1984), 'Econometric models for count data with an application to the patents–R&D relationship', *Econometrica*, **52** (4), 909–38.

Heinze, T., P. Shapira, J. Rogers and J. Senker (2009), 'Organizational and institutional influences on creativity in scientific research', *Research Policy*, **38** (4), 610–23.

IESA (2009a), 'Condiciones de generación y uso de la investigación científica en los sistemas de I+D', Internal report for Companies Survey, IESA-CSIC: Córdoba.

IESA (2009b), 'Condiciones de generación y uso de la investigación científica en los sistemas de I+D', Internal report for Research Groups Survey, IESA-CSIC: Córdoba.

Larsen, M.T. (2011), 'The implications of academic enterprise for public science: an overview of the empirical evidence', *Research Policy*, **40** (1), 6–19.

Laursen, K. and A. Salter (2006), 'Open for innovation: the role of openness in explaining innovative performance among UK manufacturing firms', *Strategic Management Journal*, **27** (2), 131–50.

Lee, C.Y. (2010), 'A theory of firm growth: learning capability, knowledge threshold, and patterns of growth', *Research Policy*, **39** (2), 278–89.

Lissoni, F. (2010), 'Academic inventors as brokers', *Research Policy*, **39** (7), 843–57.

Long, S. (1997), *Regression Models for Categorical and Limited Dependent Variables*, Thousand Oaks, CA: Sage.

Lundvall, Bengt-Åke (ed) (1992), *National Systems of Innovation: Towards a Theory of Innovation and Interactive Learning*, London: Pinter Publishers.

Merton, Robert K. (1973), *The Sociology of Science: Theoretical and Empirical Investigations*, Chicago: University of Chicago Press.

Molas-Gallart, J., A.J. Salter, P. Patel, A. Scott and X. Duran (2002), 'Measuring and mapping Third Stream activities', SPRU Report for the Russell Group of Universities, Brighton, UK: SPRU – Science and Technology Policy Research, University of Sussex.

Østergaard, C.R. (2009), 'Knowledge flows through social networks in a cluster: comparing university and industry links', *Structural Change and Economic Dynamics*, **20** (3), 196–210.

Pinto, H. (2009), 'The diversity of innovation in the European Union: mapping latent dimensions and regional profiles', *European Planning Studies*, **17** (2), 303–26.

Pinto, H., J. Guerreiro and E. Uyarra (2012), 'Diversidades de Sistemas de Inovação e Implicações nas Políticas Regionais: Comparação das Regiões do Algarve e da Andaluzia', *Revista Portuguesa de Estudos Regionais*, 29, 3–14.

Ramos-Vielba, I. and M. Fernández-Esquinas (2010), 'Measuring university-industry collaboration in a regional innovation system', *Scientometrics*, **84** (3), 649–67.

Saxenian, A. (1994), *Regional Advantage: Culture and Competition in Silicon Valley and Route 128*, Cambridge, MA: Harvard University Press.

Vuong, Q.H. (1989), 'Likelihood ratio tests for model selection and non-nested hypotheses', *Econometrica*, **57** (2), 307–33.

APPENDIX: INDEPENDENT VARIABLES: RESEARCH OBJECTIVES AND DESCRIPTIVE STATISTICS

Table 10A.1 *Companies*

Variable	Explanation	Mean	Min.	Max.
IND	Dummy variable that assumes value 1 if company is from the Industry sector and 0 if not	.264	0	1
GROUP	Dummy variable that assumes value 1 if company belongs to a group of companies	.227	0	1
AGE	Count variable with the age of the company in years	177	0	338
EMP	Count variable with the total number of employees in the company	559	1	3580
EMPQ	Ratio variable with the employees with Higher Education background and the total	.354	0	2.89
EXP	Ratio variable percentage of exports from total sales	7.05	0	100
RDDEP	Dummy variable that assumes value 1 if company has an internal R&D department and 0 if not	.251	0	1
FORM	Dummy variable that assumes value 1 if company has invested in training activities for its employees	.799	0	1
INOVACT	Dummy variable that assumes value 1 if company has developed innovative activities and 0 if not	3.370	0	7
PAT	Dummy variable that assumes value 1 if company has at least one registered national patent	.207	0	1
KTEXP	Count variable of the number of years since the first contact with a research organization	8.132	1	48

PREVREL	Dummy variable that assumes value 1 if the company respondent supports that the existence of previous relations as the crucial factor for engaging in KT activities between companies and research groups	.194	0	1
KTO	Score variable that is created with the sum of three dummy variables, one that assumes 1 if the initiative for the KT activities were from the KTO, another that assumes 1 if the KTO helped during all the processes and another one if the KTO was considered the central intermediary to KT, multiplied by the valuation of the effectiveness of the KTO (0 to 4)	.744	0	9
KTEXT	Dummy variable that assumes value 1 if company co-operates with research groups outside its region	.0841	0	1
KTVAL	Score variable with the valorization of the respondent regarding the importance of KT to the competitiveness of the company (0–4)	1.427	0	4
STP	Dummy variable that assumes value 1 if company's location is a Science & Technology Park	.0827	0	1
PROXUNIV	Dummy variable that assumes value 1 if company is geographically close to a university	.719	0	1
PROXHTMNE	Dummy variable that assumes value 1 if company is close to high-tech multinational companies	.358	0	1
CLUST	Dummy variable that assumes value 1 if company is integrated in a territorial cluster and 0 if not	.0909	0	1

Table 10A.2   Research groups

Variable	Explanation	Mean	Min.	Max.
NATLIFE	Dummy variable that assumes value 1 if research group focus is Natural Sciences and Life Sciences	.364	0	1
EXPTECH	Dummy variable that assumes value 1 if research group focus is Exact and Experimental Sciences and Technologies	.213	0	1
SOCHUM	Dummy variable that assumes value 1 if research group focus is Humanities and Social Sciences	.422	0	1
AGE	Count variable with the age of the research group in years	1.414	0	61
MEMB	Count variable with the total number of researchers in the group	1.244	2	88
MEMQ	Ratio variable with the researchers currently holding a PhD from the total	.675	.1	1
DIR	Dummy variable that assumes value 1 if strategic decision making is completely centralized in a director	.113	0	1
LIBER	Dummy variable that assumes value 1 if decision-making process is based on the individual decision of each researcher	.058	0	1
IDTOTAL	Count variable of total R&D expenditure in thousands of euros	40642.98	0	1030000
IDPRIV	Ratio variable between the budget from R&D coming from private sources from total expenditure	.110	0	1
FOCUSKT	Score variable that is the product of the sum of two dummies; firstly the main activity focused on knowledge transfer or diffusion of science, secondly the orientation of research activities towards companies with a self-assessment of ability to transfer knowledge (1–5)	.549	0	10

Variable	Description			
KTEXP	Count variable of the number of years since the first contact with a company	11.632	1	37
PREVREL	Dummy variable that assumes the value 1 if the research group respondent supports that the existence of previous relations is the crucial factor to engaging in KT activities between companies and research groups	.324	0	1
KTO	Score variable that is created with the sum of three dummy variables, one that assumes 1 if the initiative for the KT activities was from the KTO, another that assumes 1 if the KTO helped during all the processes and another one if the KTO was considered the central intermediary to KT, multiplied by the valuation of the effectiveness of the KTO (0 to 4)	.969	0	12
KTEXT	Dummy variable that assumes value 1 if research group co-operates with companies outside its region	.281	0	1
KTLARGECOMP	Ratio variable that ensures the percentage of KT activities with large firms from total number	.207	0	1
KTVAL	Score variable with the valorization of the respondent regarding the importance of KT to the competitiveness of the research group (0-4)	1.878	0	4

11. Performance measurement in business incubators: empirical evidence from Europe

Gregor H.F. Noltes, Enno Masurel and Toon Buddingh'

INTRODUCTION

The importance of small firms to economic growth, innovation and diversity is widely acknowledged. These topics are at the very centre of the policy of the European Union (EU), concentrated in the 'Innovation Union', one of the seven flagships of the EU's 2020 Strategy (European Commission, 2010). Facilitating and supporting activities in this context are seen as critical for achieving success. Because of the acclaimed success of Business Incubators (BIs), policymakers see them as a potential instrument for achieving the innovation goals (Hannon and Chaplin, 2003). Unfortunately, actual and accurate figures in this context are still lacking.

BIs are one type of vehicles that facilitate small enterprises in their growth. BIs are powerful tools set up by public, private or joint initiatives, for small enterprises to overcome the pitfalls of starting up and growing their business, both in the case of high-tech businesses and in other sectors (Voisey et al., 2006). According to benchmark research commissioned by the European Commission (CSES, 2002), BIs obtain remarkable successes in Europe. BIs come in different shapes and sizes but their common goal is to help provide their clients – or the inhabitants of the BI, best called 'incubatees'– with a strategic, value-adding intervention system of monitoring and business assistance (Hackett and Dilts, 2004).

There is a considerable growing perception among researchers as well as an increasing awareness of policymakers for more rigorous evaluations of the success of BIs (Bigliardi et al., 2006). Evaluation efforts are important to provide crucial insights into the performance of these mostly publicly funded programmes (Schwartz and Göthner, 2009). Using the classification of Grimaldi and Grandi (2003), we investigated the question whether different types of BIs lead to differences in success. Bearing in mind the acclaimed importance of BIs to the European economy, answering the question 'does type matter?' is of both practical and scientific relevance. As a working definition of BIs, we use the definition of the European Business & Innovation Network (EBN) (2010, p. 2): '[BIs] are organisations which promote innovation and entrepreneurship. They help enterprises to innovate; they drive the creation of start-ups (support to innovation, incubation and internationalisation) and they promote economic development through job and enterprise creation and development.'

This chapter starts with an overview of existing information on BIs: the main elements that constitute BIs (incubator infrastructure, management assistance, and access to networks), the typology of different BIs (Business Innovation Centres (BICs), University Business Incubators (UBIs), Independent Business Incubators (IBIs), Corporate Business Incubators (CBIs), and Green Business Incubators (GBIs)) and the different ways to measure the performance of BIs and their incubatees. Then follows the description of the empirical fieldwork among European BIs. The results of our survey are next, focusing on the differences in performance among the different types of BIs. The chapter ends with a discussion of the results, conclusions and recommendations for future research.

OVERVIEW

Elements of BIs

BIs seek to add value by offering their clients (the incubatees) a combination of facilities and services that cannot be so easily obtained from other sources (CSES, 2002). Scholars agree that a BI is not just simply a shared-space office facility, an infrastructure and a mission statement (see Aerts et al. 2007; Hackett and Dilts, 2004; Peters et al. 2004; Scillitoe and Chakrabarti, 2010). BIs should also offer access to networks to their incubatees. These networks include e.g. universities, research institutes (Mian, 1996; Vedovello, 1997), industry contacts (Hansen et al., 2000), lawyers, accountants, investors (Hackett and Dilts, 2004), and government agencies (Phillimore, 1999). Peters et al. (2004) pose that there are three BI services that affect the success of BI clients; infrastructure, coaching and networking. We agree with these authors, but for the purpose of our chapter we put networking and coaching together into access to networks, as networking and coaching have much in common, and added the constitutional element of management assistance.

Most BIs seek to provide a mix of office and workshop space to ensure that units of different sizes are available to suit incubatees at different stages of their development (CSES, 2002). These units range from only desk space for recent start-ups to larger units for more mature firms. Also, common facilities such as meeting rooms, laboratories, media rooms, lobbies and lunchrooms are offered. BIs can also choose to offer open workspace to promote interaction between the incubatees.

As managers and practitioners suggest, the quality of management assistance in the form of direct counselling enables the successful incubation of start-ups and other small businesses (CSES 2002, Hackett and Dilts 2004; Hansen et. al 2000; Lalkaka 1996). Services like assistance with e.g. business planning, presentation training, and help with raising finance are great assets to starting enterprises. BIs have the flexibility to tailor management assistance services to their incubatees' needs. The nature and range of the management assistance provided vary depending on the model and the objectives of any BI (CSES, 2002).

There is an increasing recognition in the literature that networking is a crucial element for the success of BIs (Hansen et al., 2000; Ekholm and Haapsalo, 2004; Soetanto and van Geenhuizen, 2008). Networking interactions by the BIs can be described as the extent to which the BI management provides its incubatees with access to the BI networks, in order to gain knowledge and resources not possessed by the BI management (Rice, 2002). The networking mechanism is meant to foster partnerships among incubatees and outside organizations, and also to create mutual partnerships among incubatees (Hansen et al., 2000). Hansen et al. (2000) also argue that the best BIs offer an extensive network of business connections to their incubatees. Incubatees with greater abilities to access external sources of knowledge then will have greater ability to learn and exploit this knowledge (Almeida et al., 2003). With the help of networks, start-ups and other small businesses can obtain resources and partnerships with other organizations quickly, allowing them to establish a competitive advantage. BIs can provide a valuable networking environment to incubatees by clustering firms that are in potential complementary to each other, or by exposing incubatees to possible partners. Coaching is one aspect of improving the performance of incubatees. Recent research has indicated that coaching by 'outsiders' makes an important difference in achieving organizational innovation success (Kleijn et al., 2011).

Different Types of Business Incubators

There is not one uniform format of BIs. Strategy, clientele, and being for-profit or not-for-profit organizations are but a few aspects that determine the nature of a BI. While most BIs have services and activities in common, they also offer distinct services and activities that reflect their own client-base as well as the specific resources that are available within their network (Grimaldi and Grandi, 2003). These differences lead to different incubating models. In their assessment of incubating models, Grimaldi and Grandi (2003) identified four main categories of incubators: Business Innovation Centres (BICs), University Business Incubators (UBIs), Independent Business Incubators (IBIs), and Corporate Business Incubators (CBIs). In practice, we identified also a fifth category, the so-called Green Business Incubator (GBI). Although the first four types of BIs are based on organizational principles, our attention was drawn to GBIs as well, representing a possible new line of approach for BIs. We are aware of the fact that the five categories are overlapping and not mutually exclusive, but they clearly represent different types of BIs. The five types of BIs are described below.

The first BICs in the EU were set up in the 1980s. The European Business & Innovation Centre Network (EBN) played an important role here. EBN was set up in 1984 as a joint initiative of the European Commission, European industry leaders and the first pioneering BICs. EBN is the leading non-governmental pan-European network bringing together BICs and related organizations across Europe. In 2008, EBN had 240 members including 155 BICs and 75 associate members in the 27 EU member states and in 11 other countries (Eastern Europe, Turkey, Canada, USA, Egypt and China), serving both the public interest and the interest of the private sector. BICs are set up as public–private initiatives with the aim of contributing to the stimulation of local economies in areas with industrial development and knowledge-intensive potential, by fostering the creation of new innovative enterprises (EBN, 2011). Interlocked in these goals is the main objective of BICs: to reduce the costs of doing business by offering a broad set of business support services to start-ups and other small businesses (Grimaldi and Grandi, 2003). The European Commission has a permanent team based in Brussels that provides EBN members with a number of services, e.g. a permanent quality-assurance system for the BICs, promotion of the BIC approach, and the provision of technical assistance (European Commission, 2000).

Starting in the 1980s, a number of entrepreneurial American universities longed for a more direct involvement in supporting the development of innovative new businesses (Mian, 1997), hence they founded UBIs. Scholars argue that government policymakers increasingly view science as a means for energizing national and regional economies and with increasing frequency ask universities to lend resources, faculty time and talent to economic efforts (Mian, 1994; Mian, 1996; Stankiewicz, 1994). Although universities are primarily set up to provide scientific education and research, they can make sustainable contributions to their local economy through applying scientific research, thus leading to e.g. patentable inventions and discoveries, spin-off ventures, and technology transfers (Chiesa and Piccaluga, 2000; Mansfield, 1990; Rogers, 1986; Schutte, 1999; Grimaldi and Grandi, 2003).

IBIs are a type of BI set up by single individuals or by groups of individuals who intend to help starting and growing enterprises to create and grow their business. IBIs are commercial BIs, characterized by a strong for-profit or commercial objective, although this does not eliminate motivations to generate benefits for non-commercial objectives (Von Zedtwitz, 2003). Within IBIs there is more freedom than in other BIs to develop an efficient incubation model, as IBIs are often established without the constraints of having to fit into an existing organization (Von Zedtwitz, 2003).

CBIs, also called internalized BIs, are owned and established by large companies with the aim of supporting the emergence of corporate spin-offs. These spin-offs particularly originate from research project spillover. It is quite common for the funding organization to control the new ventures by partial ownership in these ventures (Grimaldi and Grandi, 2003). CBIs have a kinship with corporate venture capital services, because both phenomena invest corporate funds in start-up companies. Management guidance is another key element in both CBIs and corporate venture capital services. The most relevant difference between CBIs and corporate venture capital is that CBIs internalize incubatees (offer them space inside their premises), whereas with corporate venture capital this is not a requirement.

The global sustainability movement that encourages climate neutral and sustainable economic activities has paved the way for a new type of BI: the GBI. This development is one movement in the trend to cluster sustainable firms (see Cohen, 2005; Schaper, 2002). These recently started incubators focus on recruiting entrepreneurs that are active in clean technologies, renewable energies, green businesses, etc. At present, there are two BIs in The Netherlands that focus on 'green-tech' businesses: New Energy Docks (Amsterdam) and Dnamo (Rotterdam). We expect future success for GBIs as the global sustainability movement is still winning ground.

Performance Measurement of BIs and Incubatees

In line with the diverse typology of BIs, we found that scholars use multiple variables in analysing the performance of BIs (e.g. Aernoudt, 2004; Hannon and Chaplin, 2003; Löfsten and Lindelöf, 2002; Rothaermel and Thursby, 2005). Given the fact that over the years different types of sponsors (public and private) have created an increasingly diversified BI landscape, it is clear that the concept of BI success is a multidimensional construct.

BIs are treated differently from most other organizations, as they are often non-profit entities or joint public–private initiatives (Hackett and Dilts, 2004). Therefore, Voisey et al. (2006) reviewed the literature to define the criteria for measuring the success of BIs. They came up with the difference between 'hard measures' and 'soft measures' for success or performance, and distinguished success measures that were BI-specific and incubatee-specific. Hard measures include 'clearly definable and quantifiable variables which show progress made, whereas soft measures represent the intermediate stage on the way to achieving the hard measure' (Voisey et al., 2006, p. 457). BI-specific hard measures include enterprise creation, growth of enterprise, job creation, and profitability. Soft measures that are specific for BIs are continued support from stakeholders, creation of goodwill between institution and community, growth in expertise of staff, increased client knowledge, knowledge valorization, and recognition by the enterprise support community. The hard measures that are specific for the incubatees are to a large extent identical to those specific for the BI: growth of enterprise, job creation, post-graduation survival, profitability, sales turnover. However, the soft measures are rather different for the incubatees than for the BI: e.g. their satisfaction with the support provided by the BI, productive networking with peers, building business skills, and growing confidence in themselves as entrepreneurs and in their business.

Schwartz and Göthner (2009) performed a literature review on success measures of BIs and found variables that can be regarded as the 'hard measures' defined by Voisey et al. (2006). For instance, survival of the incubated firms is one of the widely used indicators of BI success, since it is one of the primary BI objectives (McAdam and Marlow, 2007). Other criteria that are frequently applied in the literature are employment growth and jobs created (e.g. Löfsten and Lindelöf, 2002; Westhead and Storey, 1994).

EMPIRICAL FIELDWORK

Data was gathered in June–July 2010, by means of an online questionnaire. BI managers all across Europe were invited to fill in the questionnaire, and two reminders were sent out. Contact details were primarily obtained by employing the EBN network (www.ebn.eu). More contacts were acquired by consulting the websites of the various national business incubation associations, namely the German Arbeitsgemeinschaft Deutscher Technologie- and Gründerzentren (www.adt-online.de), United Kingdom Business Incubation (www.ukbi.co.uk), and the Dutch Incubator Association (www.dutchincubator.nl). So the population for our empirical fieldwork comes from various sources and represents an existing database.

The questionnaire included questions on basic information, general information about the BI, the success of the incubatees, and the success of the BI. See Appendix for the relevant part of the questionnaire. Expert interviews played an important role in developing this questionnaire, together with earlier research (Autio and Klofsten 1998; Voisey et al., 2006). As we did not have a strong theoretical basis to formulate explicit hypotheses this research can be seen as explorative.

Questionnaires were sent to 397 BI managers, in different European countries. 51 complete questionnaires were returned, leading to a response rate of 12.8 per cent. Regarding the organizational type, we can state that more than half of our respondents (54.9 per cent) represented a BIC. About one quarter (23.5 per cent) of the respondents represented a UBI and about a fifth of the respondents (19.6 per cent) worked within an IBI. Only one respondent represented a GBI, and the CBI was not represented in our response group at all. This absence of GBIs and CBIs indicates a gap between the theory and practice of BIs, and persuaded us to remove the GBI and the CBI from the data analysis (not from the general results), and left us with only BICs, UBIs and IBIs. In addition to this, we also removed the question on green enterprise creation from our analysis, as this was mainly expected to be an issue for GBIs. As expected, the single GBI strongly agreed with the proposition that there are many green companies that successfully leave the incubator. For the UBIs, IBIs and BICs, the successful graduation of green enterprises was much lower.

RESULTS

In our literature survey it was indicated that the first BIs were founded in the 1980s. This is confirmed in our response group: the oldest BI stems from 1980. The youngest BI stems from 2008 (two years before the survey was undertaken), which confirms that BIs are still a current phenomenon. Table 11.1 shows that most BIs are situated in Western Europe, especially in France (19.6 per cent), The Netherlands (15.7 per cent) and the UK (9.8 per cent). The remaining 54.9 per cent of the BIs are widely dispersed over Europe, including the so-called new EU countries.

Table 11.1   Country of origin of the BIs

Country	Number	Percentage
France	10	19.6
The Netherlands	8	15.7
United Kingdom	5	9.8
Austria	4	7.8
Germany	4	7.8
Belgium	3	5.9
Spain	3	5.9
Italy	3	5.9
Portugal	2	3.9
Other[a]	9	17.6
All	51	100

Note: [a] From the following countries we received back one questionnaire: Bulgaria, Czech Republic, Finland, Greece, Hungary, Luxemburg, Slovenia, Sweden and Switzerland.

The average physical space of a BI is 2,838 square meters, with a standard deviation of 2,920 meters, so there is a large variety in size of BIs. The largest BI covers 11,000 square meters and the smallest BI had no space at all (the latter concerns a so-called virtual BI). Only a small proportion of the BIs (19.6 per cent) have fewer than 25 office spaces. The remaining 80.4 per cent is made up of two categories: between 25 and 35 offices (39.2 per cent) and over 35 offices (41.2 per cent). The majority of the BIs (62.7 per cent) are located in new premises, as opposed to 21.6 per cent in converted premises and 15.7 per cent in other premises.

On the legal status of the BIs we note that 58.8 per cent are private companies, 25.5 per cent are public entities, and 15.7 per cent have another status. Furthermore, 19.6 per cent of the BIs are for-profit organizations whereas 80.4 per cent are not-for-profit organizations.

The majority of the BIs work with small management teams: 76.5 per cent of the BIs employ fewer than four managers, 15.7 per cent four to six managers, and 7.8 per cent seven or more managers. Concerning secretarial personnel, we see that the majority of the BIs (80.5 per cent) have three or less of such employees on the payroll. The remaining 19.5 per cent is subdivided into BIs that have four to six support staff (7.8 per cent), seven or more support staff (3.9 per cent) and no support staff at all (7.8 per cent).

In order to assess the representativeness of our response group, we compared the basic characteristics of the BIs of our response group with the most recent and comprehensive study on 77 BIs across Europe by CSES

Table 11.2   Characteristics of the BIs

	Our sample (2011)	CSES (2002)
Size of research sample	n = 51	n = 78
Geographical location = UK, France or Germany	64.7%	69.8%
Average space	2,838m^2	3,000m^2
Location	Urban: 88.0%	Urban: 54.4%
	Rural: 4.0%	Greenfield: 24%
	Other: 8.0%	Rural: 6.4%
		Other: 10.4%
		No answer: 4.8%
Average number of incubatees	29	27
Dependence on public subsidies	40.0%	37.4%
Legal status (private versus public)[a]	1 : 0.4	1 : 0.6

Note: [a] Only private companies and public entities were incorporated here. The category 'other status' was left out, because it was only used in our questionnaire, not in CSES (2002).

(2002). Table 11.2 shows that to a reasonable extent our findings correspond with the findings of CSES (2002), especially geographical location, average space, and average number of incubatees. The only noteworthy difference is found in the type of location. In our response group, the vast majority (88 per cent) are urban located whereas in the sample of CSES (2002) only about half (54.4 per cent) have an urban location. However, note that in our research project it was decided not to include the so-called greenfield category explicitly, as this term is ambiguous.

Data Analysis

Table 11.3 shows the mean values of the twelve different performance measures. We worked with a 5-point Likert scale (with strongly agree = 1, agree = 2, not sure = 3, disagree = 4, strongly disagree = 5), in order to identify the level of success of the incubatees and the BIs. From this it follows that the lower the score on the performance measures, the higher the level of success ascribed to it by the respondents. We detected mean scores within the range of 1.25 to 2.86, with the majority of the mean scores (69.4 per cent) being in the range of 1.25 to 2.5 (see Table 11.3). This range indicates that the BI managers are rather positive about the overall success of their incubatees and BIs. We note that job creation by incubatees among UBIs (1.25) is the performance measure with the highest rank and that achieving profitability by the incubators among UBIs (3.25) has

Table 11.3   Performance measures of the incubatees and the BIs: scores

	BIC	UBI	IBI
Incubatee-specific performance measures			
Growth of enterprise	2.71	2.58	2.00
Job creation	1.86	1.25	2.00
Post-graduation survival	1.71	1.67	2.00
Profitability	2.00	1.92	2.00
BI-specific performance measures			
Enterprise creation	1.79	1.67	2.00
Growth of the BI	2.36	1.50	2.60
Job creation	1.86	1.75	2.40
Profitability	2.93	3.25	3.00
Knowledge valorization	2.71	2.58	2.00
Societal objectives	1.93	1.58	2.00
Entrepreneurial objectives	2.86	2.83	2.80
Scientific objectives	2.36	2.17	2.00

the lowest score in success. In other words: UBIs consider their incubatees as very successful in creating new employment but they have great doubts about the profitability of their own organizations.

In Table 11.4 all three couples BICs-UBIs, BICs-IBIs and IBIs-UBIs are one-to-one compared. We found that only eight out of 36 comparisons led to statistically significant differences. Seven of the significant differences can be characterized as economic growth measures, namely job creation (by both incubatees and BIs) and commercial growth (by both incubatees and BIs). In only one situation did knowledge valorization make a difference. Thus, of our twelve performance measures, those that are concentrated around the aggregated concept of economic growth are the most distinguishing characteristics. So-called soft success measures (knowledge valorization, societal objectives, entrepreneurial objectives and societal objectives) hardly make any difference at all among the three types of BIs.

Regarding the incubatee-specific performance measures we can state that the growth of the enterprises is more successful in IBIs than in BICs. The creation of new jobs by incubatee firms appeared to happen more successfully in UBIs than in both BICs and IBIs. Post-graduation survival and profitability did not lead to any differences among the three BI types.

Concerning the BI-specific success measures, it appears that the growth of the BI is most successful in UBIs. As far as job creation is concerned, we see that IBIs are the least successful performers in this category. IBIs are outperformed by both UBIs and BICs. BICs were found to be most

Table 11.4   Performance measures of the incubatees and the BIs: differences in scores[a]

	BIC-UBI	BIC-IBI	IBI-UBI
Incubatee-specific performance measures			
Growth of enterprise	0.726	0.079*	0.213
Job creation	0.002*	0.476	0.002*
Post-graduation survival	0.855	0.306	0.304
Profitability	0.689	1.000	0.747
BI-specific performance measures			
Enterprise creation	0.594	0.370	0.231
Growth of the BI	0.027*	0.548	0.023*
Job creation	0.700	0.072*	0.064*
Profitability	0.390	0.857	0.589
Knowledge valorization	0.726	0.079*	0.213
Societal objectives	0.237	0.817	0.250
Entrepreneurial objectives	0.943	0.871	0.935
Scientific objectives	0.595	0.353	0.708

Note: [a] The LSD multiple comparison test was used to determine the significance of the differences between the scores of the three BI types. * As the nature of our research is exploratory we consider a *P* value of less than 0.10 to be significant.

successful in this respect. Looking at knowledge valorization we note that IBIs are more successful than BICs. It is striking that UBIs do not make the difference in the context of knowledge valorization, as European universities have embraced this issue recently. The other five performance measures (enterprise creation, profitability, societal objectives, entrepreneurial objectives and scientific objectives) did not lead to any differences among the three BI types.

DISCUSSION

The first striking issue from the data analysis is that only eight out of the 36 comparisons between the different types of BIs yielded significant results. This is an indication that the BIs, although they appear to represent different types, perform similarly to an important degree and that distinguishing a typology of BIs is only relevant in a very limited sense. The second striking issue from the data analysis is that seven of the eight significant differences are economic by nature: they deal with job creation and commercial growth (by the incubatees and by the BIs). Only one significant difference deals with a non-economic measure (knowledge valorization). Apparently, non-economic measures hardly differentiate among the different BI types.

Regarding the growth of the incubated enterprises, our research has shown that IBIs are more successful than BICs. This could be explained by the fact that IBIs are (partly) privately funded and they need a faster return on investment from their incubatees than their publicly funded counterparts, which puts more pressure on the performance of their incubatees. Another explanation could be that IBIs select the firms that they expect high growth from. The content of the incubation programmes might have configured in favour of realizing this objective.

The creation of new jobs by the incubatees and the growth of the BI appears to happen more successfully in UBIs than in BICs and IBIs. Apparently, UBIs represent a higher employment potential, in which scientific knowledge may play an important role.

One more interesting result that we found is that IBIs are least successful in generating jobs for the BI. Whereas UBIs and BICs are (in part) publicly financed organizations and therefore have more objectives based on the community and on the region, IBIs seem to be more focused on other goals than on creating employment, e.g. on generating sales growth of the incubatees.

Finally, it is striking that IBIs perform better than BICs when it comes to knowledge valorization. This is an unexpected finding as we anticipated BICs and especially UBIs to outperform IBIs on knowledge valorization due to their strong ties with (public) knowledge institutions. Apparently, the independent status of IBIs creates an environment in which knowledge can evolve into marketable products and services easily.

CONCLUSIONS

The focus of this chapter is on the extent to which success is different for different BI types. We distinguished five types of BIs: Business Innovation Centres (BICs), University Business Incubators (UBIs), Independent Business Incubators (IBIs), Corporate Business Incubators (CBIs), and Green Business Incubators (GBIs). The former four BIs are also distinguished in the literature but the GBI was added by ourselves. In the light of the current sustainability discussion, we consider the GBI as a valuable addition to the BI typology: for start-ups and other small businesses sustainable entrepreneurship is increasingly important, and GBIs can help them to improve their sustainable policy. Nevertheless, only one GBI was identified in our sample, which indicates that our addition apparently comes too early, but holds promise for the future. CBIs were not represented in our sample at all. Therefore, we could only distinguish between BICs, UBIs and IBIs. Our research revealed that only eight of all 36 comparisons between the different types of BIs yielded significant results. Seven of these differences were economic and only one difference was non-economic.

Based on these findings it is recommended for future research that this typology should not be distinguished a priori, but that characteristics should be collected for distinguishing a new typology. These characteristics may be, for example, the importance of different stakeholders, the size of the BI, and the kind of firms the BI wants to attract. Furthermore, it should be stressed that the performance measures of the BIs and their incubatees in this survey were measured by the perception of the respondents; new research may use more objective measures (e.g. directly from the administration). Finally, a case study approach for GBIs is recommended, because only one GBI was identified in our sample but the popularity of GBIs in the near future can be expected to increase.

REFERENCES

Aernoudt, R. (2004), 'Incubators: tool for entrepreneurship?', *Small Business Economics*, **23** (2), 127–35.

Aerts, K., Matthyssens, P., and K. Vandenbempt (2007), 'Critical role and screening practices of European business incubators', *Technovation*, **27** (5), 254–67.

Almeida, P., Dokko, G., and L. Rosenkopf (2003), 'Start-up size and the mechanisms of external learning: increasing opportunity and decreasing ability?', *Research Policy*, **32** (2), 301–15.

Autio, E., and M. Klofsten (1998), 'A comparative study of two European Business Incubators', *Journal of Small Business Management*, **36** (1), 30–43.

Bigliardi, B., Dormio, A.I., Nosella, A., and G. Petroni (2006), 'Assessing science parks' performance: directions from selected Italian case studies', *Technovation*, **26** (4), 489–505.

Centre for Strategy and Evaluation Services (CSES) (2002), *Benchmarking of Business Incubators*, Otford, UK: CSES.

Chiesa, V., and A. Piccaluga (2000), 'Exploitation and diffusion of public research: the case of academic spin-off companies in Italy', *R&D Management*, **30** (4), 329–39.

Cohen, B. (2005), 'Sustainable valley entrepreneurial ecosystems', *Business Strategy and the Environment*, **15** (1), 1–14.

Ekholm, T., and H. Haapsalo (2004), 'A profile of European incubators: a framework for commercialising innovations', *International Journal of Entrepreneurship and Innovation Management*, **4** (2–3), 248–70.

European Business & Innovation Centre Network (EBN) www.ebn.be accessed 23 February 2011.

European Commission (2000), *European Charter for Small Enterprises*, accessed

11 May 2010 at http://ec.europa.eu/enterprise/policies/sme/files/charter/docs/charter_en.pdf.

European Commission (2010), *Communication from the Commission to the European Parliament, the Council, the European Economic and Social Committee and the Committee of the Regions*, European 2020 Flagship Initiative Innovation Union, SEC (2010) 1161.

Grimaldi, R., and A. Grandi (2003), 'Business incubators and new venture creation: an assessment of incubating models', *Technovation*, **25** (2), 111–21.

Hackett, S.M., and D.M. Dilts (2004), 'A systematic review of business incubation research', *Journal of Technology Transfer*, **29** (1), 55–82.

Hannon, P. D., and P. Chaplin (2003), 'Are incubators good for business? Understanding incubation practice – the challenges for policy', *Environment and Planning C: Government and Policy*, **21** (6), 861–81.

Hansen, M.T., Chesbrough, H. W., Nohria, N., and D.N. Sull (2000), 'Networked incubators: hothouses of the new economy', *Harvard Business Review*, **78** (5), 75–83.

Kleijn, E.A., Masurel, E., and K. van Montfort (2011), 'The influence of "outsiders" on innovative behaviour by medium-sized firms', *International Review of Entrepreneurship*, **9** (2), 113–30.

Lalkaka, R. (1996), 'Technology business incubators: critical determinants of success', *Annals of the New York Academy of Science*, **798** (1), 270–90.

Löfsten, H., and P. Lindelöf (2001), 'Science parks in Sweden: industrial renewal and development?', *R&D Management*, **31** (3), 309–22.

Mansfield, E. (1990), 'Academic research and industrial innovation', *Research Policy*, **20** (1), 1–12

McAdam, M., and S. Marlow (2007), 'The university incubator: insights in the entrepreneurial process from a network perspective', *International Journal of Entrepreneurial Behaviour and Research*, **14** (4), 270–85.

Mian, S.A. (1994), 'US university-sponsored technology incubators: an overview of management, policies and performance', *Technovation*, **14** (8), 515–26.

Mian, S.A. (1996), 'Assessing value-added contributions of university technology business incubators to tenant firms', *Research Policy*, **25** (3), 325–35.

Mian, S.A. (1997), 'Assessing and managing the university technology business incubator: an integrative framework', *Journal of Business Venturing*, **12** (4), 251–85.

Peters, L., Rice, M. and M. Sundararajan (2004), 'The role of incubators in the entrepreneurial process', *Journal of Technology Transfer*, **29** (1), 83–91.

Phillimore, J. (1999), 'Beyond the linear view of innovation in science park evaluation: an analysis of western Australian technology park', *Technovation*, **19** (11), 673–90.

Rice, M.P. (2002), 'Co-production of business assistance in business incubators: an exploratory study', *Journal of Business Venturing*, **17** (2), 163–87.

Rogers, E.M. (1986), 'The role of the research university in the spin-off of high technology companies', *Technovation*, **4** (3), 169–81.

Rothaermel, F.T., and M. Thursby (2005), 'Incubator firm failure or graduation? The role of university linkages', *Research Policy*, **34** (7), 1076–90.

Schaper, M. (2002), 'The essence of ecopreneurship', *Greener Management International*, **38** (Summer), 26–30.

Schutte, F. (1999), 'The university-industry relations of an entrepreneurial university: the case of the University of Twente', *Higher Education in Europe*, **24** (1), 47–65.

Schwartz, M. and M. Göthner (2009), 'A multidimensional evaluation of the effectiveness of business incubators: an application of the PROMETHEE outranking method', *Environment and Planning C: Government and Policy*, **27** (6), 1072–87.

Scillitoe, J.L., and A.K. Chakrabarti (2010), 'The role of incubator interactions in assisting new ventures', *Technovation*, **30** (3), 155–67.

Soetanto, D.P., and M. van Geenhuizen (2008), 'Social networks and competitive growth of university spin-offs: a tale of two contrasting cities', *Journal of Economic and Social Geography*, **100** (2), 198–209.

Stankiewicz, R. (1994), 'Spin-off companies from universities', *Science and Public Policy*, **21** (2), 99–110.

Vedovello, C. (1997), 'Science parks and university-industry interaction: geographical proximity between the agents as a driving force', *Technovation*, **17** (9), 491–502.

Voisey, P., Gornall, L., Jones, P., and B. Thomas (2006), 'The measurement of success in a business incubation project', *Journal of Small Business and Enterprise Development*, **13** (3), 454–68.

Von Zedtwitz, M. (2003), 'Post project review in R&D', *Research Technology Management*, **46** (5), 43–9.

Westhead, P., and D.J. Storey (1994), *An Assessment of Firms Located On and Off Science Parks in the United Kingdom*, London: HMSO.

APPENDIX: QUESTIONNAIRE

Basic information
Name of Business Incubator
Town
Country
Contact name

1. General information about the Business Incubator

This section of the questionnaire generates more insight for the researcher into your Business Incubator.

1.1 In which year did your Business Incubator start operating?

....

1.2 How would you best describe your Business Incubator?
- ○ Business Innovation Centre (BIC). A BIC is a public–private initiative that contributes to regional economic development.
- ○ University Business Incubator (UBI). A UBI is an organization that commercializes university inventions and discoveries.
- ○ Independent Business Incubator (IBI). An IBI is a private company that helps entrepreneurs to create and grow their business and in turn receive a stake in the firm.
- ○ Corporate Business Incubator (CBI). A CBI is an autonomous business unit that is owned by a larger mother company that aims to support emerging corporate spin-offs.
- ○ Green Business Incubator (GBI). A GBI is an organization that solely focuses on 'green' companies. In this questionnaire, 'green' companies are referred to as businesses that produce goods or services without increasing resource use and environmental impact.
- ○ Other

1.3 Who are the Business Incubator's main stakeholders?
You may tick more than one box
- ○ University
- ○ R&D centre
- ○ National public authority
- ○ Regional public authority
- ○ Local public authority
- ○ For-profit business
- ○ Community-based organization (e.g. faith-based organization)
- ○ Other

1.4 What legal status does the Business Incubator have?
○ Public entity
○ Private company
○ Other

1.5 What is the Business Incubator designed to be?
○ For profit
○ Not for profit

1.6 Approximately what percentage of the Business Incubator's total revenue came from public authorities? .
...%

1.7 What sort of location does the Business Incubator have?
○ Urban
○ Rural
○ Other

1.8 What sort of premises does the Business Incubator have?
○ New
○ Converted
○ Other

1.9 What is the physical space of the Business Incubator? Please indicate in square meters.
....

1.10 How many offices does the Business Incubator have?
○ Fewer than 5
○ 5–14
○ 15–24
○ 25–35
○ More than 35

1.11 How many people does the Business Incubator employ?
Please indicate the full-time equivalent (FTE) for each category.

	0	1–3	4–6	Over 7
Managers	○	○	○	○
Secretarial staff	○	○	○	○
Other personnel	○	○	○	○

2. The success of the Business Incubator

This section of the questionnaire examines the various dimensions of success of the incubatees and the Business Incubator as an organization itself.

2.1 Please indicate to what extent your incubatees are successful at realizing the mentioned goals below.

	Strongly agree	Agree	Not sure	Disagree	Strongly disagree
Growth of enterprise: your incubatees 'grow fatter'; they realize growth in turnover, number of clients, expertise	○	○	○	○	○
Job creation: your incubates generate new vacancies in and outside their own firm.	○	○	○	○	○
Post-graduation survival: your incubatees survive after graduation from your BI.	○	○	○	○	○
Profitability: your incubates are profitable firms.	○	○	○	○	○

2.2 Please indicate to what extent your Business Incubator itself is successful at realizing the mentioned goals below.

	Strongly agree	Agree	Not sure	Disagree	Strongly disagree
Enterprise creation: your BI graduates many firms.	○	○	○	○	○

	Strongly agree	Agree	Not sure	Disagree	Strongly disagree
Green enterprise creation: there are many green companies that successfully leave your BI.	○	○	○	○	○
Growth of the Business Incubator: your BI realizes growth in turnover, premises, tenants.	○	○	○	○	○
Job creation: your BI generates new jobs.	○	○	○	○	○
Profitability: your BI is a profitable entity.	○	○	○	○	○
Knowledge valorization: your BI is good at commercializing university research and technology.	○	○	○	○	○

2.3 Please indicate to what extent your Business Incubator itself is successful at contributing to the following objectives.

	Strongly agree	Agree	Not sure	Disagree	Strongly disagree
Societal objectives; these goals include local economic development objectives, job creation, reducing CO_2, etc.	○	○	○	○	○

	Strongly agree	Agree	Not sure	Disagree	Strongly disagree
Entrepreneurial objectives: these goals include generating profit, improving sales, realizing return on investment, etc.	○	○	○	○	○
Scientific objectives: these goals include the transformation of technology and know-how into goods and services, the commercialization of university patents, etc.	○	○	○	○	○

12. The impact of human resource factors on university patent technology transfer activities in China – based on the analysis of provincial panel data

Kai Rao, Andrea Piccaluga and Xian-fei Meng

1. INTRODUCTION

In the process of technological innovation and industrial upgrading, governments worldwide have come to realize the key role that universities play in the development of the knowledge economy (Tu and Wu, 2006). The mission of universities has transformed gradually from 'teaching-oriented' to 'research-oriented', and then to 'entrepreneurial' (Lazzeroni and Piccaluga, 2003). For a long time universities have been 'ivory towers', with negligible connection with industry and society (Ndonzuau et al., 2002). In recent years, they have become increasingly entrepreneurial and are becoming network organizations in the Western countries (Butera, 2000; Lazzeroni and Piccaluga, 2003). The so-called 'entrepreneurial university' was originated in the US with the introduction of the Bayh-Dole Act in 1981 and spread to Europe later on. In spite of the popularity of such a change in university mission, moving towards a more entrepreneurial style is still difficult and is met with criticism (for instance, Gibbons, 1999; Kelch, 2002), which is mainly based on the 'corporate manipulation thesis', referring to loss of integrity and independence of universities, especially concerning their research agenda (Goldfarb and Henrekson, 2003). However, some researchers have pointed out the benefits of a more entrepreneurial university. Baldini (2006) argues that technology transfer (TT) activities and scientific excellence can mutually reinforce. Van Looy et al. (2006) find that the advantages include improved industrial innovation, additional funding opportunities or faster application of new inventions by increased patenting or spin-off activity. A report by EC (2007) also shows TT activities benefit university, industry and society.

With its new mission and closer connections with industry and government, the university becomes one of the three poles in the triple helix model (Etzkowitz and Leydesdorff, 1996), which has gained great attention through Etzkowitz, Leydesdorff and subsequently other scholars (Etzkowitz and Leydesdorff, 1996, 2000; Leydesdorff, 2000; Etzkowitz, 2003; Fujigaki and Leydesdorff, 2000; Mowery and Sampat, 2006). Etzkowitz and Leydesdorff place the university in the leading position in the innovation process in general, although in some situations, government takes the primary or dominant role in 'developing projects and providing the resources for new initiatives' (Etzkowitz, 2008). More importantly, the triple helix takes on the characteristics of a network systems type approach of a 'complex and dynamic' system of institutional spheres – academia, industry, and government (Etzkowitz and Leydesdorff 2000). Within the triple helix model, each sphere can take on the roles of another and the 'networks, arrangements, overlapping' among them spur and sustain innovation and development process.

According to a European Commission report on metrics for knowledge transfer (EC, 2009), patenting-licensing is a typical channel to activate the overlapping between universities and industries to accelerate the innovation and development process, through which inventors and universities can achieve commercial value, and technical problems of industry can be solved to enhance product innovation and industrial upgrading for greater competitiveness. Therefore, the impact factors of university patent technology transfer (UPTT) performance draw the attention of governments, industries, universities and academia all over the world.

Currently, there are a number of qualitative or quantitative researches to investigate the key success factors of UPTT (for instance, Powers, 2004; O'Shea, 2005; Fukugawa, 2009; Caldera and Debande, 2010; Muscio, 2010). Despite the variety of research methodologies and the countries, these studies all point out the importance of resources input on UPTT activities, especially the influence of human resource (HR) factors (for instance, Fukugawa, 2009; Fu et al., 2010; Wu and Dong, 2010; Caldera and Debande, 2010). In general, UPTT activities are studied from the perspectives of HR quantity and quality (Zhou and Zhu, 2007; Fukugawa, 2009; Caldera and Debande, 2010). Moreover, the scope of the HR factors includes university technology R&D staff/university faculty who generate new knowledge and new technology (Zhou and Zhu, 2007; Fukugawa, 2009), and university technology management staff responsible for the connection between university and industry, like those in university technology transfer offices (UTTOs) (e.g. Caldera and Debande, 2010).

Taking the examples of the US (Powers, 2004), Japan (Fukugawa, 2009), Spain (Caldera and Debande, 2010), and the UK (Chapple et al.,

2005), university HR factors are considered as the determinant of active university technology transfer (UTT) activities. However, researches on UPTT activities are focused on western countries. Relatively less has been done for UPTT of Chinese universities and mostly of them are qualitative (Chen et al., 2007; Liu and Fu, 2010). Few quantitative studies on Chinese universities have been done from the perspectives of university institutional type and reputation (Yuan et al., 2009; Wu and Dong, 2010). There is a literature gap of comprehensive investigation on the role of Chinese university HR. Therefore, the study of the impact of HR factors on Chinese UPTT activities and the analysis of the role of the Chinese university in promoting technological innovation and industrial upgrading has important theoretical and practical significance.

The chapter is organized as follows. Firstly, based on the relevant UPTT literature, the chapter proposes theoretical hypotheses of the impact of HR factors on the quantity of UPTT contracts and revenues, according to the actual classification of Chinese university HR. Secondly, based on the provincial panel data of China, the chapter tests the hypotheses with empirical methodology. Moreover, the impact of university HR factors on Chinese UPTT performance is analyzed and explained. Finally, a robustness check is conducted to further validate the conclusions.

2.   RESEARCH HYPOTHESES

According to the classification of university S&T personnel in China by the Ministry of Education, university S&T personnel can be divided into university faculty, research and development staff (R&D staff), and R&D results application and technology services staff (TSS). University faculty refers to the personnel responsible for both teaching and researching. Developing is their least frequent activity. Their research results are more scientifically oriented, always at the early stage of UTT procedures. Their transfer options include both commercialization and publication. Research and development staffs (R&D staffs) refer to those who focus on research and development activities. Compared with the former, this type of R&D HR is more commercially oriented, with their main activities on the mid stage of UTT procedures, and their research results are more accessible for industry. TSS is the most similar staff to UTTO staffs in Western countries. Their main task is to manage scientific research and promote technology transfer activities. The indicators of university faculty, R&D staff and TSS are selected as the independent variables in the chapter. For indicators, the quantity of UPTT contracts and their revenues are the most used (for example, Zhou and Zhu, 2007; Fukugawa, 2009; Caldera and

Debande, 2010): the quantity of contracts often represents the interest and intention of companies for university technologies, which can be seen at the initial stage of the patent technology transfer process; their revenues often represent actual demand, detectable at middle-late stages.

2.1 UPTT, R&D Staff and University Faculty

The relations of UPTT activities with university faculty and R&D staff can be analyzed with resource-based theory, which indicates that performance difference among organizations is due to the unique, difficult to duplicate, tangible or intangible resources. These resources become the sustainable competitive advantage of firms (Wernerfelt, 1984). Grant (1991) argues that the resources are the sources of capabilities, and capabilities are the main source of competitive advantage. Other scholars (Amit and Schoemaker, 1993; Michalisin et al., 1997) hold that strategic resources can be important factors of sustainable competitive advantage, and superior firm performance can be achieved only if they possess certain special characteristics. Being used initially for business studies, it was employed later in the field of UTT, according to Powers and McDougall (2005). Its application in higher education is helpful for sharpening the understanding of organizational phenomena such as UTT activities. A new line of research has thus emerged on academic entrepreneurship to analyze resources and capabilities at university level (Lockett and Wright 2005; O'Shea et al., 2005; Powers and McDougall 2005), arguing that certain resources and capabilities may provide a university with advantages in technology transfer performance.

Now it is widely accepted that the unique, scarce resources of Chinese universities are not material or financial ones, but HR, such as university faculty, R&D staff (for example, Zhou and Zhu, 2007; Fu et al., 2010). Because of the different ability of access to HR among different universities, UTT activities vary considerably, and heterogeneity of UTT activities can be expressed by different patent technology transfer performances.

At present, there are a number of western studies showing that increasing quantity or quality of university faculty (professors) R&D staff promotes UTT activities: Powers (2004) explored the relation between R&D staff quality and UPTT activities in US, and pointed out that the quality of R&D staff in life sciences, physics and engineering had a significant positive relation with UPTT activities. Fukugawa (2009) and Muscio (2010) studied Japanese public R&D institutions and Italian universities respectively, and found that the quality of R&D staff had significant impact on UTT activities. Caldera and Debande (2010) found that the quantity of Spanish university scientists had a significant positive impact on the quantity and revenues of UPTT contracts. From the perspective of both quality and quantity of HR in American universities, O'hea et al. (2005) found that the quality of S&T HR had a more significant influence on UTT activities than the quantity of S&T. As for the researches on Chinese universities, Zhou and Zhu (2007) found that the quantity of R&D staff did not have a significant impact on that of UPTT contracts and their revenues. However, the research duration of Zhou and Zhu (2007) is from 2000 to 2004, which is almost the time when the concepts of 'entrepreneurial university' and 'triple helix' were proposed in China. The Ministry of S&T of China and Ministry of Finance of China also promulgated some relevant laws and regulations, such as 'Some regulations on intellectual property management of national research programs' research results', during the period. Therefore, at that time Chinese universities were not really inspired to pursue UPTT activities and the impact of HR input cannot be observed. Based on the 2007 data of 98 key universities in China, Yuan et al. (2009) found that the quantity of university faculty was not related with that of UTT contracts; whereas Wu and Dong (2010) found a significant positive relation between the quantity of full/associate professors and the revenues of technology transfer, by studying 36 Chinese universities. Due to the fact that these two papers use only university faculty as the control variable of the researches, the classification of HR is ignored. They cannot reveal the impact of different types of HR on UTT activities, and the impact of the quality of HR was not studied either. In addition, whether the findings of these two papers are consistent with a larger sample has also become a question worthy of further study.

In the literature above there is no consensus in evaluating university R&D staff's quality. In general, the proportion of staff with an academic title or PhD degree is the widely used indicator in the studies for Asian countries (Fukugawa, 2009; Fu et al., 2010; Wu and Dong, 2010). The number of publications/citations (Zhou and Zhu, 2007) and the proportion of professors obtaining a research leave (Caldera and Debande, 2010) are also used as indicators of university R&D staff quality by some authors. However, according to the EC (2009) report, the quantity of publications or citations is more easily considered as output of knowledge transfer. Moreover, in the Chinese context, companies are more inclined to cooperate with university faculty with professorship, while young assistant professors or associate professors have more interest in academic publication activities. The same thing happens to R&D staff. So the chapter chooses the index of the title of professor for university faculty and scientist or engineer for R&D staff as indicators of their quality.

Based on the literature above, the following hypotheses are proposed:

H1   The quantity of R&D staff has a significant positive impact on the quantity of contracts

H2   The quantity of R&D staff has a significant positive impact on the revenues of contracts

H3   The quality of R&D staff has a significant positive impact on the quantity of contracts

H4   The quality of R&D staff has a significant positive impact on the revenues of contracts

H5   The quantity of faculty has a significant positive impact on the quantity of contracts

H6   The quantity of faculty has a significant positive impact on the revenues of contracts

H7   The quality of faculty has a significant positive impact on the quantity of contracts

H8   The quality of faculty has a significant positive impact on the revenues of contracts

2.2   UPTT and TSS

The relation between UPTT activities and TSS can be explored with resource dependence theory, which holds that resources are important constrained factors for enterprise development. Organizations should take all kinds of strategies to reduce dependence on key resources from outsiders (Pfeffer and Salancik, 1978). The staff positions of Chinese universities are relatively fixed, which prevents the high-speed development of faculty out of competition. Therefore it is difficult to quickly obtain a large quantity of high-quality university faculty and R&D staff. As a result, it may be more difficult to quickly obtain many new technologies with commercial value. Chinese universities need to make full use of the research results from existing university faculty and R&D staff, highlighting the importance of the university TSS. Now, many Western studies have shown that the quantity or quality of UTTO staff can promote UTT activities: Powers (2004) found that there was a significant positive relation between the quantity of UTTO staff and university licensing activities in US universities. Significant positive correlation also exists between the quantity of UTTO staff and the quantity of UPTT contracts in Spain (Caldera and Debande 2010) and the UK (Chapple et al. 2005). Siegel et al. (2008) revealed that the quantity of UTTO staff positively increased UPTT activities, but that the number of lawyers in UTTO had a significant negative influence on the number of license contracts. Similar studies include O'Shea et al. (2005), Belenzon and Schankerman (2009) and so on. As for the studies on Chinese universities, only Zhou and Zhu (2007) studied the impact of the quantity of TSS on patent technology transfer activities based on the data of 58 universities from 2000 to 2004. The results demonstrated that the quantity of TSS does not have obvious influence on UPTT contracts and the revenues. Whether the findings of the paper would be consistent with a larger sample, and the impact of the quality of TSS on UPTT activities, are questions worthy of further study. Based on the literature above, the following hypotheses are proposed:

H9   The quantity of TSS has a significant positive impact on the quantity of contracts

H10   The quantity of TSS has a significant positive impact on the revenues of contracts

H11   The quality of TSS has a significant positive impact on the quantity of contracts

H12   The quality of TSS has a significant positive impact on the revenues of contracts

The control variables that the literature suggests are R&D investments and the quantity of universities in one region. A number of recent empirical studies have found that the R&D funding of universities is positively related to technology transfer activities (e.g. O'Shea et al., 2005; Landry et al., 2007). So R&D funding for universities in their region is selected as one of the control variables. Previous research has shown that competitive government R&D programs also matter. Bolli and Somogyi (2011) observe that a larger number of competitive government R&D programs generates more technology transfer contracts and higher contract revenues. So the control variables also include the quantity of national R&D programs in China. Moreover, the regions with more universities are more knowledge-based, which provides a better environment for inventing and developing technologies, sharing technology transfer experience and interacting with high-tech companies. So the quantity of universities can be another control variable.

3. METHODOLOGY

3.1 Regression Model

Regression models are designed to test all the hypotheses proposed. When the dependent variable is the quantity of UPTT contracts, because it is a counted variable and its distribution is skewed, baseline regression cannot be chosen. Poisson regression or negative binomial regression is chosen for this reason. The most critical assumption for the asymptotic efficiency of Poisson regression is that the conditional mean is equal to the conditional variance. This is usually violated in applications, as it is likely to be with our sample of patent counts. In most cases, negative binominal regression is applied because of the situation of over-dispersion. Nevertheless the Poisson estimates will still be asymptotically consistent. Thus, Poisson regression is also chosen in some cases (such as Hu and Jefferson, 2009), and is used in this chapter.

$$Y'_{it} \sim Poisson(\lambda_{it}); \ Pr(Y'_{it} = y_{it}) = e^{-\lambda_{it}}\lambda_{it}^{y_{it}}/y_{it}!; \ E(Y'_{it}) = \lambda_{it} = \exp(X_{it}\beta)$$

When the dependent variable is the revenues of UPTT contracts, baseline regression (e.g. Caldera and Debande, 2010) and frontier analysis (e.g. Chapple et al., 2005) are the two regression models widely used. Usually two methods are used to estimate the best practice frontier: data envelopment analysis (DEA) and stochastic frontier estimation (SFE). However, DEA is sensitive to measurement errors and outliers, which can lead to upwardly biased estimates of the technical efficiency scores. SFE requires strong assumptions about the functional form of the production function and about the structure of the error term. Thus, linear regression analysis is chosen as follows:

$$Y_{it}'' = \beta_0 + \beta_1 TEN_{it} + \beta_2 TEL_{it} + \beta_3 RDN_{it} + \beta_4 RDL_{it} + \beta_5 SSN_{it}$$
$$+ \beta_6 SSL_{it} + \alpha_i + \varepsilon_{it}$$

In the two models, the dependent variable Y'_{it} and Y''_{it} attempt to measure the quantity and the revenues of UPTT contracts in region i at year t, respectively. X_{it} represents each of the independent and control variables, including TEN_{it}, RDN_{it}, SSN_{it}, TEL_{it}, RDL_{it}, SSL_{it}, GOV_{it}, NUM_{it}, PRO_{it}. Independent variables TEN_{it}, RDN_{it}, SSN_{it} represent the quantity of university faculty, R&D staff and TSS in region i at year t respectively. TEL_{it}, RDL_{it}, SSL_{it} represent the proportion of university faculty with the title of professor, the proportion of R&D staff with the title of scientist or engineer title, the proportion of TSS with scientists or engineers in region i at year t respectively. GOV_{it}, NUM_{it}, PRO_{it} represent the funding from government, the quantity of universities surveyed and the quantity of the completed national governmental programs in region i at year t. α_i represents the fixed effect from regional difference to avoid omitted variable bias.

3.2   Variables

Dependent variables are indicators of UPTT performance. Following western research, the quantity of UPTT contracts and their revenue (in million Yuan) are selected as dependent variables. In order to estimate the impact of R&D investment on UPTT activities of Chinese universities accurately, R&D funding and UPTT revenue are deflated on the 2004 base according to the *China Statistical Yearbook* of the National Bureau of Statistics of China.

For independent variables, two groups are selected. One is the quantity of university HR (in thousands), including the quantity of university faculty, full-time equivalent R&D staff and full-time equivalent TSS. The other is the quality of university HR, including the proportion of university faculty with the title of professor, R&D staff with the title of scientist/engineer and TSS with title of scientist/engineer.

For the control variables, the respective amount of government funding, of university and of national governmental programs is introduced. Government funding (in 100 million Yuan) includes general research expenses, special funding from administrative departments and R&D funding from non-administrative departments. The number of universities is the quantity of universities surveyed in each region. The national governmental programs include those of the 973 Program, national S&T pillar program, 863 Program and National Natural Science Foundation of China.

3.3   Data Sources

Considering that universities' merging basically happens within province, municipality and autonomous region, provincial level data can be used. All data are sourced from the 'S&T Statistics Compilation of High Education' for each year, published by the Science and Technology Department of the Ministry of Education of China. Twenty eight provinces, municipalities and autonomous regions in the years of 2004–10 (196 in total) are selected to build provincial panel database. As universities in Tibet, Xinjiang and Qinghai account for only a tiny percent of all Chinese universities, they are usually excluded by empirical studies, and are excluded by this chapter. In spite of the exclusion, on average more than 700 Chinese universities were surveyed each year.

4.   RESEARCH RESULTS

4.1   Descriptive Statistics and Correlation Analysis

The descriptive statistics of each variable and the correlation analysis between HR and UPTT activities in China are shown in Table 12.1. Pearson coefficients show the significant correlations between the quantity of three types of university HR and UPTT activities (significance level 1 percent), but not all types of HR quality have significant relevance with UPTT activities.

From Table 12.1, in terms of the quantity factors, it is easy to find that faculty is the largest part of university S&T human resources. The faculty quantity accounts for 65.7 percent of all the three types of S&T HR. R&D staffs and TSS are 29.4 percent and 4.9 percent, respectively. In terms of the quality factors, the proportion of faculty with professor title is the lowest of all three types of university S&T HR. Only 15 percent of university teachers have the title of professor. However, R&D staff and TSS with the title of scientist/engineer account for a very high proportion, 97.5 percent and 96.0 percent respectively.

4.2   Regression Results

The chapter utilizes Stata 10 to model and analyze the panel data. First, the Hausman test is used to check the endogeneity of the data. The result of Hausman test shows that panel data do not have endogeneity. For example, the Hausman check for the quantity of R&D staff shows that Prob>chi2 equals to 0.9862, which means the variable has no endogeneity. Then as for the impact of HR factors on the quantity of UPTT contracts, due to the log likelihood comparison between Poisson random effect regression and Poisson fixed effect regression, the fixed effect model of poisson regression is selected in this section. The numbers in brackets represent the standard error of explanatory variables. In order to exclude multicollinearity, Table 12.2 takes the method of introducing independent variables into the regression model one by one and observing the changes of independent variables' significance and coefficients, as shown from Model 1 to Model 6. Model 7 includes all control variables.

As for the impact of HR factors on the revenue of UPTT contracts,

Table 12.1   Means, standard deviations and Pearson correlation coefficients of variables

Variables	Mean	Std	1	2	3	4	5	6	7	8	9	10	11
1. Y′	32.88	43.48	1.00										
2. Y″	14.96	30.68	.56***	1.00									
3. RDN	5.83	3.93	.64***	.54***	1.00								
4. SSN	0.98	0.91	.54***	.45***	.73***	1.00							
5. TEN	13.03	6.97	.55***	.35***	.78***	.69**	1.00						
6. RDL	0.98	0.02	-.29***	-.10	-.30***	-.30***	-.22**	1.00					
7. SSL	0.96	0.08	.05	.04	.13*	.07	.17**	.13*	1.00				
8. TEL	0.15	0.04	.47***	.48***	.72***	.47***	.43***	-.23**	.10	1.00			
9. GOV	8.33	10.47	.70***	.61***	.82***	.61***	.60***	-0.23***	.08	0.71***	1.00		
10. NUM	27.33	12.44	.39***	.16**	.48***	.41***	.84***	-0.09	0.18***	0.08	-0.14**	1.00	
11. PRO	59.26	78.71	-0.10	-0.01	-0.01	0.11	-0.10	0.02	0.10	0.03	0.79***	-0.14*	1.00

Note: ***P<0.01, **P<0.05, *P<0.1.

Table 12.2 Effect of HR factors on UPTT contract quantity

Variables	Y'						
	Model 1	Model 2	Model 3	Model 4	Model 5	Model 6	Model 7
RDN	0.219***	0.228***	0.146***	0.141***	0.143***	0.142***	0.130***
	(0.013)	(0.013)	(0.015)	(0.015)	(0.015)	(0.015)	(0.016)
SSN		0.255***	0.155***	0.160***	0.156***	0.155***	0.189***
		(0.032)	(0.033)	(0.033)	(0.033)	(0.033)	(0.034)
TEN			0.074***	0.077***	0.078***	0.078***	-0.010
			(0.007)	(0.007)	(0.007)	(0.007)	(0.012)
RDL				-4.370***	-3.766***	-3.729***	-4.652***
				(1.229)	(1.282)	(1.287)	(1.311)
SSL					-0.794	-0.822*	-0.502
					(0.476)	(0.482)	(0.495)
TEL						0.497	2.251
						(1.489)	(1.745)
GOV							0.011***
							(0.003)
NUM							0.024***
							(0.003)
PRO							-0.001***
							(0.000)
Wald chi2	292.59	340.30	477.60	484.24	486.14	486.24	574.45
Log likelihood	-1505.57	-1474.37	-1410.30	-1403.96	-1402.66	-1402.60	-1356.6196
Prob > chi2	0.0000	0.0000	0.0000	0.0000	0.0000	0.0000	0.0000
Observations	196	196	196	196	196	196	196

Note: ***P<0.01, **P<0.05, *P<0.1.

after the Hausman test, the results show that chi2(6) equals to 4.55 and Prob>chi2 equals to 0.6032, so the random effects model of panel data is selected. The regression results can be seen in Table 12.3. The numbers in brackets represent the standard error of explanatory variables. In order to exclude multicollinearity, Table 12.3 uses the method of introducing independent variables into the regression model one by one and observing the changes of independent variables' significance and coefficients, as shown from Model 1 to Model 6. Model 7 includes all three control variables.

To explore regional differences, regional dummies are introduced into the regression models. As for the regression model with the quantity of UPTT contracts as independent variable, the effect of regional dummies on the quantity of UPTT contracts is revealed by Table 12.4.

As for the regression model with the revenues of UPTT contracts as independent variable, the regional difference is revealed by Table 12.5.

5. DISCUSSION

From the regression results of Model 6 in Table 12.2 and Model 6 in Table 12.3, parts of the theoretical hypotheses are supported (H1, H2, H5, H9, H10), while some are not (H3, H4, H6, H7, H8, H11, H12). The regression results Model 7 in Table 12.2 and Model 7 in Table 12.3 are mostly in line with the regression results of the former models. Only H2, H5 and H11 turn to insignificance.

5.1 Impact of the Quantity of HR factors on UPTT Activities

Models 1–6 of Table 12.2 and Table 12.3 show that R&D staff has a considerable positive influence on UPTT contracts and their revenues at the level of 1 percent significance. The results support the model's hypotheses H1 and H2. Model 7 of Table 12.1 also supports hypothesis H1. Several reasons can explain this. First, the increase of R&D staff helps the development of new knowledge and technologies with commercial potential. As a result, the UPTT activities are facilitated. Second, UTT requires not only new knowledge and technology which is generated in universities, but also the supporting R&D. The more R&D staff there are, the more the availability of successful supporting R&D. Thus, the success rate of UPTT increased. In the end, the increase of R&D staff is often accompanied by the diversification of R&D academic background. Multiple R&D academic background facilitates the inventing of a large number of new cross-disciplinary knowledge and technologies, leading to rapid increase of UPTT contracts and their revenues. Therefore, unlike Zhou and Zhu's

Table 12.3 Effect of HR factors on UPTT contract revenues

Variables	$Y^{//}$						
	Model 1	Model 2	Model 3	Model 4	Model 5	Model 6	Model 7
RDN	4.207***	3.173***	4.092***	4.258***	4.254***	2.993***	1.559
	(0.652)	(0.867)	(1.042)	(1.054)	(1.069)	(1.334)	(1.309)
SSN		6.701*	7.872**	8.229**	8.200**	8.290**	7.788**
		(3.609)	(3.677)	(3.691)	(3.731)	(3.726)	(3.589)
TEN			−0.815	−0.843	−0.806	−0.605	−1.231
			(0.565)	(0.567)	(0.576)	(0.589)	(0.941)
RDL				152.988	160.709	166.909	154.570
				(130.282)	(132.229)	(131.986)	(122.722)
SSL					−11.412	−13.673	−9.203
					(22.952)	(22.906)	(22.649)
TEL						144.988	64.474
						(92.483)	(89.780)
GOV							1.181***
							(0.341)
NUM							0.184
							(0.369)
PRO							−0.009
							(0.023)
R-sq	0.2948	0.2990	0.3192	0.3266	0.3276	0.3390	0.4048
Wald chi2	41.66	43.25	48.66	49.77	48.46	50.83	83.62
Prob > chi2	0.0000	0.0000	0.0000	0.0000	0.0000	0.0000	0.0000
Observations	196	196	196	196	196	196	196

Note: ***P<0.01, **P<0.05, *P<0.1.

271

Table 12.4 *Effect of regional dummy on the number of UPTT contracts*

Y^1							
Beijing	0.292	Tianjin	1.196***	Hebei	0.549	Shannxi	0.220
	(0.408)		(0.362)		(0.349)		(0.351)
Shanxi	0.653*	Neimenggu	-0.218	Liaoning	0.069	Gansu	1.609***
	(0.339)		(0.423)		(0.356)		(0.343)
Jilin	-0.434	Heilongjiang	0.276	Shanghai	0.590	Ningxia	0.655
	(0.361)		(0.358)		(0.385)		(0.551)
Jiangsu	-0.089	Zhejiang	2.411***	Anhui	1.576***	Guangdong	0.535
	(0.382)		(0.340)		(0.331)		(0.355)
Fujian	1.388***	Jiangxi	-0.647	Shandong	0.801**	Guangxi	0.827**
	(0.342)		(0.412)		(0.350)		(0.350)
Henan	0.030	Hubei	0.592*	Hunan	1.210***	Chongqing	1.851***
	(0.365)		(0.353)		(0.336)		(0.334)
Sichuan	0.512	Guizhou	-0.386	Yunnan	1.166***		
	(0.348)		(0.456)		(0.347)		

Note: ***P<0.01, **P<0.05, *P<0.1.

Table 12.5 *Effect of regional dummy on the revenues of UPTT contracts*

Y'

Beijing	-11.902	Tianjin	-39.263	Hebei	-34.110*	Shannxi	-58.075**
	(39.492)		(24.170)		(19.657)		(23.397)
Shanxi	-24.849	Neimenggu	-9.786	Liaoning	-46.801*	Gansu	-6.029
	(15.470)		(13.981)		(26.297)		(14.308)
Jilin	-40.899**	Heilongjiang	-48.301**	Shanghai	-50.846	Ningxia	-2.199
	(20.721)		(24.319)		(34.433)		(13.889)
Jiangsu	-57.786	Zhejiang	-27.295	Anhui	-23.316	Guangdong	-38.784
	(35.664)		(21.747)		(17.963)		(25.837)
Fujian	16.802	Jiangxi	-24.259	Shandong	-46.034*	Guangxi	-21.171
	(16.441)		(16.236)		(25.396)		(16.956)
Henan	-12.417	Hubei	-53.851**	Hunan	-29.724	Chongqing	-25.255
	(20.691)		(27.500)		(20.286)		(17.574)
Sichuan	-43.895*	Guizhou	0.821	Yunnan	-11.144		
	(23.606)		(14.963)		(15.028)		

Note: ***$P<0.01$, **$P<0.05$, *$P<0.1$.

results on Chinese UPTT from 2000 to 2004, the R&D staff in Chinese universities have begun to realize the importance of protecting the new knowledge and technology in the laboratory and of transferring them to industry via patenting/licensing. The traditional channels, which include reporting to the superior administrative departments and application for various awards from government, are not the only ones to be selected any more. So R&D staff has significantly facilitated UPTT activities. Although R&D staff quantity can promote UPTT activities, compared with government funding, the influence of R&D staff quantity on UPTT activities is not as strong as that of government funding, which may be the dominant factor for UPTT in China. Thus, H2 is not supported by Model 7 of Table 12.2.

Models 2–6 of Table 12.2 and Table 12.3 demonstrate that the quantity of TSS has a significant positive impact on the quantity of UPTT and its revenues at the level of 1 percent and 5 percent significance, respectively. Regression results support hypotheses H9 and H10. Model 7 of both tables also fits well with the results. A considerable portion of Chinese universities have set up TTOs controlled directly by the universities. The staff is responsible for registration of S&T results, intellectual property protection and UTT activities, etc. Other universities without specialized TTOs set up positions to perform relevant UTT activities in the S&T department of the universities or similar departments. Although there is a gap between Chinese TTOs and their analogues in Western countries such as the UK and Denmark, Chinese TSS have already reached a certain level of technical management and accumulated some experience. Their commercial awareness is growing, which facilitates the contact channel between university and industry. Moreover, with the increase of TSS, the proportion of those with a law or business background is increasing. The forming of a more rational structure of TSS accelerates the UPTT process.

Models 3–6 of Table 12.2 and Table 12.3 show that the quantity of university faculty has a significant positive impact on that of UPTT contracts at the level of 1 percent significance, without exhibiting significant impact on revenues. Regression results support the model's hypothesis H5, but not H6. Model 7 does not show significant impact in either table. The reason for Models 3–6 of Table 12.2 is that university faculty is the main body of university knowledge and technology innovation. The increase of university faculty quantity significantly increases the potential to generate new knowledge and technologies. Hence the quantity of UPTT contracts increased. However, the significant improvement of the potential of UPTT activities does not predict the commercial success of universities. Lacking a business background, university faculty find it difficult to evaluate the commercial value of technologies correctly. The price for technologies frequentlydeviates from the real commercial value. Moreover, many R&D programs are undertaken by a program responsibility system. The commercial value of technologies is often determined by the program leader. Thus a close relation between the quantity of university faculty and the revenue of patent technology transfer contracts is absent. Hypothesis 6 is not supported. Comparing the regression results of Model 6 and Model 7 in Table 12.2 reveals that the impact of the quantity of university faculty is not very robust. This may be attributed to the indirect involvement in UTT activities of university faculty in most cases, given their more science-oriented mission. The understanding of 'entrepreneurial university' could be strengthened among university faculty in order to turn the potential to generate new knowledge and technologies into real UTT activities.

5.2 The Impact of the Quality of HR Factors on UPTT Activities

Models 4–6 of Table 12.2 and Table 12.3 show that the quality of R&D staff has a significant negative impact on the quantity of UPTT contracts at the level of 1 percent significance, without showing significant impact on revenues. Regression results do not support hypotheses H3 and H4. Model 7 of both tables also fits well with the results of Models 4–6 of Table 12.2 and Table 12.3. The reasons may be as follows. First, R&D staff with the title of scientist/engineer have obtained some achievements in a particular subject area. They need to maintain their advantage in academic society by publication, so they cannot focus too much on UTT activities. Secondly, it is much easier for R&D staff with this title to obtain financial support. In China's case, government is the biggest financial source for university R&D staff. Considering the huge amount of R&D funding from the Chinese government and the availability of the funding for R&D staff with the title of scientist/engineer, the incentives for these staff are insufficient. Finally, R&D staff with the title of scientist/engineer usually have more working experience. They have already formed their own understanding of their mission and responsibility, and their habits of work. It is not easy to accept the changes brought about by the new concept of 'entrepreneurial university'. Thus, it is difficult for them to carry out UTT activities immediately.

Models 5–6 of Table 12.2 and Table 12.3 show that the quality of TSS has a significant negative impact on the quantity of UPTT contracts at the level of 10 percent significance, but it does not show a significant impact on revenues. H11 and H12 are not supported by regression results. In both tables, Model 7 shows insignificant impact on the quantity and revenue of UPTT contracts. This shows that the proportion of TSS with the title of scientist/engineer should not be the only indicator for TSS quality, despite Ministry of Education of China's practice. Table 12.1 shows that Chinese TSS with science/engineering background accounts for 96 percent at the average level and that the proportion of staff with any other academic background is far lower. Such an imbalance hinders UTT activities because staff with a law or business background could also be helpful. Referring to the academic background of UTT staff in Western countries, the successful achievement of highly efficient UTT requires not only staff with a science/engineering background, but also those with a law or business background. Therefore, the quality of TSS relies on the formation of multi-disciplinary background staff. Chinese universities should increase the proportion of TSS with other backgrounds, gradually decreasing the proportion of those with an engineering background. By this means, the optimal structure of TSS can be achieved. The regression results of Model 7 also reveal that it is inappropriate to evaluate the quality of TSS only by the title of scientist/engineer.

Models 6 of Table 12.2 and Table 12.3 show that the quality of university faculty has no significant impact on either the quantity of UPTT contracts or their revenues. H7 and H8 are not supported by regression results. The regression results of Model 7 are consistent with this. University professors cannot be engaged only in UTT activities; they have also scientific and didactic duties, which are more easily encouraged and recognized by society. Therefore, the proportion of university professors does not have a significant impact on the quantity of UPTT contracts or revenues.

5.3   The Impact of the Regional Dummies on UPTT Activities

The dummy variables of Tianjin, Shanxi, Zhejiang, Anhui, Fujian, Shandong, Hubei, Hunan, Guangxi, Chongqing, Yunnan and Gansu have a significant positive on the quantity of UPTT contracts. These regions locate all around China, except the Northeast area, showing the popularity of UTT activities in China. Nearly all universities have realized the importance of transforming into an 'entrepreneurial university'. These regions are not the traditional knowledge-based ones such as Beijing, Shanghai, Jiangsu, where the companies usually have their own labs or R&D centers to satisfy their technological needs. In the less knowledge-based regions, the opposite phenomenon emerges: in these regions, such as Anhui and Fujian universities' technology arouses the interest of industries because it is the only source of technology. So UPTT activities are very active here. Table 12.5 shows that there is no significant positive impact of dummy variables on the revenues of UPTT contracts. Eight dummy variables, including Hebei, Liaoning, Jilin, Heilongjiang, Shandong, Hubei, Sichuan and Shannxi, have significant negative impact on the revenues. All the regions in the Northeast area of China, namely Liaoning, Jilin and Heilongjiang, are among the eight regions, which reflects the poor interaction between university and industry in Northeast China. Usually the three regions are deemed the old industrial bases of China, with traditional industries accounting for a large percentage of their economies. But the universities' research results are almost all high-tech, which attracts little interest from the industries there. Furthermore, the results also reveal that areas with famous universities, but not developed economies, such as Hubei, Sichuan and Shannxi, have a significant negative impact on revenues. Although they have quite a few high ranking universities, research results cannot easily be transferred into real values, due to the inactive economy and lack of high-tech industries.

6. ROBUSTNESS CHECK

To further validate the robustness and effectiveness of regression results, as for the impact of HR factors on the quantity of UPTT contracts, the Poisson regression model with random effects (Model 2), negative binomial regression with fixed effects (Model 3), negative binomial regression with random effects (Model 4) and OLS model (Model 5) are all chosen for the robustness check. The results are compared with the results of the Poisson regression model with fixed effects (Model 1) in Table 12.6.

The regression results in Table 12.6 and Table 12.2 are consistent: all models show that the quantity of R&D staff has a significant positive impact on UPTT contracts and the robustness of the impact is very stable. Two Poisson regression models and two negative binomial regression models demonstrate that the quantity of TSS and university faculty has a significant positive impact on the quantity of UPTT contracts. The Poisson regression model with random effects verifies the significant negative impact of R&D staff quality on the quantity of UPTT contracts. As for the quality of university faculty, no regression reveals significant relevance.

In terms of the impact of HR factors on the revenues of UPTT contracts, fixed effects panel data model (Model 7), OLS model (Model 8), between estimator regression model (Model 9) and XTGLS model (Model 10) are chosen to check the robustness of random effects panel data model. All the regression results are shown in Table 12.7.

The regression results in Table 12.3 are consistent with those in Table 12.7. The OLS model, estimator regression model and XTGLS model all show that the quantity of R&D staff has significant positive impact on

Table 12.6   Robustness check of the effect of HR factors on UPTT contract quantity

Variables	$Y^\prime$				
	Model 1	Model 2	Model 3	Model 4	Model 5
RDN	0.142***	0.138***	0.121***	0.110***	4.229***
	(0.015)	(0.015)	(0.038)	(0.033)	(1.394)
SSN	0.155***	0.153***	0.167*	0.163*	5.440
	(0.033)	(0.033)	(0.096)	(0.085)	(4.029)
TEN	0.078***	0.077***	0.062***	0.063***	0.775
	(0.007)	(0.007)	(0.021)	(0.017)	(0.599)
RDL	−3.729***	−4.038***	−0.243	−3.823	−234.525
	(1.287)	(1.278)	(4.406)	(4.119)	(152.150)
SSL	−0.822*	−0.763	0.529	0.364	−15.183
	(0.482)	(0.473)	(1.347)	(1.219)	(30.426)
TEL	0.497	0.777	1.466	2.924	86.436
	(1.489)	(1.430)	(3.506)	(2.747)	(91.991)
Wald chi2/F	486.24	519.52	92.39	175.07	24.34
Log likelihood/	−1402.60	−1569.61	−588.80	−751.88	0.42
Adj R-squared					
Prob > chi2	0.0000	0.0000	0.0000	0.0000	0.0000

Note: ***P<0.01, **P<0.05, *P<0.1.

278

Table 12.7 *Robustness check of the effect of human resource factors on UPTT contract revenues*

Variables	Y$^{//}$				
	Model 6	Model 7	Model 8	Model 9	Model 10
RDN	2.993***	2.933	3.631***	4.475**	3.631***
	(1.334)	(2.290)	(1.063)	(1.815)	(1.044)
SSN	8.290**	14.960**	6.858**	4.922	6.858**
	(3.726)	(5.903)	(3.071)	(5.512)	(3.016)
TEN	−0.605	0.429	−0.842*	−1.087	−0.842*
	(0.589)	(1.029)	(0.456)	(0.766)	(0.448)
RDL	166.909	93.537	180.027	186.846	180.026
	(131.986)	(166.901)	(116.004)	(236.735)	(113.914)
SSL	−13.673	−12.726	−13.332	−9.870	−13.332
	(22.906)	(24.319)	(23.198)	(74.796)	(22.780)
TEL	144.988	207.080	125.472*	98.113	125.471*
	(92.483)	(184.684)	(70.137)	(113.811)	(68.872)
R-sq	0.3390	0.3081	0.3205	0.3379	N.A.
Wald chi2/F	50.83	2.16	16.33	7.00	101.59
Prob > chi2	0.0000	0.0498	0.0000	0.0003	0.0000

Note: ***P<0.01, **P<0.05, *P<0.1.

UPTT contract revenues. The fixed effect panel data model, OLS model and XTGLS model show that the quantity of TSS has a significant positive impact on UPTT contract revenues. As for the hypotheses that fail to be verified by Table 12.3, none of the other models can show the impact of the quality of TSS on the revenues of UPTT contracts, either. Both the OLS model and the XTGLS model reveal that the quality of university faculty can significantly improve the increase of UPTT contract revenues. In addition, both the XTGLS model and OLS model show a significant negative relation between the quantity of university faculty and the revenues of UPTT contracts.

7. CONCLUSION

The chapter has studied the impact of HR factors on UPTT activities in China. Using provincial data for the period 2004–10, empirical research has examined the influence of HR factors on UPTT activities, from the perspectives of the quantity and quality of HR. Hypotheses were proposed based on the theoretical analysis, and were tested with regression models.

The regression results were then analyzed and rechecked. The main research results are as follows:

1. University HR factors have significant influences on UPTT activities in China, and the influences on UPTT activities are not always the same. UPTT activities in China are still basically in a situation of extensive growth. The improvement of UPTT performance depends on the increase of the quantity of HR, especially that related directly to UTT activities, such as R&D staff and TSS. However, the quality of HR factors does not have significant influences on the performance of UPTT. Indeed in some cases, negative relations are observed.
2. The quantities of R&D staff and TSS have significant positive impacts on both the quantity of UPTT contracts and revenues. The increase of university faculty can also significantly increase the quantity of UPTT contracts. Therefore, Chinese universities should increase investment in the quantity of HR, and should actively encourage university faculty to be engaged in R&D activities and support the growth of TSS.
3. As for the quality of HR factors in each university, none of them show a significant positive impact on either the quantity of UPTT contracts or the revenues. This indicates that Chinese universities do not fully exploit the enormous potential of high quality HR. For TSS, Chinese universities should not take the title of scientist/engineer as the only criterion for evaluating the quality of their HR. TSS qualified as lawyers, economists or other professionals related to technology transfer can also facilitate efficient UTT activities. Concerning R&D staff and university faculty, Chinese universities should encourage them not only to publish papers or books and constantly improve their academic level, but also to be engaged actively in UTT. With increasing awareness of intellectual property protection, the channel of patenting/licensing can be used intensively to perform UTT for new knowledge and technology with commercial value.
4. Regional differences exist among Chinese universities. Although there is a general tendency to pursue UTT activities in China, those in the northeast lag behind. Moreover, some regions with famous universities but less developed economies are shown to be hindered in UTT activities. To take advantage of universities' research, the transformation from traditional to high-tech economy is urgent for these regions. Furthermore, knowledge-based regions with the most developed economies do not show significant positive impact on UTT activities either. This is attributed to the high R&D capabilities of their

companies. Guiding universities' research to fit the needs of industry and paying more attention to applied research should be an option to encourage UTT activities in these regions.

REFERENCES

Amit, R. and P. Schoemaker (1993), 'Strategic assets and organizational rent', *Strategic Management Journal*, **14** (1), 33–46.

Baldini, N. (2006), 'University patenting and licensing activity: a review of the literature', *Research Evaluation*, **15** (3), 197–207.

Belenzon, S., and M. Schankerman (2009), 'University knowledge transfer: private ownership, incentives, and local development objectives', *Journal of Law and Economics*, **52** (1), 111–44.

Bolli, T., and F. Somogyi (2011), 'Do competitively acquired funds induce universities to increase productivity?', *Research Policy*, **40** (1), 136–47.

Butera, F. (2000), 'Adapting the pattern of university organization to the needs of the knowledge economy', *European Journal of Education*, **35** (4), 403–19.

Caldera, A., and O. Debande (2010), 'Performance of Spanish universities in technology transfer: an empirical analysis', *Research Policy*, **39** (9), 1160–73.

Chapple, W., A. Lockett, D. Siegel and M. Wright (2005), 'Assessing the relative performance of university technology transfer offices in the UK: parametric and non-parametric evidence', *Research Policy*, **34** (3), 369–84.

Chen, H., Z. Song and M. Yang (2007), 'Factors analysis and primary study on the patents implementation in Chinese universities', *R&D Management*, **19** (4), 101–6 (in Chinese).

EC (2007), 'Improving knowledge transfer between research institutions and industry across Europe: embracing open innovation – implementing the Lisbon agenda', EC publication no. SEC(2007) 449, Luxembourg: Office for Publications of the EC.

EC (2009), 'Metrics for knowledge transfer from public research organisations in Europe. Report from the European Commission's Expert Group on Knowledge Transfer Metrics', accessed 28 October 2009 at http://ec.europa.eu/invest-inresearch/pdf/download_en/knowledgde%20transfer_web.pdf.

Etzkowitz, H. (2003), 'Research groups as "quasi-firms": the invention of the entrepreneurial university', *Research Policy*, **32** (1), 109–21.

Etzkowitz, H. (2008), *The Triple Helix: University–Industry–Government Innovation in Action*, New York and London: Routledge.

Etzkowitz, H., and L. Leydesdorff (1996), 'Emergence of a triple helix of university-industry-government relations', *Science and Public Policy*, 23, 279–86.

Etzkowitz, H., and L. Leydesdorff (2000), 'The dynamics of innovation: from National Systems and 'Mode 2' to a triple helix of university–industry–government relations', *Research Policy*, **29** (2), 109–23.

Fu Y., L. Zhang, Q. Ma and Q. Chen (2010), 'Impact of R&D resource input on patent output of various types of colleges and universities', *R&D Management*, **22** (3), 103–11 (in Chinese).

Fujigaki, Y., and L. Leydesdorff (2000), 'Quality control and validation boundaries in a triple helix of university-industry-government relations: "Mode 2" and the future of university research', *Social Science Information*, **39** (4), 635–55.

Fukugawa, N. (2009), 'Determinants of licensing activities of local public technology centers in Japan', *Technovation*, **29** (12), 885–92.

Gibbons, M. (1999), 'Science's new social contract with society', *Nature*, **402** (6761), 81–4.

Goldfarb, B., and M. Henrekson (2003), 'Bottom-up versus top-down policies towards the commercialization of university intellectual property', *Research Policy*, **32** (4), 639–58.

Grant, R.M. (1991), 'The resource-based theory of competitive advantage: implications for strategy formulation', *California Management Review*, **33** (3), 114–34.

Hu, A.G., and Jefferson, G.H. (2009), 'A great wall of patents: what is behind China's recent patent explosion', *Journal of Development Economics*, **90** (1), 57–68.

Kelch, R.P. (2002), 'Maintaining the public trust in clinical research', *The New England Journal of Medicine*, **346** (4), 285–7.

Landry, R., N. Amara and M. Ouimet (2007), 'Determinants of knowledge transfer: evidence from Canadian university researchers in natural sciences and engineering', *Journal of Technology Transfer*, **32** (6), 561–92.

Lazzeroni, M., and A. Piccaluga (2003), 'Towards the entrepreneurial university', *Local Economy*, **18** (1), 38–48.

Leydesdorff, L. (2000), 'The triple helix: an evolutionary model of innovations', *Research Policy*, **29**, 243–55.

Liu, Z., and Z. Fu (2010), 'Analysis on influencing factors of technology transfer in local colleges and universities', *Scientific Management Research*, **28** (3), 26–9 (in Chinese).

Lockett, A., and M. Wright (2005), 'Resources, capabilities, risk capital and the creation of university spin-out companies', *Research Policy*, **34** (7), 1043–57.

Michalisin, M., R. Smith and D. Kline (1997), 'In search of strategic assets', *International Journal of Organizational Analysis*, **5** (4), 360–87.

Mowery, D., and B. Sampat (2006), 'Universities in national innovation systems', in J. Fagerberg, D.C. Mowery and R.R. Nelson (eds), *The Oxford Handbook of Innovation*, Oxford: Oxford University Press, pp. 209–40.

Muscio, A. (2010), 'What drives the university use of technology transfer offices? Evidence from Italy', *Journal of Technology Transfer*, 35, 181–202.

Ndonzuau, F., F. Pirnay and B. Surlemont (2002), 'A stage model of academic spin-off creation', *Technovation*, **22** (5), 281–9.

O'Shea, R.P., A.J. Thomas., A. Chevalier and F. Roche (2005), 'Entrepreneurial orientation, technology transfer and spinoff performance of U.S. universities', *Research Policy*, **34** (7), 994–1009.

Pfeffer, J., and G.R. Salancik (1978), *The External Control of Organizations: A Resource Dependence Perspective*, New York, US: Harper and Row.

Powers, J.B. (2004), 'R&D funding sources and university technology transfer: what is stimulating universities to be more entrepreneurial?', *Research in Higher Education*, **45** (1), 1–23.

Powers, J., and P. McDougall (2005), 'University start-up formation and technology licensing with firms that go public: a resource based view of academic entrepreneurship', *Journal of Business Venturing*, **20** (3), 291–311.

Siegel, D., M. Wright., W. Chapple and A. Lockett (2008), 'Assessing the relative performance of university technology transfer in the US and UK: a stochastic distance function approach', *Economics of Innovation and New Technology*, **17** (7–8), 717–29.

Thursby, J., and S. Kemp (2002), 'Growth and productive efficiency of university intellectual property licensing', *Research Policy*, **31**, 109–24.

Tu, J., and G. Wu (2006), 'Triple Helix model and its application in China', *Science Research Management*, **27** (3), 75–80 (in Chinese).

Van Looy, B., J. Callaert and K. Debackere (2006), 'Publication and patent behavior of academic researchers: conflicting, reinforcing or merely co-existing?', *Research Policy*, **35** (4), 596–608.

Wernerfelt, B. (1984), 'A resource-based view of the firm', *Strategic Management Journal*, **5** (2), 171–80.

Wu, F., and Z. Dong (2010), 'The influencing factors of university technology transfer ability and the empirical analysis', *Science & Technology Progress and Policy*, **27** (10), 137–40 (in Chinese).

Yuan, C., Y. Jia, K. Fang and C. Liu (2009), 'Effects of university type on university knowledge transfer in China: a resource-based view', *Science of Science and Management of S&T*, **30** (7), 134–8 (in Chinese).

Zhou, F., and X. Zhu (2007), 'A study on the resource factors and the performance of university technology transfer', *R&D Management*, **19** (5), 87–94 (in Chinese).

Index